Emilio Pettoruti

A Painter before the Mirror

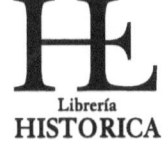

Pettoruti, Emilio
    A painter before the mirror - 1a ed. - Buenos Aires : Stock Cero: Librería Histórica, 2006.
    260 p. ; 23x15 cm.

    Traducido por: Cristina Soares Gache

    ISBN 987-1136-53-6

    1. Petorutti Emilio-Biografía. I. Soares Gache, Cristina, trad. II. Título
    CDD 927

Copyright © Fundación Pettoruti
Traducción Christine Castro Gache © Librería Histórica - Buenos Aires
De esta edición © Stockcero 2006

1º edición: 2004 - Librería Histórica - Buenos Aires
1º edición traducida: 2006 Stockcero
ISBN-10: 987-1136-53-6
ISBN-13: 978-987-1136-53-7
Libro de Edición Argentina.

Hecho el depósito que prevé la ley 11.723.
Printed in the United States of America.

Ninguna parte de esta publicación, incluido el diseño de la cubierta, puede ser reproducida, almacenada o transmitida en manera alguna ni por ningún medio, ya sea eléctrico, químico, mecánico, óptico, de grabación o de fotocopia, sin permiso previo del editor.

stockcero.com
Viamonte 1592 C1055ABD
Buenos Aires Argentina
54 11 4372 9322
stockcero@stockcero.com

Emilio Pettoruti

A Painter before the Mirror

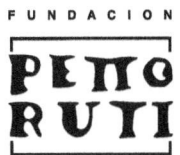

The memoirs of Emilio Pettoruti (La Plata 1892-Paris 1971) "A painter before the Mirror" was published a few years before the painter's death. Not only do we witness the vicissitudes of his struggle in order to impose his works, but we also find key aspects of his aesthetic convictions. His ties with Futurism and Cubism, his appreciation of color and light, in short a conception of art that led him to evolve towards an original abstraction, as his last paintings so well demonstrate.

His essential concepts about art and life are highlighted by an existence defined by his beliefs and passions".

To María Rosa

Contents

Introduction ix
A landmark in Argentine art

A Painter before the Mirror
Part One
Chapter 1 3
La Plata- First Steps
Chapter 2 15
Florence- First Impressions
Chapter 3 29
The "Lacerba" Futurist exhibition
Chapter 4 33
The Study of New Forms
Chapter 5 37
Nella
Chapter 6 43
Mosaics and Collages
Chapter 7 49
Italian Neutrality
Chapter 8 53
Towards an Expression
Chapter 9 59
War. Trip to Sicily
Chapter 10 65
Meeting Balla
Chapter 11 71
First Solo Exhibition
Chapter 12 75
Rome
Chapter 13 83
Milan

CHAPTER 14 91
Artistic life and struggles
CHAPTER 15 101
1921: In Munich
CHAPTER 16 105
Meeting with Mariátegui
CHAPTER 17 109
Exhibition at «Der Sturm» art gallery, Berlin
CHAPTER 18 115
Paris
PART TWO
CHAPTER 19 127
In Buenos Aires
CHAPTER 20 137
The «Witcomb» Exhibition
CHAPTER 21 147
First years in my home country
CHAPTER 22 161
Appointment, Dismissal, and Replacement at the Museum
CHAPTER 23 171
My first painting at the National Museum
CHAPTER 24 179
The treasure
CHAPTER 25 187
On both sides of The Andes
CHAPTER 26 199
Home and Friendships
CHAPTER 27 209
In the United States
CHAPTER 28 219
Years of hardship
CHAPTER 29 229
My Trip to Europe
THE PETTORUTI FOUNDATION (FUNDACIÓN PETTORUTI).....................243

Introduction

A landmark in Argentine art

Memoirs represent an essential source of documentary reference. They amplify and complement the vision we have of the author, often surprising us. Through them, not only do we better grasp his personality, but also the historical context in which he moved. Events in which the author played the main part, people he knew, significant circumstances: they are all reflected here, akin to multiple gazes in a fresco.

By entwining both personal and world history, often in remarkable ways, memoirs also pertain to the realm of fiction. They kindle the reader's imagination, motivating him to recreate a vast and complex existential framework. His own knowledge is thus enriched, through the accumulation of facts and opinions he is not likely to forget.

«In the community of men, everything is recollection and fantasy», declares Giambattista Vico in his «Principi di scienza nuova», published in 1774. In 1589, almost two centuries earlier, Montaigne reminds his readers, when publishing his essays, that he is the one hiding behind them. Emphatically, he affirms, «I am the subject of my book». And in the same vein, Anatole France considers «all novels to be ultimately autobiographical», adding that «the good critic is the one who can tell the adventures of his soul through works of art».

These memoirs by Emilio Pettoruti (1892–1971) were first published in 1968, while the author was still living in Paris. They saw the light a few years after the major exhibition that was held at the Buenos Aires National Museum of Fine Arts in 1962, celebrating the artist's international achievements, and after his last significant shows at the Charpentier Gallery and the Museum of Modern Art in Paris, respectively held in 1963 and 1966.

In part, the interest that «A Painter Before The Mirror» awakens is due to Pettoruti's theories on the laws of painting, as the artist is considered to be one of the major exponents of modern art in Argentina. His controversial exhibition at the Witcomb Gallery on Florida Street in October 1924, upon his first return from Europe, marks an important turning point in Argentine art, revolutionizing both the intellectual and artistic world of Buenos Aires. Atalaya (pen–name of Alfredo Chiabra Acosta), a distinguished critic of those decades, saw in this exhibition a new «Hernani», comparable to Victor Hugo's romantic and liberating cry that had resounded in Paris in the 1830s. In the seventh issue of the «Alfar» magazine, published in Montevideo in 1931, Atalaya reports: «excited crowds burst into the halls arguing loudly».

From that moment onwards, Pettoruti became the leading figure of 20th century artistic transformation in Argentina and Latin America.

The book reflects the course of his life, beginning with his childhood in his native city of La Plata, and ending with his last years in Paris. We witness the first manifestations of his vocation, his friendship with the writers Benito Lynch and Rafael Alberto Arrieta, his studies and artistic training, his first exhibitions in La Plata. We see him, too, as a perfectionist, a characteristic that led him to systematically destroy a large part of his work.

In 1913 he travels to Europe, only to return in 1924. This European phase is crucial, as Pettoruti is at once an observer and a major figure of a particularly rich and vital period of avant–garde art.

His first objective is Italy: he travels across it, attracted by its grandiose artistic past and by the effervescent creativity present everywhere. In Florence he meets Pappini, Pallazzeschi and Marinetti, with whom he eventually develops a close friendship, and immerses himself in the Italian way of life. On November 30, 1913, he attends the renowned «Lacerba» exhibition, in which the Futurists are paid fervent homage, and the show has a decisive impact on him. At the same time, he visits Florentine museums, carefully analyzing the works of great Italian Renaissance painters. This age–old way of learning, favored by artists such as Cézanne, van Gogh, Kandinsky, Mondrian and so many others, allows him to study their pictorial techniques in depth.

In 1914 he begins to participate in collective shows, presenting oils and drawings, and in July 1916, holds his first solo exhibition at the Gonnelli Gallery in Italy, where the Futurists exhibit their art. He meets Xul Solar in Florence, with whom he becomes close friends, and in October he travels to Rome, where he remains up until the middle of the following year. There he becomes acquainted with Balla, De Chirico, Melli and Pampolini, among others, eventually settling down in Milan, where he joins the Equ group, composed of the painters Marussig, Sironi, Ungaretti, Bontempelli, Martini and Sartoris. In 1919 he holds another solo show, and participates in various collective exhibitions, not only in Milan, with artists from Lombardy, but also in Bologna and Trent.

In 1920 he exhibits at the Arte de Milan Gallery, together with Sironi, Carrá, Carpi, De Chirico, Russolo, Funi and Martini, among others, totally identified with the artists that embody the Italian avant–garde movement. It proves to be a successful show: after selling all of his work, he exhibits, for the first time, at the Venice Biennial.

In 1921 Pettoruti continues to exhibit in Italy: ironically, the Buenos Aires National Salon, inaugurated in 1911, rejects one of his paintings. He travels around Germany and Austria, exhibiting once again in Rome in 1922.

In 1923, in Berlin, the famous Der Sturm Gallery exhibits thirty–five of his paintings, while in other halls hang the works of Paul Klee, Zadkine, Marcousis and Archipenko. As a result, Pettoruti is hailed both by German and Italian critics. In Paris, he holds a collective show at the Galliéra Museum.

Through Marinetti, leader of the Futurist movement, he meets the art dealer Léonce Rosenberg in Paris. The latter proposes to manage his career in Europe, advising him not to return to Buenos Aires. However, due to family circumstances, Pettoruti decides to go back home.

During his stay in Paris, he becomes acquainted with Picasso, Juan Gris, Lohte, Gleizes, van Donghen, Zadkine and Tristan Tzara, among many others. In that respect, the book is filled with observations on what was going on in art in Europe in those days, revealing a wide array of anecdotes that reflect both people and circumstances.

When Pettoruti returns to Buenos Aires in 1924, after eleven years of absence, the staff members of the «Martín Fierro» magazine receive him with open arms. The publication considered itself the local exponent of a «new avant–garde sensitivity» prevalent in Europe, interlaced, however, with the defined characteristics of «Criollismo». Both Pettoruti and Xul Solar, the latter returning to the country after twelve years of absence, became paradigms of that movement, and the magazine is more than willing to publish their articles.

In October of that same year, the gallery on Florida Street exhibited eighty–six of Pettoruti´s paintings that had arrived from Europe. The show caused such an upheaval amid local artists, that it provoked disturbances on the streets calling for police intervention. «They fought for my cause, which was also theirs, like true lions», observes Pettoruti in his book. These anecdotes not only evidence the painter´s struggle for greater freedom of expression, but also the painstaking introduction of aesthetic modernity in a society in which, according to the author, «a rhetorical and obsolete Impressionism reigned».

In 1925, Pettoruti exhibits in the halls of the prestigious «Amigos del Arte» association, holding a show a year later in the province of Córdoba. Its governor Ramón J. Cárcano purchases «The Dancers» for the collection of the Córdoba City Museum of Fine Arts. Meanwhile, the artist and his work are relentlessly criticized, revealing an unprecedented aesthetic intolerance. To crown it all, a Futurist show exhibiting counterfeit works is held in Buenos Aires, and Pettoruti, taken unawares, presents two paintings that eventually vanish.

In 1927 he is appointed director of the La Plata Provincial Museum of Fine Arts. He is dismissed at the beginning of 1932, only to resume his post in that same year. He remains at the museum until 1947, year in which political reasons oblige him to renounce after almost twenty years of distinguished labor.

After important shows held in Montevideo (1939) and San Francisco (1941), and a two–year tour exhibiting at different American museums, Pettoruti's reputation strengthens abroad. The artist also exhibits at the Museum of Fine Arts in Santiago de Chile (1950).

In Buenos Aires he holds a retrospective at the «Amigos del Arte» association (1940) and at the Peuser Salon (1948). At the Witcomb Gallery a commemorative exhibition takes place, presenting eighty–six of his paintings (1962). Acclaimed by everyone, his name resonates throughout Europe and the United States. In the 50s he holds shows in Milan, Rome, Paris, Lausanne, Valencia (Venezuela), Washington, London, Florence and Minneapolis, now considered a master of 20th century art.

In 1956, the «Fondo Nacional de las Artes» (National Fund of the Arts) presents to him the prestigious Guggenheim Continental Award of the Americas, and in 1967, the Great Award of Honor. Widely acclaimed, he is appointed Doctor Honoris Causa by the La Plata University, and holds successive shows over the years. In 1968 he travels to Germany, where his work is exhibited in different cities, and in 1969, when in Switzerland, presents a retrospective at the Rath Museum in Geneva.

In 1971 Pettoruti represents Argentina at the XI San Pablo Biennial, with works ranging from 1914 to 1917. Finally, as a result of a liver and kidney trouble, the artist dies in Paris.

In «A Painter before the Mirror», not only does Pettoruti describe his struggle in order to earn recognition, but also discloses his views on aesthetics. His identification with Futurism and Cubism, his understanding of color and light, progressively lead him towards the creation of original abstract art, especially evidenced in the last years of his life. His fundamental concepts on art reflect an existence defined by his beliefs and convictions.

Fermín Fèvre
Buenos Aires, November 2003

A Painter before the mirror

By Emilio Pettoruti

Although Emilio Pettoruti was honored with the First Prize by the National Fund of the Arts (only granted to the most outstanding Argentine artists), rewarded with the Guggenheim Award, fêted and warmly welcomed in France, Italy, Germany and the United States, he continues to be a relatively unheard–of artist in Argentina: his resonant triumphs are received in vast circles with incomprehensible reticence and his human qualities remain in the shadows. Today, this great artist publishes his memoirs spanning six decades of his remarkable life. We are witnesses to his meticulous investigation, to his intense creative activity, to his heroic battles against adversity. With elegance and simplicity, in a pleasant conversational tone, he evokes long years fecund in works of singular perfection, his friendship with notable intellectuals, interspersed with humorous or dramatic episodes. These recollections, at times bitter, at times amiable, often moving, possess a two–fold significance: on the one hand, we behold the intimacy of the painter himself, entirely devoted to the artistic activity with ardent passion and strict discipline, and on the other, the brilliant cultural atmosphere present in both Europe and the United States.

The memoirs of Emilio Pettoruti, that now see the light, comprise his childhood period to the day he took up residence in Paris in 1953. Consequently, nothing or relatively little is said about his most recent and memorable achievements. Rather, his memoirs often delve into moments of great importance in the history of contemporary art. Historians would greatly benefit from them, particularly if interested in the birth, development and decline of Italian Futurism, as they contain substantial detail in that respect. Pettoruti's observations are sharp, and his opinions categorical, of a forthright frankness. Though not all readers might agree with him, all of his reflections are significant, bearing the seal of competence and sincerity. Funny anecdotes, quaint portraits of celebrated artists –Marinetti, Yrurtia, Greta Garbo and so many others– enhance a text throbbing with richness of thought and extraordinary considerations on pictorial technique. While Pettoruti´s writing fascinates, what truly strikes is the deep sensitivity, the cordial and passionate nature, the capacity for loving and the incomparable humanity of one of the greatest masters of Argentine abstraction.

December 1967
Julio E. Payró
From the first edition: Solar Hachette, 1968

A Painter before the Mirror

Part One

Chapter 1

La Plata- First Steps

The story of a life course, viewed through so many years of work and struggle —that haven't yet come to an end nor seem to want to— has no justification other than the hope that there might be those interested in closely following the development, at times universal, at times local, of one aspect of Modern Art. These memoirs also reflect my arduous attempts at combating prejudice, so embedded when it came to accepting novel ways of comprehending art.

It will not be easy to fulfill the task, nor do I know whether I will ever be able to complete it. Let me begin, however, by thanking my parents, Carolina Casaburi and José Pettoruti: my good health and will of iron I owe to them, and these aspects, together with some others, have allowed me to act decisively, enabling me to accomplish most of my goals: all I did was carried out with determination and with the utmost rejection of any influence foreign to my feelings and conscience.

I am indebted to my parents for their tact and exceptional common sense. They did not oppose themselves to my vocation with observations of any kind; much to the contrary, I have always received their full and solicitous support. To my maternal grandfather, José Casaburi, for having contributed, through his affection, temperament and wisdom, to the detection of my inclinations and favoring them in the best of manners.

I lived with him and my beloved grandmother from childhood, my days filled with long conversations and my nights with activity. In effect, I was a sleep–walker, sign, perhaps, of my inability to demonstrate all that I felt during the day; I went to see them, it seems, during my unusual slumber, or headed for the stable to feed my horse some grass and water.

My grandfather —wide–brimmed hat and long frock coat, in the guise of President Bartolomé Mitre —was a slender, proud man, and not as tall as he seemed, with smiling eyes, and rosy cheeks. He stood with his hands folded behind his back, the left foot slightly forward, drumming an inaudible beat. He was extremely kind to me and never gave me a toy, for he knew, watching me grow, that toys did not amuse me; the ones I had been given by my parents piled up in the corner. Instead, he gave me paper and colored pencils, the «toys» that truly made me happy. It was he, when I was an eleven–year old child who had never seen a painting before, nor knew how to use color, who made me paint a large basket of flowers on the top of a patio wall. His words were categorical: «You have to invent the flowers, not copy them».

He had bought colors in powder form and prepared them while explaining how to use them; as far as the choice of color was concerned, that was up to me. He then improvised the scaffold: two stepladders joined by a pair of planks, upon which I had to «work». This is how I achieved my first painting, a wide blue basket, brimming with yellow flowers. This painting accompanied my grandfather until his death, at the age of eighty–six, a few months after my return to the country, in 1924. I think it needless to mention that the large house with a double patio was painted more than once in the course of two decades; it was grandfather who on every occasion closely supervised the work so as to keep the first mural by his grandson undamaged and spotless.

Singular being, this José Casaburi: intelligent, curious, intransigent, always tormented and dissatisfied with everything, who seemed to have concentrated his love on the child that I was and on the adolescent and the man I became. All the while I was gone, from 1913 to 1924, he yearned to see me, and when I stopped sending him so many letters, he turned my portraits against the wall.

Originally from Polla, he and a close friend of his had studied together: both belonged to families that had settled in the city, bonded across generations with ties of friendship stronger than those of blood. Yet life separated them, for his friend entered the seminary, while my grandfather, a staunch liberal, became a passionate Garibaldi partisan. Both of them men of principles, the moment came when one preached from the pulpit and the other in the canteen.

In the small–town atmosphere, my grandfather's exhortations were inappropriate and scandalous. To be a liberal, in those times, especially when surrounded by narrow–minded people, was worse than being an ultra–communist in countries under conservative regimes today. My grandfather found himself in an adverse condition, and that is how his father, assessing the situation, decided to give the couple part of the family inheritance for the unruly youth to «come to his senses» elsewhere.

Married quite young, in the course of time father of six children, José Casaburi set out for Argentina, and landed, by a whim of fate, in the newly-founded city of la Plata, where he acquired lands that soon became valuable. There his children grew and were educated; there his eldest daughter Carolina, my mother, married a generous and kind-hearted young Italian, who after squandering the small fortune he had brought along in order to progress in the sparkling city of Buenos Aires, was able to intelligently rekindle it in La Plata. At the time, José Pettoruti not only owned a productive cigarette factory, but also represented an Italian store in Buenos Aires that imported oil and wine from the distant Peninsula.

It was a prolific and happy marriage, which began its «brood» with me. I was born on October 1, 1892, at a quarter past four, and apparently, my coming into this world was held by my family to be of singular importance. At my grandfather´s request, the umbilical cord barely cut, I was bathed in one the most exquisite wines from Italy, while my father, prodigal by nature and always ready to enjoy himself, declared three days of merriment in a row to properly celebrate the event. As a result, they forgot to record my name at the register office within the time allotted by the law, reason why my birth certificate reads October 3.

Eleven more brothers joined the household in which abundance reigned for a quarter of a century. From a very early age I lived in the home of my grandparents, for they wanted to spare my mother the exhausting attention that my sensitive nature required. For reasons I will never know, if my days were placid, my nights were restless, assailed by terrible dreams that obliged my grandmother to stay at my bedside.

When I returned to my parents´ home, old enough for school, it wasn't in a continuous manner either; often my grandfather came to fetch me under the pretext of going for a horse ride or an outing in his convertible, that he affectionately called a «birloche»[1]. I spent weekends, as well as the short and long holidays, in his company.

Many are the cities I love, either for the beauty they store, the memories they bring to mind or the way they have influenced my life; among them, and in the first place, stands Florence, then Rome, Milan, Munich, Paris, Buenos Aires. Above all there is one I feel deeply attached to, imbued with memories that are very dear to me; it is La Plata, my country´s youngest city, a square urban plant crossed by open diagonals, situated on an endless plain on the banks of the widest river in he world, with its thick and dazzling oxide or silver-colored waters, forever changing hues.

The colors and forms that I observed as a child I took along wherever I went and are still present in my work. This city had squares of incomparable greens and a magnificent eucalyptus forest where my grandfather´s «birloche» or our horses slowed down in order to better inhale the perfume of

---

1 *Birloche*: Type of sled pulled by oxen, used to carry potatoes or timber.

the leaves; dream–like forests later devastated by ugly constructions and the gigantic trees felled.

When I turned fourteen or fifteen my grandfather, though knowing I was strong on mathematics, believed Art, rather than Humanities, to be my vocation, and asked one of my uncles, whom he knew to be on cordial terms with Pío Collivadino´s brother –the former had recently been appointed director of the National Academy of Fine Arts– to try to enroll me at that Academy. My uncle´s reply was not promising: his friend had let him know that my admission would be difficult, for his brother was very strict.

That was lucky for me. Indignant at the answer– and possibly to please my father a little, who preferred to see me pursue my secondary education– my grandfather remembered that there existed an Academy of Fine Arts within the city itself, founded and directed by a painter named Antonio del Nido, a Spanish artist brought to La Plata in order to teach at the «Colegio Nacional», financed by the Provincial government.

I was registered for the evening class, but did not meet the director right away for we had been told he was ill. However, his helpers gave me pictures to copy: I meticulously reproduced mouths, ears, noses, eyes, something I did with exemplary regularity. At one point the director stopped by the classrooms, and that was the only time I saw him. He was a tall and pleasant man, with a pale face framed by a bushy black beard. He kindly stood next to me and stroked my head, asking me whether I truly loved art. Then he told his helper to show him my drawings, ordering him to immediately bring me a model of a plaster foot. He died some days later.

Two young painters, Atilio Boveri and Enrique Blancá, took charge of the Academy. The former was a conceited talker, who behaved and dressed accordingly. He addressed himself to others arrogantly, twirling his walking stick, and with his long hair and tinted glasses, was a well–known figure in the calm and sunny town. The latter was a postal employee, member of a distinguished and musical family –where I had often enjoyed exquisite concerts– who disliked appearing in public, preferring to sit alone on a café corner or exchange views with a good friend rather than walking along 7th Street.

After Professor del Nido´s death, my grandfather went to see Boveri in order to interest him in my progress, and the latter recommended to enroll me in the afternoon classes, for they had longer hours. I tackled still–lifes without a single indication from my new teacher, observing how he spoke to others and corrected their work with a paintbrush, while to me he would say: «Carry on...»

I sweated blood trying to add volume to an orange, and though he noticed and listened to my difficulties, he never revealed to me that if I continued to apply touches of light on the edges, I would never be able to reproduce the corpulence nor the sensation of solidity present in fruit.

However, Boveri took me into account. Friends in common told my mother what he used to say in the intimacy of his home; he had spotted in me no ordinary conditions. He also trusted me –probably relieved by my young age– and was determined to teach me painting according to his methods.

There are beings that do not realize that children grow, soon turning into men that judge. He often rambled on about how to act in life and how he always came out on top. For instance, he insisted on me wearing black glasses like the ones he wore, telling me they «made it easier to observe without others noticing it». One afternoon, with his thumb on his chest discreetly pointing at a student talking to a young girl in a corner, he demonstrated his point: «Watch this. While we speak, without even turning my head, I am observing him».

One of his most shocking confidences concerned his citizenship. He disclosed he had been born in Italy, but that he had needed a grant from the Provincial government in order to study in Europe. He thus declared having been born in a certain provincial village in which, he said, the register office had burned down, his documents disappearing in the blaze. «Only a wizard would find out the truth», was his comment.

At the Academy I had nothing to do and stopped attending it. I stayed a couple of months, during which time no one taught me anything; the little I learned came from drawing the plaster foot over and over again. All things considered, it was better to study at home, and decided to work on my own just as my childhood friend Carlos Scotti was doing, or Humberto Causa, another companion, born in Montevideo. This youth was later awarded a scholarship so as to study painting in Germany. That was his downfall, and after spending a few months in Mallorca, he returned to La Plata, where he literally let himself die of hunger. These friends were intelligent young men, inquisitive, yet without means or motivation, smothered by their environment.

Causa's death plunged me in bitter reflections. It wasn't the first time that someone close died, but it was the first time that I grasped a man could die when he loses his will to live. From that moment onwards, I told myself that one has to think about life and never about death, only way to conquer both.

Once I had made up my mind, I began to skip school often without my parents realizing it; I went to the woods to draw trees and plants, or to the Museum of Natural History, where I stealthily copied the extraordinary birds that were kept there. But my true models, from that time up until my departure to Italy, were «The Skinned Man» by Brancusi and my sister Aída, who with infinite patience, posed hours on end. The oval of her face and the expression of her eyes became so engraved in my memory that my later portraits always had something of her. With respect to the «The Skinned Man», I knew it so well I could draw it from memory, entirely or in parts, foreshortening it most daringly.

At the La Plata Natural Museum, known to scientists all over the world, there functioned a School of Drawing where the painter Martín Malharro had taught for a while. I enrolled in a perspective course in charge of the architect Emilio Coutaret. Before or after this class, provided with a special permit, I walked about the museum halls copying, here and there, stones, minerals and birds, developing a collection worthy of an ornithologist. I also often copied Michelangelo's Moses, and its magnificent plaster reproduction, placed on the landing of the main stairs leading to the second floor, was an imposing sight.

A personal friend of my father's, Coutaret became particularly interested in my studies, and many of the problems related to perspective, so complex they had to be solved in class, he explained to me at his home. I studied with him for a year, and believe I did not disappoint him as a student.

Little by little and due to my own activity —my drawings were frequently exhibited in the shop windows at the «Gath & Chaves» department store, and reviewed by the press— I got involved in La Plata's artistic and intellectual scene, composed mainly of writers and poets. I frequented Benito Lynch, reputedly the surliest of writers. However, I believe he sought the company of people who wouldn't bother him in any way.

He made appointments to see me, or we met by chance at the Jockey Club where he enjoyed taking his baths, and we spoke about many things there. In the evenings we took strolls along the solitary streets or reached the edge of the wood. I think that at the time I was a young acquaintance with whom he felt comfortable, for our true friendship was to develop later, upon my return from Europe, when by age differences no longer matter.

I recall, however, he took me into his confidence. I thus learned that the reason he shunned intellectual circles was due to an interview in which a reporter had made him speak nonsense. Of what nature I ignore; I only know that he paled when remembering the episode.

I saw little of Rafael Alberto Arrieta, who also enjoyed leading a solitary life, and in general we met at the newspaper for which he worked. Our relations were cordial; he was a cultured man, of a refined spirit. I once drew a caricature of him, displayed at my first solo exhibit, in 1911. Upon returning to the country, I saw him even less; he already lived in Buenos Aires, and his life, just like mine, was quite busy. He wrote the preface to the catalogue of one of my exhibitions in La Plata, in 1925.

I visited the poet Almafuerte at his home, a small house with rooms in a row all facing the patio, similar to those existing in the outskirts of the city; today it is situated downtown.[2] This ordinary house had no personality other than the one generated by the negligence of a man living on his own. I can still see him with his worn out canvas sandals walking along the forlorn corridor.

---

2 66 Street, no. 530. Presently a Museum Library.

The frankness of his language was proverbial, and, let me add, frightening. I heard him complain with unspeakable violence against the frequent felling of the eucalyptus in the forest and other offenses perpetrated in our young city. Yet what he was fond of talking about, at least with me, was painting. One fine morning, he said he had been born to be a painter, and told me about a grant that the legislature had refused to award to him.

He believed the destiny of a painter to be much more viable than that of a writer, especially in a country like ours. «Here –he told me– people are uncouth. You portray a handsome head or a beautiful landscape, and the painting is sold. Images are immediately understood. However, you write the «Divine Comedy» and you are nothing but a mangy dog, doomed to starvation».

My regular friends were the poets and writers Rafael de Diego, Alcides Graca, Raúl Oyanaharte, José María Rey, Aníbal González Ocantos, Antonio Gellini among others, and art students or painters, such as Ernesto Riccio, Pepe Fonrouge, Carlos Dillon, Carlos Scotti, Enrique Blancá, and Humberto Causa.

From the end of 1909 to 1911 I became quite active; I drew and painted profusely, contributing to the «La Ciudad» and «Rayos de Sol» magazines, of which I was the artistic director until 1923, when I was replaced by Carlos Scotti. In December 1910 Enrique Blancá and I opened a free studio, where we taught drawing and painting.

Among my paintings of this period, I recall numerous portraits and still–lifes, a large quantity of forest scenes, and depictions of the Pereira estate, which I often visited to paint on Sundays, together with Scotti or Dillon. I often portrayed the cathedral still under construction, its left wing barely roofed, the columns on the ground where they were still being worked on. The whole scene reminded one of antique ruins.

Only two still–lifes remain of all these paintings: both are drapery studies, with an ancient candlestick placed on top. Wistfully, I still recall a basket full of onions lit by sunlight pouring through the window, which I destroyed myself, clumsily, because an angle had failed. My ignorance at the time had me believe that a painting, in order to be perfect, had to be accomplished my way, and this can be seen in the studies, which were all executed in one brush stroke.

In July 1911 I exhibited caricatures in the halls of the «Buenos Aires» newspaper, today no longer in existence. Actually, they were pseudo–caricatures, for I never was a caricaturist, nor was I interested in my models to be well known: I drew my companions, my hairdresser and the salesman on the corner. This exhibition was well received by the press, yet the reason for my comment is to stress the benefic consequences of the show.

I recall that the young La Plata artists met at the «Bazar X». We held conversations there and exchanged views on art. The owner, a friend of ours, gave us loans, and at times, generously exchanged paintings for frames.

Previous trips to Córdoba had kindled in me the desire to paint its surroundings and its beautiful hills. I went there to spend a month in the fall of 1912, reproducing landscapes, as well as portraying local men and women. The days were mostly gray, or rainy, and I barely saw the sun, which didn't help my work much. Upon my return, while preparing a show where I would display these works, I went, as I regularly did, to the House of Deputies to listen to political speeches. On one occasion it was deputy Rodolfo Sarrat's turn to speak, and I became interested in both his discourse and the man himself. I decided to sketch him, later transforming the drawing into a caricature, though I cannot remember whether I sent it to the «La Ciudad» or to the «Rayos de Sol» magazines. Once published, painter Pepe Fonrouge came to see me, telling me that Sarrat had wanted to know, in his capacity as an artist who knew his milieu, who had been the «gentleman» that had caricatured him. He was surprised to learn it had been done by a «kid, a word that some months ago was used by almost all who had reviewed my exhibit and which some months later, as a result of my Córdoba landscapes, was to be repeated in almost all newspapers. I did not look my age, and everyone believed me to be younger.

Sarrat had asked Fonrouge if I deserved to be helped, something that encouraged me. I was then asked to visit him, which I did, and after countless questions, he saw me out in the most amiable of ways, inviting me to have coffee with him at the House someday.

I continued to see him often, almost always at his home, for he quite grew to like me and I him. He became used to my company, and the week I stopped visiting him, for my show [3] «A Month in Córdoba» was about to open, he sent an office boy to find out what had happened to me. Through the same messenger I invited him to the exhibit, to which opening he came.

Of the thirty some paintings exhibited, I only know the fate of one, currently in my possession. I reckon that «Bad day», donated to the «Circle of Journalists», might still belong to them, and that the third one, «Río Primero», donated to the «Circle Ars», (at the time directed by José María Rey), might be in the hands of some of his descendants.

Months went by without Sarrat mentioning the possibility of me being awarded a grant. Nonetheless, he would often ask me very paternally whether I wanted to study in Europe, to which I replied enthusiastically. It was probably in the month of March 1913, though I cannot recall the exact date, when an office boy brought me a card in which Sarrat asked me to see him around ten in the evening.

At the time he was a deputy and president of the Budget Commission. I found him working, alone. We had some coffee, chatted for a while, and

---

[3] The show opened on 8 July 1912, in the hall of the "Buenos Aires" newspaper.

he immersed himself once again in his thick open books, not before handing me a volume he had promised me. I understood something was in the air and waited for the news. The telephone then rang in an adjacent room (I later learned it was the direct line to the manor of the Provincial Governor, Marcelino Ugarte, an imposing residence situated in the woods facing the Museum of Natural History).

When Sarrat returned to his office, I realized, by the sadness on his face, that something unfortunate had happened. He told me: «I wanted to bring you good news tonight, Emilio, yet they are bad. I had hoped for a grant, and the governor asks me to economize …». Again he sat down in front of his big books, pondering, when I heard him triumphantly exclaiming: «That's it! I will award you a grant and still economize!»

When reviewing the province's long list of scholarship holders, all of them in Europe —many of them without any merit other than being spoiled brats— he had stumbled upon abnormal amounts that called his attention. In effect, some scholarships were worth one hundred and fifty pesos, while others were only worth one hundred. He instantly figured that if some students could live on one hundred pesos, so could others who had been awarded one hundred and fifty. Fairly distributing the amount so as to give each scholarship holder one hundred pesos, he awarded me a grant while contenting the governor at the same time.

That same night he came to the conclusion that it wasn't appropriate for so many students to remain unchecked in foreign countries; and since it was impossible to nominate a special inspector due to financial reasons, he managed to get the Government to see to it that its Scholarship Patronage, then directed by Ernesto de la Cárcova, also inspect Provincial grants.

This outstanding measure would not last long. In 1914 the war was declared, and the bridge that had once linked Buenos Aires to Europe narrowed for aspiring painters. At any rate, when I arrived in Florence in August 1913, and met my colleagues, some of them wondered how I had managed to be awarded a grant, considering both the state of the economy and the reduction of their monthly pay, reduced to a third.

I only told one student who had become my friend and who had received a hundred pesos from the very beginning; he thought it amusing and we both laughed madly every time someone complained.

At home, the news of me leaving for Europe was received with both joy and consternation. My mother, taciturn, resigned, began the preparations taking care of the linen (I had the impression a trousseau was being put together), and when our gazes met, her moistened eyes revealed ineffable tenderness. My father, for whom crossing the Atlantic held few secrets, (he often traveled to Europe), disclosed details of my future journey, or spoke to me about the New World.

I personally went to tell my grandfather the news; unfortunately, at the time, my grandmother had already died. He fell silent, tightening the muscles of his face, trying to be brave. He motioned for me to sit down, and disappeared from the room. When he returned, he was carrying a tray with two cups of steaming chocolate with a hint of coffee, named by him «the drink of the Popes», and a dish with pastry.

He was quite unstinting in his advice, much of it heard since I was a child: «You have to eat well but not a lot, and sleep little. Sleep is a question of habit. Great men have been able to achieve wonderful things because they barely rested; it is the lazy who came up with the idea that man needs to sleep eight or ten hours daily. If you don´t make good use of your time, you won´t accomplish anything». And he added: «The main thing, remember, is not to be thrifty when acquiring useful things. You always have to buy quality shoes, regardless of how much they cost, and sleep in good beds. With good shoes you will be able to walk without tiring, and in comfortable beds, your rest will be complete».

I had a slight squint in my left eye, present since childhood; as it didn´t bother me, the operation was postponed. In the course of time, however, my sense of aesthetics overrode any apprehension, and I presented the following dilemma to my parents: either the operation was to be performed before my departure, or carried out in Florence, city of my destination. Considering I would have no–one there to accompany me, I went to see an oculist recommended by our physician. Established in Buenos Aires, he also had a practice in La Plata, where he saw patients three times a week. He recommended the operation and performed it, assisted by our family doctor.

For fifteen days I remained in darkness, my head enveloped in bandages that were taken off a few at a time. When they removed the last one, not only was my left eye poorly aligned, my vision was also badly impaired. The oculist that had operated on me, Dr. Raúl Argañaraz, assured me that with the help of a device that exercised the eye, I would fully recover. Not being an expert, I believed him.

Still convalescent, I was welcomed home by my friends, happy for me I was leaving; all of them dreamt of imitating me and said they envied my luck. Fonrouge arrived home one day with ten kilos of coffee asking me whether I could deliver them to his teacher, Tito Lessi. My father advised me not to, for it was too bulky, and hence I only took with me the cardboard box upon which the brand name was printed so as to fill it up in Florence with the best of coffees. I was also bringing along three letters of introduction: one for Tito Lessi, another for Cesáreo Bernaldo de Quirós and the third one for Arturo Dresco, our consul stationed in the city of the Medici, and who was also a sculptor. The latter was working on a monument dedicated to Columbus, situated today on the promenade named after it. It was thus as light as a feather that I traveled to Europe.

Around that time, a friend who was also an artist, had difficulties in accomplishing a painting he wanted to send to the National Salon, and came to me for advice. It was a true aesthetic conundrum, and as my friend offered no resistance, I painted it all over again. I also put aside one of my works in order to send it to that Salon, which opened in September, after my departure. My small painting was rejected, yet the one that belonged to my friend, accepted.

When the day came to leave, I went to say goodbye to my grandfather, early in the morning. He saw me coming and froze, unable to utter a word. Tense and quiet, he urged me to remember his recommendations, advising me to speak as little as possible to strangers, to listen a lot and above all, to ask questions. His voice faltered and he stopped talking. Overcome with emotion, we hugged each other.

Here and there some handshakes, and I returned home, where my father was waiting for us to leave; the rest was confusion. My older brothers didn't know what to do and some cried; the younger ones gripped my trousers. Overwhelmed, I embraced my mother who, inconsolable, could not release her embrace. My father was astonished to hear me tell him in a whisper not to accompany me: I told him Juancito, a childhood friend would be there.

Someone shouted the train was leaving, and I jumped into the coach. We arrived in Buenos Aires at two in the afternoon. Not far from the North Dock, where the steamboat Città di Torino was moored, I asked the driver to stop in order to see Quiros' exhibition. Then, we headed towards the harbor.

I thus left La Plata, city where I saw the light, and where I spent my childhood and my youth up until August 7, 1913, when I embarked for Italy, land of my parents and forefathers.

Chapter 2

Florence- First Impressions

On the Cittá de Torino, the small, old ship that crossed the ocean with me for the last time, there existed only two classes. My cabin had two beds, and was beautifully situated; I had obtained it thanks to a friend of my father's, who was a travel agent, and did not have to share it until Rio de Janeiro. From the first night, my table companion was an Italian gentleman who also traveled by himself, a very intelligent mathematics professor, so tall he seemed infinite. He visited his country every two years and knew every port like the back of his hand.

While we anchored at the harbor, we explored the quaint town of Santos. With its black people dressed in curious garments, the loud voices, its markets overflowing with color, its strange fruit and its striking and extensive beaches, Brazil dazzled me.

We set sail at nightfall, while a furious storm broke out. Far from being alarmed, the spectacle captivated us. When we went down to the dining room, the tables were already set, each one with its own violinist. Unfortunately everyone abandoned the room, seasick, except for my companion, a fat gentleman and me. At one point everything rolled around the floor. Sailors ran about, helping out other passengers. In Rio de Janeiro the ship anchored for a day. The impression this city made on me is beyond description. Listening to my guide, I couldn't get over my surprise, and felt like someone whose eyes open to a magical world. He took me to the most beautiful and to the most sordid places that clustered high up on the hills: the famous «favelas». Together we walked through a neighborhood situated a few minutes away from the glittering city center, named «Mangue». The name, he told me, was a tribute to a foul–smelling river delimiting our district: there the nights were day and the days were night... It was at sunset that we explored its dilapidated streets, while barely dressed women of every kind and color exhibited themselves in the doorways and behind windows, like dolls in glass cases.

From Rio de Janeiro to Genoa the sea was magnificent and the dusks unforgettable. The beauty of it all led me to reflect upon the vulgarity of the enriched bourgeoisie that traveled with me, fussing about everything, but never having time for contemplation. Whenever I could, I exercised my eyes with the help of the device recommended by the oculist. Remembering my grandfather's advice, I rarely held full–fledged conversations: my sole interlocutor was the mathematician, who in practice was the only one that spoke, for I assailed him with questions. The rest of the time I read books by Ruskin and Taine, given to me by my grandfather at the last minute.

The arrival to Dakar was spectacular. As if by enchantment, an infinite number of slender canoes surrounded the ship while it reached the harbor, filled with gesticulating young black men displaying minuscule loincloths or completely naked. They dove like fish towards the bottom of the sea to pick up the coins that travelers tossed to them. When we disembarked, I realized that a ship's deck is altogether different from dry land; for a while, I found it impossible to regain my sense of balance.

My companion and I then took a car, and the driver offered us a screen to protect us from the blazing sun. As we drove through the city, we saw people walking by, tall and black, who wore vivid earrings and necklaces, their swaying bodies enveloped in flamboyant cloth.

Sailing into the Gulf of Naples on a radiant day was simply fantastic. The distant silhouettes of the Ischia and Procida islands stood out against the sky, with Capri on the right and the Vesuvius facing us. We finally had reached Italian soil, and that changed my mood for the better. We remained there almost all day, and my travel companion showed me many remarkable places.

On September 3 we disembarked in Genoa where I remained for ten days; the first four I spent with my friend, the mathematician. After he left, it was easy to orient myself, and took in every detail of the city. The Chiassone Museum was closed, but I visited the Palazzo Bianco and the Staglieno cemetery. Contrary to what I had heard, I found it uninteresting, though stunningly situated.

From Genoa to Florence I took the train, skirting the shore. How wonderful and varied the landscape for a young man like me, born in the plains! Tunnels succeeded each other without interruption; I opened and closed the window, at times to avoid the smoke and at times to behold the novel scenery. Passengers protested loudly, but I paid no heed to them. Only later did I realize the smoke suffocated them. The Tower of Pisa came into view unexpectedly, but it was just for an instant, lasting as long as a flash of lightning does, or a sudden brightness. I held my breath, like a child from whom something is snatched, stretching my neck in vain to see whether the miracle would repeat itself.

In Florence (it was September 13), I stayed at the Stella d'Italia e San Marco Hotel, on the Via Calzaioli. I had noticed some people furtively gazing at me, and standing in front of the mirror I understood why: my face was as black as that of an African from Dakar. I washed it immediately, and went out for a walk.

Night fell, and I began to explore the city feverishly, craving to find out all of its secrets. It is difficult to describe how much I saw; all I remember is that this mad race, not even interrupted to eat, wore me out, and I collapsed from exhaustion on a chair in a café on Piazza Vittorino Emanuele II [4] well past midnight. It was the Caffé delle Giubbe Rosse, served by four waiters wearing, as the name indicates, light red livery, where I gobbled up a couple of eggs and greedily drank a cup of coffee with milk.

For a few days I did nothing else than visit the city, knowing its topography as well as its artistic and political history, entering churches that lay on my path, without even thinking about museums. The city itself was a work of art, and its monuments and palaces entranced me. My first «formal» visit was Lorenzo the Magnificent's tomb, where I stumbled upon Michelangelo's marble blocks. Never before had I had a close encounter with the masters, and God knows how thrilled I was. My second visit was the Academy, where I had the opportunity to behold «The slaves», achieved by this brilliant Renaissance artist. I was overcome by emotion, for it was the first time in my short life that I stood face to face with the originals. This certainly had nothing in common with the reproductions I had seen in La Plata.

Running as if pursued, I crossed Piazza San Marco and entered the convent named the same way, burning with curiosity to see Beato Angelico's work. His small «Annunziazione» overwhelmed me. What exquisite spirituality! I must have been enraptured, for I lost all notion of time until a guard tapped me on the shoulder telling me they were about to close.

In order to calmly digest everything I had seen, the following day I changed my itinerary. I visited our consul, the sculptor Arturo Dresco. He wasn't in, but I obtained his personal address. He received me very kindly, and trying to be helpful, asked me to accompany him to Pablo Curatella's studio. Besides being a sculptor, Curatella was also his art student. Through him, Dresco suggested, I would meet both Argentine and Latin American artists that met to eat at a neighboring «trattoria».

Curatella greeted me warmly. He was a short and lively young man,

---

[4]   Today, Piazza della Repubblica.

with abundant black hair. At the time, he was finishing a life–size clay sculpture [5]; facing each other, stood a worker and his wife, the latter holding a baby in her arms. After we had exchanged a few words, Curatella offered me a stool: I was elated to find myself in Florence, and in a studio similar to the one of my dreams.

The sculpture, on the whole, did not seem beautiful to me, but it was there and I glanced at it every time it wasn´t hidden from sight by the silhouettes of both teacher and student. At the same time, I was listening to Dresco´s comments. Suddenly, I heard something that seemed hard to believe. Dresco said: «Look, Pablo, it´s getting late for lunch and I don´t see any other solution than to eliminate the man: let´s keep only the woman and the kid» [6].

Curatella had no defect in his youth other than giving out advice, regardless of how people took it. The rest of the time he was pleasant. That noon I went with him to the «trattoria» Dresco had recommended. It was late and many people had already left. He introduced me to the sculptors Nicolás Lamanna, Miguel Angel Negri, and José Luis Zorrilla de San Martín, as well as to the tenor Antonio Codegoni, from Lomas de Zamora [7]. I took to the latter as soon as I met him, and soon we became excellent friends. That same afternoon he asked around and obtained the address of a good oculist. Then, he accompanied me to look for a suitable studio. Fortunately, we found one on 6 Via Degli Artisti, not fifty steps away from the «trattoria»: the owner rented it to me for 450 lire a year. It was exactly what I wanted, and as it wasn´t very large, the cost of the heat could be kept down.

On the following afternoon, Antonio went with me to the oculist´s. I exposed my situation briefly, and after telling him I was a painter, begged him to be honest. After a thorough examination, he assured me my right eye was completely normal, but that the left one had been poorly operated on. He did not think the exercises would in any way bring about a modification, and suggested corrective surgery at some point in the future. For the time being, I had to continue strengthening my eye.

Needless to say his answer terrified me: it was the most horrendous thing he could have told me. Yet, candidly hoping that the practitioner might have made a mistake, I carried on, more determined than ever, with the annoying exercises. Every fifteen days I went to see him; he never asked for a cent, and we became good friends. Then the war broke out, and he disappeared in the turmoil.

Codegoni was of great assistance when I first arrived in Florence. In order for me not to spend a penny on hotels, he found me a room that ended up being even more expensive: at one point, all the garments my mother had lovingly bought me vanished. In dismay, I noticed the landlady´s sons wearing them, but I felt too embarrassed to say anything: their impudence baffled me.

---

5   The photograph of this sculpture, which I had seen at the end of 1913, is published in "Curatella Manes", by Osvaldo Svanascini (Ediciones Culturales Argentinas, 1963), who mistakenly dates it 1911.

6   Curatella complied. In effect, three years later, when walking through the felled forest of La Plata, I ran into the sculpture " Woman with child in arms", seen in Curatella´s studio in Florence.

7   Neighborhood in the City of Buenos Aires.

Endowed with solid common sense, Codegoni also accompanied me to look for second-hand furniture that he helped me paint white. I believed, and still do, that cleanliness never opposed itself to art, and decided to whitewash the walls for them to harmonize with the furniture. I then realized that many of my best friends (de Chirico, Archipenko, Juan Gris, just to name a few), were even tidier than I was. Although not many people are aware of this, hygiene is especially recommended to painters, as dust is particularly damaging to paintings, particularly oils.

Though I could have easily painted the studio gray or any other color, my choice of white was due to some kind of emotional response. All the other studios I had seen were gloomy, and I was always under the impression they were filthy. It was hard to understand how an artist could work in those conditions. However, I soon realized that painting in an entirely white space was a tricky thing, for light reflected off the walls. As months went by, and in spite of my warnings, my idea became popular, especially among some young Italian painters. All in all, the experience proved to be quite useful, in terms of the «recherche de la lumière», as it is now called.

Almost immediately after arriving in Florence, I bought the ten kilos of roasted coffee for professor Tito Lessi. I carried them in the same cardboard bag my father had given me in La Plata. Pleased with his letter and his gift, the professor received me with open arms, and upon my request, showed me some of his work. However, I immediately discarded the idea, suggested by Fonrouge, of becoming his pupil. It wasn't the type of painting that suited my temperament, nor was it my style. Quite by chance, I saw Lessi again on the street, and he thanked me on the occasion for the exquisite coffee I had brought him from America.

Carrying Fonrouge's third letter in my pocket, I went to visit Quirós, who lived in Ponte a Mensola, halfway down the road to Settignano. From where I got off the streetcar up to the large gates of the splendid villa in which the artist lived, it was all uphill. When I arrived I felt slightly weary; the weather in Florence becomes clammy when summer draws to a close. Standing before the imposing entrance, provided with a bell-pull, I hesitated for a while, pondering on whether to meet the artist whose work I had recently seen in Buenos Aires. The mansion and the man intimidated me. Through the gates I saw a large park, and in the background, in between the clearing flanked by trees, Settignano's landscape delineated by a winding river. After meditating for a while, I returned home.

I repeated the visit, with the same results: shyness has always plagued me. The third time, I closed my eyes telling myself that it was «now or never», and pulled as hard as I could on the heavy ring attached to the rope. Bells chimed in the distance and I felt like running away. Yet I couldn't move, feeling I had been nailed to the ground. I saw a maid walking towards the entrance, wearing a starched uniform, and I took a deep breath. I handed her the letter through the gate, and followed her silhouette crowned by a white headdress until she was out of sight. A few moments later, I saw a gentleman approaching, tall, strong, carrying a child in his arms. From afar his face looked odd. When he got nearer, I realized it was a mustache cover. Before reaching the gate, the masked gentleman sermonized me for a long time. I shook like a leaf, and a crimson one at that. He described Argentines as being pedantic and ungrateful, vehemently affirming he had grown tired of their company and that if he received me, it was only because his friend Pepe had recommended me. This much said, we shook hands and he let me in. I later found out he was right in criticizing our compatriots thus. Once in the villa, he introduced his wife to me, a beautiful Roman woman. We talked for a while, and he offered me white vermouth and pastries. Apparently I made a good impression on him, for he invited me back to paint in his park, kindly proposing to guide me in my work. At the time, he was still at work on a family portrait, which he worked on in the open air: his wife, his oldest daughter and the infant I had seen in his arms. I ran into this painting some fifteen years later, at the National Museum of Fine Arts in Rio de Janeiro.

By the end of September, I had already settled in my brand–new studio. Already I had visited many places, starting with the museums. I woke at cockcrow, (just as I had in La Plata, where I used to read) and exercised my eye for an hour. Then, I had breakfast, and either went to visit the Il Duomo cathedral to admire the variations of light shining through the tall stained–glass windows or the Del Carmine church, where only in the early morning can the magnificent Masaccio´s frescoes be seen without any electric light. I also enjoyed going to Santa Croce to see Giotto, or to Settignano or Fiesole with my little paint box, first tool bought in Florence. Other mornings I worked in my studio, especially since I now owned it.

Libraries, galleries, venerable monuments, nothing escaped my fervor and I felt the stones confided in me. Asking, often insisting, my determination opened doors; I had even obtained a special permit to copy paintings in museums. I began doing so at the Hall of Prints and Drawings at the Degli Uffizzi Gallery, where I studied the preparatory drawings the great masters had used to guide themselves in their work. Depending on the seasons, I copied many of them with numb hands, for in those days even important Italian museums lacked heating.

I had no idea what an official academy was like in a country that possessed a high artistic tradition, and reckoned I was better off studying regularly. I headed for the «Reggio Istituto delle Belle Arti», intending to attend classes in a disciplined way. I took the Nude Model examination under the condition to be tested every three months on the rest of the course load, until completion. My admission depended upon the results, and I anxiously awaited the outcome. Fortunately, having copied «The Skinned Man» so often in the past came in handy, and I passed the test successfully. One of the judges, however, not quite satisfied with the result, whispered to his neighbor that he found it «troppo parigino»: too Parisian. Turning towards me he inquired if I had studied in Paris, and upon replying I had been educated in La Plata, he looked at me incredulously.

In the end I was accepted, only to find out I had knocked at the wrong door. The students became angry for I insisted on understanding the teacher's corrections and they made my life miserable: he was regarded as a god, never giving any explanations, and all he modified in charcoal was deemed perfect.

One day, after he had corrected my work, I told this Eternal Father that my nude was not standing straight. Rather, I remarked, she seemed to be stooping. That was too much for the students, horrified by my impertinence. To make matters worse, they called me «the Indian», and I decided to quit the Academy. I felt sorry about one thing, however: I would no longer attend my engraving class, taught by Celestino Celestini. This teacher had grown fond of me, and had made it possible for me to participate in his classes. Relatively young, Celestini wasn't only an excellent teacher, but also a delightful person and a friend to the boys: he gave them advice and in some cases, his own money.

Around that time, I became a member of a sports club. I wished to continue with my boxing practice and take hot baths.

I enrolled at the Reggio Istituto, and wrote a letter to the Budget Inspector, Mr. Ernesto de la Cárcova, who was posted to Paris. I knew I was breaking the rules, since my obligation was, as a grant holder depending on the Buenos Aires Provincial Government, to travel directly to Paris, and await his indications. Though the decision was up to him, I wished with all my might to study in Florence, for it held a special attraction for me. I was drawn to its history, its gentle tranquility, and truly believed there was no better place to study and take care of my eyes. They were my major worry, and ever since, the fear of losing them has always obsessed me.

I wrote him an explanatory letter, informing him about my health and of my reasons to remain in Florence. Since Dresco had told me the inspector was a fine painter and a sensible man, I believed the matter was settled, and I awaited his response with a clear conscience.

Among the first things I did in Florence, was to browse through books likely to interest me. I had been told the Ferrante Gonnelli bookstore, on Via Cavour, was provided with the largest supply of art books. At the same time, it functioned as an art gallery. I bought a book by Ruskin on drawing (it taught me many useful things and recommend it to young painters and in particular to drawers), and discovered a magazine edited in Florence named «Lacerba», dated September 15. The store attendant encouraged me to buy it, telling me I was lucky to find the last two copies, as no more issues would be published.

I browsed through it at home: what an exciting discovery! So much audacity seemed incredible to me. On the front page there was an article written by Papini, whose name at the time was still new to me. In capital letters, it read: «Frankness when Addressing Imbeciles». In brief, it stated that all men were imbeciles, except for the Futurists. Signed by Marinetti, «liberated words» peppered the text, such as «pataplum–pluff», «fraaaaaaah», «plupluflac», and intertwined with the absurd language, beautiful poetic language not always easy to understand. The other texts were a hymn to the new movement, to dynamic pictorial forms. No photographs illustrated the ideas, however, and I was left eager to know what these new forms meant. I bought the following number, dated October 1 –it was published every fortnight– written in the same incisive tone, but this time hinging on vaudeville and politics. It included an off–text drawing by Carrá that I did not grasp: probably, no–one had.

The owner of the library, a young man of about thirty, tall and corpulent, used to my presence or to the avidity of my search (I rummaged through a lot but bought little), suggested two small books containing reproductions that had just arrived from France: one portrayed Van Gogh and the other Gauguin. Noticing I was interested, he mentioned that a brief essay on the French painter Cézanne was being published in Florence. I did´t dare inquire who Cézanne was, lest he´d think I was an ass. Moreover, he said, more books of the same series would be published on Futurist painters and sculptors. He seemed to be quite informed about everything, and I had heard him say he was a friend of Ardengo Soffici´s, who advised him on the selection of art and literature books coming from France. However, he himself gave me the impression of being a man well versed in artistic matters.

Often, I had dinner at the Caffè delle Giubbe with Codegoni, when my day´s work had ended. I enjoyed its atmosphere and the quaint charm lent by the waiters´s old–fashioned attire: short breeches, white socks and buckle shoes. After our meal, I sometimes stopped by a large café, on the Piazza San Gallo, where a rather small group of students and Argentine artists working in Florence gathered around Dresco. Their meetings lasted past midnight: Lamanna, Donis, Curatella, Amadeo and González Roberts were some of the regular members; the names of the others I cannot recall. One night I referred to the «Lacerba» magazine in order to support a certain argument, yet as no one knew of it, I kept quiet.

On the grapevine I heard that the International Academy was in Lungo il Mugnone. A nude model session was held there every morning, from eight to half past twelve. It was inexpensive, the admission was free, and if one so desired, two professors, one academic, the other «modern», corrected the work twice in the week. I enrolled in the class taught by Augusto Giacometti. Sturdy, with enormous feet and hands, his mouth was shaped like a crescent. He had a wide and good-natured face, tapered-off by a pointy red beard, and tiny eyes. He came in on Tuesdays and Fridays, and he corrected my work right away. One day, as I stood next to my easel, he asked me point-blank why I didn't use a spatula. My reply was flippant: «Because I don't like them. The only frescoes I like are those made by masters who do not resort to texture and yet produce quality-work». «Bravo!» he answered, while disconcertedly stroking his chin.

I understood my reaction had been out of line. The truth is that I did not expect his question nor knew the language well enough to use it with more subtlety. At any rate, I regretted having been so harsh with such a pleasant and good man. However, I disliked him as a teacher, for all students painted uniformly, using only spatulas and shrill colors.

Though I felt reluctant to follow his indications, I didn't want to give up this real bargain that working on nudes meant, practically at no cost. I thus decided, since both Giacometti and the students always arrived late, to reach an understanding with the only two students who, just like myself, arrived at 8 in the morning. One was Russian and the other Japanese, and barely spoke Italian. With our limited vocabulary and through signs, we agreed to work together from 8 to 10 in the morning, time at which the first students turned up. For a small amount of money, a model would show us a new pose every morning, different from the one studied every week in class. Imperceptibly, fall settled. It was cold, and still somewhat dark when we reached the Lungo il Mugnone studio, but nothing discouraged us.

Domingo Candia, an artist originally from Rosario [8], had his studio in the other wing of the same building. His teacher was the mediocre painter Giovanni Costetti, who worked in the studio facing his. I visited Candia's studio only once, often meeting him quite by chance in Florence, together with his brother. Our friendship developed much later, in Buenos Aires, upon his first return to the country.

Augusto Giacometti, an artist especially versed in decorative arts, occupied a studio on 6 Via degli Artisti. We all used the same entrance, a large iron door, and the concierge we had in common, a woman named Beppa, had a splendid collection of works given to her by artists. Almost immediately, to the left, stood my studio, totally isolated and surrounded by a garden. To the right, in a vast two-storied building —each floor had a large corridor that allowed access to the studios— stood the one belonging to a Swiss painter. Being neighbors, we could not help but meet, and soon grew to like each other.

Giacometti was twice as old as me, and he was a connoisseur of primitive art. We often chatted, for I was attracted to his great his kindness. In spite of his age, deep down he was an innocent child, easily tricked. However,

---

8   City in the Province of Santa Fe.

he was careful in choosing his acquaintances. At first, I believed that if he so generously offered me his friendship, it was because he appreciated youthful company. Once, I invited him to join all the young painters for a bite at the «trattoria» on the corner of Via degli Artisti and Masacchio, instead of going to Paoli´s. He replied the restaurant was too close by, and that living in such a confined space, he needed to exercise his legs. «Jogging whets my appetite», he said smiling, and added: «and on the way back it helps me digest».He draped his cloak around his body and nearing his mouth to my ear as if to arouse my gastric juices, he opened up his heart: «At Paoli´s one can eat great «faggioli»: they´re delicious». He must have been persuasive, for at times I ended up imitating him.

All in all, I must have visited Quirós five times, to paint in his park. Among other reasons, I stopped going for it was a long way to Ponte a Mensola. The second time we met I brought him, upon request, a few sketches of Florence. He studied them attentively, only to say: «You are wasting your time in this city; you must leave for Paris immediately».

His advice was of no avail, for Florence filled me with such enthusiasm, that his words lost all meaning. I respected him, and this admiration remained unchanged over the years. I believe he felt the same way, in spite of our diametrically opposed temperaments and our very different conceptions of art. Though he was already a consummate painter when I first met him, and despite the fact that he greatly intimidated me in the beginning, my anxiety dwindled as soon as I discovered the man beneath it all.

That day, Quirós showed me work he had accomplished in the summer, and we held our first —and last— discussion on art. The argument began when he handed me a sketch he intended to use as the basis for a large historical painting. I objected that his approach contradicted that of the preparatory works I studied and copied with so much care in the Hall of Prints. Quirós was taken aback: I still recall the startled look in his eyes. «I don´t understand why I don´t ask you to leave», he mumbled, referring to my impudence.

In Florence his arrogant silhouette was familiar. They called him «il bel pittore», the handsome painter. On one occasion, as I was walking along Via Calzaioli towards Piazza della Signoria, I witnessed the most incredible sight: a gentleman, canvas in hand (or rather, his drape, for it measured no less than two meters long by two meters wide), stood holding a palette and brushes. A curious crowd of all ages recoiled whenever the painter stepped back to contemplate his work from a distance, only to draw closer like a tide when he neared his canvas, paintbrush extended like a foil. It was Quirós, abandoning himself to his task, and probably unaware of the commotion he was causing.

De la Cárcova did not take long to reply. His letter arrived one morning, dry and peremptory: I had to leave for Paris and place myself under his orders. The unexpected request upset my day. I wrote back at once, more explicitly, if that had been possible, than the last time. In my letter I explained I was in the hands of a skilled specialist who possibly saw the need of another operation. Furthermore, and among other things, I told him I was working well and a great deal, and that Florence quite suited me.

I wrote my mother a letter every week, not failing her once in the eleven years my absence lasted. Perhaps I should say I wrote to her a little bit every day, the way one keeps a diary, telling her all I had seen, perceived, suffered or enjoyed. Knowing she understood how much I loved Florence, a safer city in a mother's eyes than Paris, so full of perilous temptations, I justified my insubordination in advance. Only after getting everything off my chest did my peace of mind return, and I headed towards the post office.

At the hall of Prints, I began by copying Bassano: a head belonging to his «Family Portrait», a few hands and fragments of fabric. I believed it useless to copy the entire painting, the way other students did, for I had neither time nor patience to reproduce a painting for months on end. Besides, I believed that copying part of it –without its patina– led to the same result. In this case, my intention was to study the Venetians' technique.

Since Bassano had been Tiziano's disciple, and Tiziano, Giorgione's, I thought their most skilled followers would reveal their technique. A great artist is rarely methodical while executing his work, and it this ineffable quality that copiers have to face. Disciples, on the other hand, adjust themselves to this method. This explains the large production achieved by painters living from their art, for they knew how to begin a painting and when to finish it. If the disciple was talented, and the case is not rare, his painting revealed his talent, and if he wasn't, his art always possessed the dignity or the poise of the well–accomplished work. All museums in Europe are full of this type of painting, some of them admirable, achieved at times by unknown authors who follow either their masters or their school.

I think a sixth sense guided and taught me these things, for I had no teacher. This holds true in my life as well: my intuition never led me astray.

I hardly rested, but did not mind because the work was varied. Each activity provided a respite from the previous one, and I only wished to learn other useful things in order to support myself one day without having to give up the arts: too often had I seen the squalor in which many painters lived, limiting their actions to easel painting. As far as my profession was concerned, there was no duty I disdained, as long as it would allow me to earn my living. I believed and still do that the poetry the artist carries within can express itself regardless of whether he decorates a wall, a floor or builds a chimney. Only renowned artists sold their paintings, and I wondered if someday I would make a name for myself.

Finding myself at the Baptistery one morning, where Ghiberti's famous Door of Paradise can be seen, I noticed an artisan restoring the mosaics that decorated the floor. This prompted me to ask him whether he had a studio, for there was something I had in mind, but he replied he was following orders and gave me the address of the workshop that had engaged him.

I went to see the owner who also happened to be a master craftsman, and offered him part of my afternoons for any kind of work that had to be done in his studio. In return, they would reveal the secrets of their trade. The man looked at me suspiciously, but after telling him I was a student interested in learning about mosaics –not in schools, I emphasized, where this technique was poorly taught, but with artisans who transmitted this tradition from father to son– he immediately understood and accepted my proposal. I went to his workshop every day from 1.30 to 4.30 in the afternoon, from mid–October to the first days of November. I learned so much, that I adopted the system, and eventually presented myself to the painter and decorator Galileo Chini, a rather mediocre artist, but quite knowledgeable about the fresco technique, who also accepted my services.

Exchanging time for instruction, in the course of the months I learned the ropes of many trades: frescoes, mosaics, and stained glass, as well as the rudiments of their technique and manufacture. I reflected upon the fact that I would have had to attend a technical school for a number of years in order to learn as much as I had in such a short time.

My new arguments did not convince my patron, Ernesto de la Cárcova. In a brief letter, this time not signed by him but by his secretary, I was told to head immediately towards the French capital, within the stipulated period. This lack of understanding on the part of the bureaucracy filled me rage. I replied at once that I felt quite comfortable in Florence, and that consequently I would not be traveling to Paris. That night, considering my rash behavior, I weighed the gravity of the situation, and realized it could cost me the grant. Once it expired, would they stop sending me money? Though my anxiety had worn me out, I was unable to fall asleep. I thought about Rodolfo Serrat, and his almost fatherly love, and told myself my attitude was bound to upset him. To make matters worse, he was the only person who could intercede, if that proved to be necessary. I jumped out of bed and wrote him a long letter, telling him all that had taken place, without concealing any detail of my violent reaction and apologizing for it. I also told him about the intensity of my work in Florence, my apprehension with regard to my eyes, and the inspector's lack of interest in the face of it all. At the time, Sarrat was a Secretary of State and the grants depended on his department. I posted my letter the following day, and resigned myself to waiting, knowing that it would not reach La Plata before twenty–five days.

No one knew about my worries in the long days that followed. Fortunately for me, I had so much work that it required my constant attention, preventing me from drifting towards my personal problems. I have always disliked paying attention to my troubles, and never have I deemed it necessary to share them.

I usually got together with the other grant holders at the «trattoria», where trivial conversations were held in between bites. Sporadically, I saw them at the Café on the Piazza della Libertà, and listened to them speak with complacency about their work. One had just created a group sculpture, the other boasted about having painted three pictures in a month. «And you, Pettoruti, what is it you do?» one of the students once asked, provocatively. Shrugging, I replied I had done nothing, and as he insisted, I quietly observed, «Well, what can I say? I visit museums, churches, libraries; I go to galleries, bookstores; I observe paintings, illustrations; I talk to people. This is how I spend my life, and in the mornings, I try to achieve something, but it takes a lot of work».

Actually, I didn´t want to hear any confidences, and wasn´t keen on establishing relationships that would make me lose my precious time, for one always has to devote some attention to them. I was convinced that an artist, in order to improve himself, has to tackle it all, without limiting himself to what he likes best, and I had arrived to Florence, alas, knowing practically nothing.

One day Giacometti came to my studio announcing that he would teach a night class after dinner on ornamental composition at the academy in Lungo il Mugnone, based on the method introduced by the Frenchman Gasset. I signed up and told Curatella and Lamanna, who did the same. The course began with approximately thirty students, who jotted down all Giacometti wrote on the blackboard. After our second or third class he asked us to solve certain problems at home, yet after he had corrected the tasks, many students quitted, including Curatella and Lamanna. Soon, there remained only five or six left. Almost at the end of the month, Curatella announced the course had finished. It had lasted exactly four weeks, and I had attended eight classes, finding them to be of great help in my composition studies, which I undertook later on my own.

It is through the observation of nature, its plants, its animals, and the infinite prodigies it encloses –skies laden with oddly shaped clouds, powerful and alive– that one learns composition. One must always keep, however, a spiritual and physical discipline. Harmony is present in all our eyes can behold; it is a question of discovering it, analyzing it with all of our determination, for without study there is no practice, and without practice beauty cannot be interpreted, no matter how deeply we experience it.

I soon became friendly with Ferrante Gonnelli, an intelligent, enthusiastic and good man. He wished to visit my studio, something that encouraged me deeply, for he had taste and great intuition. It was through him and the third copy of the Lacerba magazine bought in his bookstore, that I was introduced to this particular art called «Futurism». The copy included a drawing by Boccioni and represented a cyclist. I realized this novel and dynamic way of understanding form did not leave me indifferent.

Some time later, I learned from Gonnelli that the Futurists were holding a show at his gallery, funded by the «Lacerba» magazine, and of course, I decided to go. Concurrently, «La Voce», an important Florentine literary magazine, published a monograph on Cézanne, and I felt compelled to buy it. The monograph did not include any text, only several black and white illustrations. Seen on paper, Cézanne's paintings transmitted solidity, ampleness: in effect, the forms expanded, but at the same time the works seemed incomplete, as if unfinished. Tradition was not overlooked, however, and I found his paintings to be superior to those of Van Gogh and Gauguin, who had definitely left convention behind.

These impressions did not vary substantially when I finally found myself face to face with the work of these two painters, but they did in Cézanne's case. I realized his first paintings were perfectly finished, and they opened up my understanding of modern works. So much so, that my incipient monograph collection grew, and Manet, Monet, Renoir, Douanier Rousseau and other painters were readily incorporated.

Fall had drawn on and Quirós was leaving Florence to establish himself in Majorca. He had bought an abandoned church and he adapted it to his needs: he assured me it was paradise. Before his departure, he organized a farewell party for his friends at his Ponte a Mensola villa. It was a splendid day and the table had been set in the open air. All the guests were Argentine, yet I only knew Amadeo. The latter introduced me, among other people, to the sculptor Luis Falcini, a petulant youth if I ever saw one. He inquired what I was doing in Florence and invited me to his Porta Romana studio.

The day we met, I noticed he was working on a sculpture, but cannot recollect which. However, I do remember he showed me some folders packed with drawings and said: «This is for you to see how they study in Paris. The drawings in this folder took me one minute to achieve, those in that one over there, two and those in the third folder, a quarter of an hour. Believe me: it's great exercise». I then showed him some sketches I had made in La Plata based on Brancusi's «The Skinned Man». Instead of only working with pencil, something Falcini had done and which conveyed a certain monotony, I had also used charcoal, as well as a pen and brush. I did not see my interlocutor again for another ten years.

One afternoon, before the grant expired, I found a telegram upon my arrival home. It came from Serrat and read: «Do not leave Florence. Take care of your eyes. Work if you can. Don't worry about your grant». As can be imagined, my satisfaction and relief were indescribable.

Chapter 3
The "Lacerba" Futurist exhibition

On November 30, 1913, a singular art show opened in Florence, at 48 Via Cavour, named the «Lacerba Futurist Exhibition». I went there that same afternoon, but such pandemonium reigned that I decided to return the following day. There still was a crowd, yet I was able to see the show, and the experience had a profound effect on me. It was the first time in my life that I was exposed to avant–garde work, for La Plata was a city that revered romanticism, and where the writer Vargas Vila and the likes of him were worshipped.

I left the exhibition with a splitting headache and experienced a spiritual turmoil difficult to explain. It was as though everything were spinning inside. I had just turned 21, and my artistic training was practically non–existing –fortunately, in retrospect–. Granted, I loved the classics, yet I had no particular preference, and there was something about the Moderns that spoke with the voice of logic.

I mused upon the fact that if those older artists, more knowledgeable than I about artistic problems, sought to impart another sense and shape to form, their argument could not but be valid. It was the rest of the world that wasn´t ready to appreciate such painting.

The Futurist group had displayed their manifestos, provocative but intelligent, at the entrance of the show, which they presented as being «the most important, the most modern, the most novel ever held in this medieval town». Moreover, the front page of «Le Figaro» newspaper, dated February 20, 1909, ran a story on the «First Futurist Manifesto», signed only by Marinetti. Other cuttings revealed the importance and the activities of the group, and I arrived at the conclusion that if Giacomo Balla, who was 42 years old and famous in

Rome for his paintings and portraits, shared the ideals of a young poet deemed mad, he certainly had a reason to do so.

These thoughts so preoccupied me that I was unable to fall asleep. At the time I was copying a Beato Angelico at the Hall of Prints, sufficient proof to demonstrate how removed I was from all that was novel in art. Fortunately, I was quite young when I became exposed to novel concepts: it is an age in which contradictory realities are rapidly understood, learned and assimilated.

I returned to the exhibition the following day, and didn´t miss one of the forty–seven days the show lasted.

One afternoon, as I was talking to Gonnelli about exciting art–related topics, a group of «troublemakers» burst into the gallery. It was the Futurist group, led by Marinetti and backed up by other key figures: Boccioni, Carrà, and Russolo. Both Balla, who had not left Rome, and Severini, who lived in Paris since 1906, participated from afar, contributing their work to the cause. Noticing my curiosity, Gonnelli introduced them to me.

Before long, Marinetti revealed his enthusiastic and vivacious character. Always keenly on the lookout for new promises to join his movement, he inquired right away whether I was a Futurist. Taken aback, I uneasily replied I was a student, but Gonnelli, butting in the conversation, told him he had seen my work and that I was truly an avant–garde artist. Marinetti immediately wished to visit my studio, and in effect, he whizzed in one afternoon, together with four or five more people, all of them, I believe, belonging to the world of letters. The only name I recollect is that of Aldo Palazzeschi, a fine Florentine poet that lived in the city and whom I befriended.

What I showed Marinetti and the others were studies, more or less successfully accomplished: they could not be taken for paintings, for I was fully conscious I was a raw beginner. But Marinetti, an excellent and impassioned writer who did not have the faintest idea about fine arts declared I was a Futurist, and adopted me as a member.

That same night we all went to the Delle Giubbe Rosse café, meeting place of all the Florentine avant–garde and consequently, of the intellectual youth, both Italian and foreign. The group was also composed of writers and artists who were not Futurists, but who stood out either because of quality, insubordination or zeal. Old friends like Achille Lega, Ottone Rosai, and Tulio Garbari fraternized with Papini, Soffici or Palazzeschi, and it was through these meetings that I became initiated into the intellectual circles of both Italy and the world.

On December 12, I attended the Great Futurist Soirée, held at the Verdi Theatre. I don´t believe having ever witnessed such an uproar, nor seen anything that absurd: on the stage were eight men desperately attempting to make themselves heard in a theatre teeming with people of all ages and belonging to different social classes. Students, workers, professors, officials, bourgeois, aristocrats, perfectly level–headed when working at the office or resting at home, had become a mad pack of dogs.

Everyone was standing, hurling abuse from the first balconies, boxes or stalls. They whistled and uttered angry curses, while tomatoes, cabbage, eggs and cooked noodles were flung onto the stage with the ferocity of a machine gun´s rattle. It was chaos. I watched the mouths of the orators move with boiling rage, yet could not hear a single word they were saying.

When everything was over, and no one had even tried to understand what these men believed in, the crowd went out into the street, scattering amid screams, gesticulations and comments. That night I even forgot to visit my new acquaintances: I was devastated. Human bestiality manifesting itself collectively has always made me miserable and my grief lingered for days on end.

Almost the entire Futurist group left Florence after the singular soirée. Only once, in 1915, did I see Puccini again, and he died in 1916. I met Balla a year and a half later in Rome and we became excellent friends. Rissole and Carr I ran into in Milan, but only became friendly with the latter. Aldo Palazzeschi, Ardengo Soffici, and Giovani Papini remained in Florence, together with Lega, Rosai, and Garbari. None of us lost touch with each other, regularly meeting either at the Giubbe Rosse, or at our respective studios.

A «physical and spiritual» review of the battle held at the Verdi Theatre came out in the «Lacerba» magazine on December15, review that I translate and copy for I believe the story has to be divulged as accurately as possible, and with precise dates:

Great Futurist Soirée

Succinct (physical and spiritual) review of the battle

On one hand (on stage)
2 poets (Marinetti, Cangiullo)
3 painters (Boccioni, Carrà, Soffici)

1 anti-philosopher (Papini)
1 inmoralist (Tavolato)
1 occasional volunteer (Scarpelli)

On **the other hand** (in the auditorium)
5000 enemies:
Clerics (on behalf of morality and re ligion)
The bourgeois (in defense of banalities)
Students (in defense of Manzoni, spurred on by their professors)
Liberals (to avenge their president, etc…)
Aristocrats (ruder than others)
Virtuists (Christians (?), abusive and vengeful)
Journalists (indifferent, ironic)
Policemen (inactive)
Boors (hired)

Arms: Courage, Poise, Confidence, New Ideas, Necessary insults, Sound advice, Original poetry.	**Arms:** Potatoes, carrots, onions, anchovies, sardines, eggs, polenta, spittle, apples, chestnuts, pastasciutta, electric lamps, beans, chickpeas, small trumpets, car horns, bones, rattles, keys, etc…
State of Mind: Disgust at the reigning stupidity Aesthetic satisfaction derived from the infuriated opponents' magnificent spectacle Thrill at feeling superior	**State of Mind:** Urge to be rowdy, Incontrollable rudeness, Vulgarity on the verge of impunity, Feelings of hate and resentment, Furious imbecility, Unbridled malice, The weak taking their frustration out on the strong, Fear of allowing others to speak. Revenge against old and new blows. Asinine and bovine attitudes. Stupidity, Piggishness.
Allies: Groups of friends and supporters (youths, workers) in two or three boxes and in the orchestra, A lot of noise and little energy, Din made in order to cover up confusion, Disorganization, Flowers hurled at people, Applause without continuity, Punches wanted, Ousting offensive people from the boxes.	**Allies:** criminals outside and guards inside.
Casualties: One wounded (Marinetti).	**Casualties:** Many wounded in the orchestra by their box companions).
Results: Irritation on the part of the public that wanted to listen, Futurism becomes more popular, Many citizens feeling belatedly ashamed, Spectators rebuked by the press for their malice. Satisfaction felt by the Futurists.	**Results:** Boredom, Weariness, Costs, Screams, Spectators insulting each other Massive flight, (on the way out, the Futurists did not find a single enemy, not even in the city or cafés)

Chapter 4

The Study of New Forms

While I record the memories of an epoch on tape, perhaps to be published some day, I realize that the young man I was in the years described, could easily have drifted towards the easy life and ended up, like other avant–garde members, in the most ordinary *Pompiérisme*, rejecting all they had done and sustained in their conversations, manifestos and even books.

It wasn´t easy, contrary to what it might seem, to resist the persuasive eloquence displayed by Marinetti when addressing himself to the youths; he spoke well, his arguments were seductive and his personality almost irresistible. But I have always believed that imposing oneself without merit is akin to emerging victorious without glory. True, I was looking for a modern art, but as solid as the one practiced by the artists I most admired: the Quattrocentists. I had noticed, without exception, that they reduced the elements of their painting to clear and legible expressions.

More than once, upon contemplating their works, I told myself that, had they been born in our century, they would have been avant–garde artists. It is likely they were considered as such in their time, just as Carpaccio, Velázquez and Rembrandt were in theirs. After having studied the Italian Renaissance artists in depth, one becomes conscious of the numerous deformations existing in the composition as a whole, as well as in the details; deformations that few people notice and which all things considered do not exist, for they obey a certain rhythm, which is the general rhythm of the painting.

These deformations, that many attribute to a lack of perspective and other laws, I felt deliberately portrayed an epoch, just as Cubists and Futurists, when representing the object from various angles, sought to understand theirs. Perspective and mathematics were certainly not unknown in the century of Paolo Uccello.

The «Lacerba Futurist Exhibition» taught me a great deal, in the sense that it forced me to reflect on a thousand things that ordinarily would not have moved me. In the first place, it compelled me to work in different ways so as to «find myself», golden dream, I believe, of every young artist. In order to avail myself of more time, I stopped making the habitual copies, though I still recognized their effectiveness. Still today, I feel they were extremely useful, in terms of technique and coloring.

Freed from my activities at the museum, I began to work on something that really interested me. What obsessed me the most was the idea of movement: day after day I visited the remarkable exhibition with the hope of grasping the idea of movement, something that still escaped me. I finally discovered that it was achieved by repeatedly drawing the profile of a leg, or the wheel of a bicycle, the whole process reminiscent of a cinematographic sequence.

I discussed this point with Rosai, and later with Balla, in Rome. Rosai, without being a Futurist himself, defended the movement, and tried his hand at it for a short while: as far as the concept of movement was concerned, he replied that in cinema the figures engaged in movement, while in painting, they remained static. Needless to say his simplistic explanation did not satisfy me, but I wasn't ready at the time to refute such arduous topics. I preferred to tackle them in practice and completed many drawings, searching for movement and velocity the way I conceived it. It was only in the middle of the year 1914, after many attempts and a lot of tearing up, that I managed to produce work that eased my mind somewhat. However, it did not have much in common with what the Futurists were doing, and only Balla, among the painters of the group, worked in the same direction, even though I saw his works only much later.

Today, when looking at some of my first paintings, people say they are abstract, and certainly they are, though they weren't meant to be. The word «abstraction» itself was not used at the time to define a certain art movement. What I intended to express was an interaction that could not be conveyed through known forms, resorting to the subterfuge of superimposed lines.

While working on these exercises I did not lose sight of others, and attempted to increase my knowledge through all possible means. When tackling composition, for instance, I first painted the objects the way we see them, recreating them later with new forms and different arrangements. They were the same objects, natural in one painting and recomposed in the following, with the same hues, yet the light, the atmosphere I had managed to impart to the first, were absent in the others. Logic told me that if natural light suited forms in nature, that same light would seem artificial when applied to invented forms. It was therefore necessary to invent autonomous light that matched the autonomous object: the light of the invented painting.

My search began thus: I placed a white paper in the sun, that is to say, beneath a perfectly even light; upon the white paper, a cube or rectangle, fully black, and another, intensely red, then a blue element and a yellow, attempting to capture the luminous color from each one of these objects, always considering the original hue conveyed by sunlight. Hence, by incorporating light in the non–objective composition I had created, all the colors, though maintaining their independence, yielded to the same hue, to the same harmony. Think about the instruments in an orchestra, tuned to a single note. They all maintain their voice, but in keeping with the harmony this note establishes. In painting, this is called *tone*.

This modulation of colors playing within a same tone was what I admired, without even being conscious of it, in the great paintings throughout history; but it was the works by the Futurists, which, through contrast, revealed the essence of the question to me. In these paintings, excepting those that were predominantly gray, I clearly realized that though the drawing was carefully composed, the colors, bearing no relation between each other, existed on their own. People were not able to understand, as is often the case today, that when the artist strays from nature, he must necessarily sublimate the expressive means.

Some months later, after achieving some studies on color, seeking the light of the painting, I set my easel once more at the Hall of Prints, in front of another Beato Angelico painting. What I intended to do this time around was not to copy the picture or some of its details, but to study color, its associations and harmonies through its quantities. For example, the painting that hung in front of me enclosed two parts of vibrant light blue (the sky), two parts of black (dispersed), four parts of white (distributed among various points), eight parts of bluish grays, three parts of green, two of gold, and one of pale red.

I took the smallest proportion of color as I possibly could, and distributed it on my cardboard, starting off by centering the blue; then, I disposed the other colors in accordance with my taste, their quantities broken up or not. I used that same study when at the studio to perform other drawings, focusing on composition or color, respecting at all times the proportions of the latter.

The result was paintings that today would be called abstract. Through these studies, I greatly refined my taste and sense of composition, especially that of coloring. However, the works I produced from then onwards greatly differed from those studies. *Tachisme*, so popular in the 50s, would have borne a resemblance to them if it had possessed order; I mean, the mental elaboration that all work requires, particularly the abstract one. Giacometti kept many of those paintings, as did other friends and artists.

The funny side of the matter lies in the commotion my system caused among the copiers at the Hall of Prints and the public of 1914. They watched me studying a painting for hours, only to end up not copying anything at all. In general, the first few minutes they kept an intrigued silence; then, they smiled and walked away, whispering, probably imagining I was a Futurist. For a while, in Florence and in the whole of Italy, the term «Futurist» designated the mad.

I stopped by the Piazza della Libertà café one night, where Dresco and his group always met. I recall I had just seen a Futurist show, for when I brought up the topic in conversation, I was amazed to find out that none of the artists and art students present even knew what this group represented.

Later, when Futurism imposed itself as an important artistic movement of our century, more than one bragged about having experienced and participated in the glorious event. There even were those who affirmed and wrote down, so as to demonstrate their degree of perspicacity or precocious inclination towards all things modern, having seen a Futurist Sculpture Exhibition in Florence in 1911, with works by Carrà, Russolo, and Balla. This truly is quite an exaggerated fantasy, for no Futurist sculpture show was ever held in Italy nor in any other part of the world in 1911, much less with works by the aforementioned artists.

In those days, in Rome, Balla made wooden painted toys that he sold for a few lire, so as to earn his living. Boccioni was the only one among the Futurists that sculpted, and quite well, but he didn´t produce any sculptures before 1912, year in which the Technical Manifesto of Futurist Sculpture, written and signed by him, was published. The document laid the foundations of a new conception of sculpture that only he was able to sustain, for too brief a time. In March 1914, a show displaying work by Umberto Boccioni was held at the Gonelli gallery, and it so thrilled me, that I decided to tackle this art myself, albeit temporarily.

I consider Boccioni to be a sculptor only: his works as a painter, already mediocre when Futurism was popular, degenerated into an ill–digested «*Cézannism*», expressed with sharp colors. Few people are aware these paintings exist, for as far I know, they were never exhibited. I saw them in Milan, at the home of his sister, towards 1917 or 1918, when Boccioni had already passed away. As the apartment she lived in was small and crowded, she was selling some paintings and tools left by the artist; I bought her a press.

In his short life, Umberto Boccioni created a small but substantial series of sculptures that represents the Futurists at their best. His «Walking man» [9] alone suffices to do credit to his name and justify this movement.

---

9   "Forme uniche della continuità nello spazio", 1913

Chapter 5

Nella

Recalling the Futurist exhibition moves me. It was there, in effect, some days before it closed, that I met Nella, a young Florentine woman studying Humanities.

There were very few people in the halls at that early hour, and yet, moving back to better appreciate a painting, I bumped into someone. When I turned round to apologize, I saw a young woman I had often noticed at the show, and whose face and figure were typically Florentine: her features were identical to those seen in paintings at the museums.

Smilingly, she forgave my clumsiness, and we both started a conversation that would last over ten years. We first spoke about the paintings on show, later, about a thousand other topics. She was a refined girl, sensitive, polite, eager to learn, and because she was well-read, she taught me a great deal. Together we attended a course on Florentine architecture, then, another on Dante Allighieri and yet another on the history of Florence, in the days of the Medici. With her, I practiced my Italian, which I got to speak as fluently as I did Spanish. On the other hand, she told me I helped her correct certain Florentine idioms that sneaked in her conversation without her realizing it.

At times she accompanied me to churches and museums, and when I suggested getting up early in order to better see Masaccio's frescoes at the Del Carmine church, she readily accepted. On the days we did not meet, she would inform me, either personally or through messages, of all that went on in Florence with regard to music or culture; they were all opportunities to be together, nourish the spirit and exchange impressions. We could talk about everything, for we shared the same taste and because, just as I did, she was an avid learner. We used to walk up to Piazzale Michelangelo, or along the

Arno River, and more than once our steps led us to the distant Le Cascine Park. For these walks (she had adopted my grandfather's ideas), she used comfortable low-heeled shoes.

At my suggestion she now dressed in a more sporty way, prompting her family to call her «l'Americana», completely unaware that the young man she was friendly with came from a South American country.

I liked her independent attitude with respect to her family, and her discreet reserve: she never asked any questions or interfered in my private life, nor did she request more time than I could give her. This is perhaps why our friendship lasted for such a long time.

As I tell you these things, I recall a moving episode, something so unexpected it engraved itself forever in my memory. On a wintry dawn (it was January 14, on the eve of the Futurist exhibition's formal closing), as I drew the curtains of my bedroom windows that gave on to the garden, I noticed everything was white. I panicked, for I thought I had gone blind. Once I had calmed down, however, I perceived some black figures amid the whiteness and let out a scream of joy. For the first time in my life, I was seeing snow.

I got dressed and in spite of the cold went out into the garden to touch it with my hands, the way I would see some children do a few hours later in the squares. After lunch, Amadeo, Codegoni and I took the streetcar on the corner and went to Fiesole to behold Florence from atop: it was an extraordinary sight, for everything was sparkling like diamonds.

One morning around eleven o'clock –I had just retuned from the Lungo il Mugnone Academy, where I was still drawing nudes with my Russian and Japanese companions– someone rang my studio's doorbell. As I opened the door, I saw a pleasant-looking gentleman, of medium height, dressed in elegant clothes. He inquired whether a painter named Pettoruti lived there, to which I replied: «It's me, sir.» Holding out his hand, the gentleman then said: «Pleased to meet you, my name is Ernesto de la Cárcova». I almost had a fit. Unable to utter a word, I let him in, and he walked straight through the first room, which I used as a wardrobe, bedroom, office and library, while discretely looking about. Finally he planted himself in the center of the studio, as if he'd found the essence of his search.

The walls, stridently white, were mostly covered by carelessly pinned drawings; cardboard sheets, some painted, some not, were standing on the floor facing the wall. On the easel, there was an unfinished work. My visitor turned around, walking with short steps around the paintings, exactly as if he were alone. Meanwhile, rather nervous, I fiddled with some cardboard pieces, attempting to regain my composure.

As I placed one work on the easel, he asked me to see the others as well. They were small self-portraits, portraits of friends, still-lifes, and views of Florentine surroundings. I told him not to feel surprised at their size, explaining that «the smaller studies require less time. Before solving the problem on a large scale, it has to be solved on a smaller one. Besides, I spend less money on color and it saves me from buying canvas, stretchers and prepared cardboards: I apply the fixative myself». I illustrated my point showing him two surfaces: one intended for a rapid exercise, the other for a more meticulous way of working.

I was eager to hear his opinion on my study methods: instead of answering, he asked me to show him my other paintings, which I did. Once he had seen the series, I presented my copies to him: when I got to the detail of the Bassano painting, I explained why I had not copied the entire picture. He neither objected nor approved. Then, I let him see him my latest studies, pure patches of color based upon works by Beato Angelico, telling him in advance I had been seeking autonomous light for paintings that did not base themselves on natural sources. I did not dare show him the studies on movement and velocity, in charcoal and pencil with some touches of color, nor those oils where I attempted to decompose the real forms: they did not satisfy me and therefore did not believe it was prudent. However, I let him know that in exchange for some of my time, artists had let me in on the technique of mosaics, frescoes and stained glass at their studio.

My patron listened with great attention. When he felt I was done, he mused: «So this is the work you have been doing since your arrival, in spite of your eye condition…»

This reflection made, he inquired about my health, and whether I had kept up with my exercises. Upon leaving, he invited me for dinner at the hotel at seven thirty. I vividly remember that evening, not only because De la Cárcova somehow managed to make me feel at ease, but because, somewhat dazed by his visit, I had forgotten to tell him that in January, which had just come to an end, I had exhibited two sketches at the «Esposizione Annuale di Bozzetti», organized by the Fine Arts Society of Florence. I brought him the catalogue for him to see my name and the name of the works I had sent. «Excellent», he muttered absent-mindedly, but I noticed he was pleased.

He remained in Florence two more days: both nights we had dinner together. He then left for Rome announcing he would be back in three days, that I shouldn´t tell anyone about it and that on the night he arrived he expected me at his hotel around seven thirty for dinner.

During his stay in Florence, in which we held lengthy conversations, I accompanied him to the museums and churches. He knew them, but wanted to see them again. One afternoon, upon noticing I always carried my pince–nez along, he laughed wholeheartedly, but I remarked that it was quite practical, for in churches and museums, even when I sat down to rest, I was able to perceive the most minute details of the works from afar.

On the night he left Italy for good, I accompanied him to the station.

Only then did he disclose he was quite satisfied with my work, adding that if I wanted to remain in Florence, I should, considering it made me so happy. «But please», he then said with a smile of infinite goodness, and referring to our correspondence, «please, Pettoruti, if you need to communicate any more decisions to me, do so more courteously». As the train departed I was filled with sorrow, feeling a friend was leaving.

A little after the pleasant visit I have just described, I proposed to both Curatella and Lamanna to make full use of that still hour preceding dinner: we could work on the nudes together, between seven and eight in the evening, when the models weren´t as busy. Certainly we could find one that would come for an hour, if we increased her pay somewhat. The costs would be split proportionally, and this included heating. I offered my studio but Curatella proposed his, which was larger. With the exception of holidays, we worked from sunrise to sunset for some time. One night, Curatella received two Argentine gentlemen in his studio: he introduced them to me, but I didn´t catch their names. It turned out they were the writer/ painter José León Pagano and the physician/ sculptor Enrique Prins.

Pagano, still a young man at the time, tall, thin, high–strung, with a very long neck, posed his inquisitive gaze upon our works. Suddenly, he placed himself in front of my nude, and with the tone of one who is never wrong, asked me the question that already enclosed its own and self–assured answer: «I gather you must be a sculptor?» When I replied I studied painting, he exclaimed, without getting flustered: «Ah, but this drawing could have been made by a sculptor!» something I recognized as being possible, considering I was very keen on sculpture.

Our evening occupation was interrupted by Curatella´s weariness, but Lamanna and I continued to work. This was the only period in my life in which I used charcoal to create my drawings, in true–to–life sizes. It took me about six sessions to complete one drawing.

I forgot to mention that before starting on the nude sessions, Curatella, Lamanna and I took a short trip that lasted three days. We visited Sienna, San Gimignano and Pisa. It was a fruitful journey. I needed to travel: partly to rest (I painted a lot at night and my oculist had forbidden me from doing so) but especially to study the mosaics of Ravenna and Venice.

We left Florence on May 10 and returned on the 19th. Our journey included Bologna, the city of the two towers and arcades, whose glorious university gave the world so many scholars; its important museums gave me a clear idea of the Bolognese art school.

I learned a great deal in Ravenna and Venice about mosaics —how much the Byzantines knew— and reflected deeply upon the need to express myself differently: in harmony with the present, yet remaining true to myself. It was in Venice, a dream–like city, where we spent most of our time, visiting the city, its churches and museums. I saw Carpaccio's impressive works, and greatly admired Verrochio's statue «Il Colleone».

One morning I took the steamboat to the island of Murano, where they sold enamel for the decoration of mosaics. Basing my selection on samples, I bought a large quantity of those colors and sizes I deemed necessary for the work I had in mind. Without delay, they dispatched the material to Florence.

On the way back we stopped off in Padua, where among other things, I saw the Scrovegni Chapel with the frescoes by Giotto, and the «Gattamelata», the famous equestrian statue by Donatello. This sculpture, together with the splendid work by Verrocchio, which I had recently contemplated in Venice, and «Marco Aurelio», which I later admired at the Roman Campidoglio, make up the most marvelous trio on earth as regards equestrian monuments; at least, among those I have seen so far.

After Padua, we went to Verona and Vicenza where we admired magnificent works of art, and whose enumeration would prove tiresome; we also traveled across a part of the Lago di Garda.

As soon as I was back in Florence, I went to see the First International «Black and White Exhibition», organized by the Fine Arts Society of Florence. To my surprise, the jury had accepted, not one, but the four works I had submitted. Browsing through old newspapers Nella had kept for me, I saw my name was mentioned with particular deference.

I felt quite comforted, for at that international exhibition, that remained open from May to June 1914, the best Italian and foreign artists exhibited their work. Auguste Renoir, Auguste Rodin, Jacques Villon and Félix Vallaton represented France, harmonious–sounding names I already knew. I immediately wrote my incomparable patron Ernesto de la Cárcova a few lines announcing him the good news, and sending him the catalogue.

Chapter 6

Mosaics and Collages

When I first felt the call of the arts, I believed the term just meant painting, and that the only tools required were cardboard, planks, canvas on stretchers, colors and paintbrushes. Yet, how horizons widen if one possesses a sense of the aesthetics, and what an infinite variety of materials one can fully take advantage of! I am alluding to the compositions created after my trip to Murano, in which pieces of paper supplanted color, and to the way I put in practice all I had recently learned about mosaics.

I had begun making sketches that would not necessarily lead me to original conceptions, but to an idea of simplicity I strived for, given that every support requires a particular drawing. It is obvious that a picture intended for mosaics will never do for stained glass, and the other way round.

By dint of designing arabesque on paper, I discovered that the flat surfaces of traditional mosaics could well convey an illusion of movement, provided I applied my technical knowledge differently and resorted to materials of diverse quality, form and thickness.

With the eyes of imagination, I saw «my» mosaic, unique, hanging on the wall, framed by its own architecture, the sinuous parts of its undulating surface and the arabesque bathing in light. With this idea in mind I painted numerous cardboards in tempera, [10] almost all of them with simple motifs, as I believe this art requires. And since one thought leads to another, it occurred to me that I could perfectly well add other materials, namely glass, porcelain and ceramic, to my stock of Venetian mosaics. I had cut these into irregular shapes so as to convey a stronger vibrancy, and realized that if I combined larger pieces with smaller ones, I would be able to create other rhythms, a new series of arabesque that would entwine with the ones already conceived.

---

10   Some cardboards still exist and are owned by my brothers.

This unique stuff could only be gotten in the refuse dumps. A brilliant idea then occurred to me: I bought strong and ordinary cloth, made a few rectangular bags, of about thirty centimeters by ten centimeters, and gathered a couple of children of the neighborhood. By means of one lira, as well as twenty cents for the streetcar, my «helpers» dispersed in the outskirts of Florence, where rubbish piled up. There, they filled up their small bags with bits of terracotta, thick crystals and porcelain.

It is unbelievable how many wondrous things people break in a city. The children came to me with their load: I can still see them, emptying their accumulated treasures onto a cardboard sheet lying on the floor. With the help of a small stick I separated what I could use from that which I could not, returning the rest to them. This is how the children spent their day, carrying and bringing back their little bags, while I collected exceptionally valuable materials.

My first works in mosaic, three in all, were accomplished upon iron stretchers on which I had laid a wire netting. Upon this structure I applied thick cement, and stage by stage, as my work progressed, I superimposed a fine layer of cement of different colors, upon which I placed the enamels: these were set according to the requirements of the design, taking into account whether the plane was convex or concave or whether the surfaces were flat or sinuous.

This allowed every stone or glass fragment to be equivalent to one or more brushstrokes, the cement also acquiring a purpose insofar as color was concerned. The frame was included in the composition so as to enclose the arabesque, and the light that enveloped the work produced an impression of change whenever the spectator moved about.

It is obvious that working with mosaics the way I wanted could not be entrusted to a worker. I couldn't merely hand him a design on cardboard, no matter how experienced he might be. I thus started on my first work, «Spring».

In this sense it is worthwhile to recall an anecdote, which, at one point was divulged by journalists, causing quite an attraction: in the foreground and to the right, a cluster of cypresses was set upon a background reminiscent of the hills of Fiesole and Settignano, and to the left, there sat a young woman (Spring), for whose garments I was seeking a certain shade of blue. Then again, the same thing always happened to me: the hue was impossible to define until it became concrete on the canvas.

I had repeatedly sent the children to look for anything that color. Again the bags traveled to and fro, but the blue of my dreams was nowhere to be found. On the brink of giving up, chance had me walk into a large bazaar on Via Larga one afternoon, and there, in the store window, I saw a jug of just the tone of blue I was after. It had four minute triangles painted on it, enclosed within a square that splendidly absorbed and refracted the light.

My dream had come true. Overcome with emotion, I entered the crowded shop, telling the salesclerk I wished to buy it. Yet as he started to wrap it up, I realized the package would be too bulky to carry it comfortably, and asked him to break the jug so as to make the parcel smaller. The clerk smiled and kept on wrapping. I repeated my request. Annoyed at his smile and at the little attention he was paying to me, I snatched the jug from his hands and smashed it into smithereens against the counter. Chaos ensued. The salesclerk, opening his eyes wide, drew back instinctively, people fled before me, panic–stricken mothers ran towards the door with their children and a gentleman, perhaps the storekeeper, walked towards me, trying to calm me down, assuring me that not only would I not have to pay for the jug, but that they would give me another. I realized they believed me mad, capable of destroying the whole store, including the shelves and the glassware.

As quick as lightning I grabbed my package and ran off into the street. Fortunately an empty carriage passed by and jumping upon the footrest I gave the coach driver my address. He must have thought he was carrying a thief, for he whipped his horse ever so intensely.

That night, while having dinner at a restaurant and fully conscious that I had narrowly escaped a frozen shower at a police station, I told my tale. A Florentine journalist overheard me, and the story came out the following day. Amused by the account, several Italian dailies reproduced it, with versions of their own: this is how I became the hero of a preposterous episode.

Once I had finished the mosaic, I sent it to Buenos Aires. It was exhibited at the National Salon of 1914, in the decorative arts section. A first, second and third prize were assigned. Enrique Prins won first prize for his figurative oil landscape; I have no idea who took the other awards. Once the exhibition was over, the mosaic left in a truck to La Plata. It arrived unharmed but because of its enormous weight no one was able to unload it. I heard someone called the fire brigade: four firemen on duty showed up, upsetting the calm neighbors. The mosaic remained ten years at my parents's home and in 1924 I donated it to the La Plata National University, where it now decorates its main patio.

Very soon I began to experiment with both collage and mosaics. Besides using newspapers, magazines, and colored or painted papers, I also used bits of cardboard, cloth, sand, colored pencils, oils, and postcards. Among the first collages I made, I recall one called «City/country»; it portrayed houses of Florence and its environs, while the Ponte Vecchio and a main street are depicted on two postcards. I made collages on and off for years, in part to help relieve my mind from so much painting. The last ones I did in Buenos Aires in 1925 and 1926, but then lost sight of them. I only know Doctor Felipe Gil, of Montevideo, has one of them.

Don't think for a minute these tasks absorbed all of my days for I still found enough time to play pranks. This is the description of one of them: among my painting companions who came to visit me, there were two artists from Rosario [11] that I remember with a great deal of affection: Manuel Musto and Augusto Schiavoni. They shared a room in the Duomo area, a splendid place on the second floor, luxuriously furnished. Two large windows overlooked the street and the door gave to a corridor.

Schiavoni trusted me greatly, and consulted me about everything, or so I thought, for one day Musto told me his friend had made it a habit to borrow some money from him every third week of the month. The thing was he also borrowed money from me, despite receiving a much more generous grant than I did. Musto also revealed that Schiavoni frequented ladies of the street quite assiduously; the women, besides leaving him penniless, distracted him from his work and both his health and his pocket had deteriorated.

Together with Musto and the sculptor Miguel Angel Negri, we decided to effectively tackle the situation. This was our plan: one night, most surreptitiously, Musto let us in the room they both shared. Negri, covered up with a large sheet, hid behind a couch, while I squeezed myself under Schiavoni's bed. The latter arrived, got undressed, and lay down. Musto was reading, lying face upward on the bed. Both friends used the same lamp standing on the table, which they turned on or off thanks to a double wire connected to a switch. Schiavoni began to doze off, and Musto announced in a loud voice that he was going out to buy cigarettes. He rose from his bed, and as he turned off the light, he loosened the light bulb. The room was left in the dark, its ceiling eerily illuminated by the light of a solitary streetlamp. From our hiding places, Negri and I waited for Schiavoni to fall asleep. And the plan unfolded: ever so slowly, using my shoulders, I raised the metallic bedstead on which the mattress rested. Schiavoni kept on sleeping. At the third attempt, my movement startled him; I sensed he sat up on his bed with a start. At that moment, Negri appeared from behind the couch, slowly flapping his soft tunic and I began to moan. Our friend desperately groped for the light switch, while Negri, slowly extending his arms in a ghostlike manner, intermittently emerged from behind the couch. Terror–stricken, Schiavoni pressed the light switch, a futile thing to do. For a second he curled up beneath the blankets, hiding his head, but when the light pressures against the mattress resumed, the man just couldn't stand it any longer: he jumped up and darted out of the room, dressed in his nightgown that reached to his calves. The landlady, who through Musto knew all about the prank, lived at the other end of the corridor. Negri and I then ran downstairs where Musto was waiting for us.

The following morning at seven, Schiavoni knocked at my door. He came to tell me what had happened, and described the incident in detail. I

---

11 City in the Argentine province of Santa Fe.

gravely answered that since I didn´t believe in ghosts, I attributed all that had occurred to a hallucination on account of overwork: for him not to have any more visions it was imperative to discover the causes and put a brake on abuses. In effect, Schiavini put order in his life and his health improved.

I was no saint, and could understand Schiavoni. Around that time I had met a Russian woman, delightful and enterprising, at a large studio stylishly furnished by Gino Sensani, then one of the best modern Italian xylographers. He had just arrived from Paris, and received his friends once or twice a week. The inclinations of the young man were no secret to anyone, and the people who surrounded him were also quite liberal.

The Russian woman was quite appealing; she spoke Italian poorly, granted, but that minor detail didn´t concern us in the least. She loved to walk, just as I did, and we often went to Fiesole on foot together, for she loved nature, the solitary paths and the cypress woods carpeted with dry leaves.

Everything would have been perfect had it not been for her obsession to see me, as her tenacity prevented me from concentrating on my work. As she could not be brought to reason, I decided to disappear one day, so as to give her a chance to direct her affection towards another responsive heart. I first intended to go to Vallombrosa, where I enjoyed taking down notes, but I suddenly changed my mind and decided to travel to Sienna.

The following day, after a good night´s rest, and celebrating my recovered freedom, I went for a walk through the city of The Three Hills. After admiring, once again, «Guidoriccio Fogliani about to lay siege to Mount Massi», the monumental fresco by Simone Martini, and another one by Il Sodoma, I comfortably sat in the sun at a café on Piazza del Campo. This square is particularly memorable as every year, on July 2 and August 16, it is the stage for the unforgettable «Corsa del Palio»: a multicolored array of people dressed up in 15th century attire. Lost in my daydreams, I unfolded my newspaper, but an imperative hand snatched it away: it was my Russian woman.

The explanation? Very simple: I remembered that the day before, on my way to the Florentine station, a friend of mine had hailed me, and in passing, I had told him I was leaving for Sienna. She ran across him, and my friend, unaware of my ulterior motive, revealed our conversation. Peace of mind? I had already given up hope, but fortunately one of her brothers arrived to the city of the Medici from distant Russia, whisking her off to Paris a few days before the outbreak of the European conflict.

And since amusing anecdotes spring to mind, here goes another, that took place approximately at about the same time: I met a Florentine youth, older than I was, who always sought the company of other artists. He enjoyed drawing and was quite pleasant, and though he talked too much, his conversations were so entertaining it was a pleasure to listen to him. He became fond of me and used to visit me once in a while so as not to interrupt my work. Whenever I was busy, he would enter and leave the room as if on tiptoes. It was through him that I learned the tango was in fashion in Europe and that in cities like Paris it was all the rage. He took lessons so as to learn the latest steps, and rehearsed in front of me, knees limp, elbow pointing upwards, his right hand upon his chest. One afternoon he interrupted his dance, stealthily when advancing, swiftly when moving backwards, to express his admiration. It seems the passion I demonstrated when working was unique in his eyes, and he was filled with awe. At a given point, and akin to one who decides to take a helpless being under his wing, he said to me: «Pettoruti, don't worry about anything, that's why I'm here; if you need any money, just ask, and if someone bothers you, tell me who it is and I will immediately get rid of him. I will solve all your problems; you just keep on working».

When he left, I felt bewildered. I had seen him having cordial conversations with people in the neighborhood, including our own doorkeeper Beppa. I decided to ask her, in the most discreet of ways, what sort of character I was dealing with. She told me he was an excellent young man, and that he had often been sent to prison, though she didn't know why.

Although he never stayed long, he came often. One day this extraordinary friend found out I was leaving for Venice, and came running to offer to look after the studio. I felt like refusing, yet accepted, so as not to upset him. Deep down I felt irritated, imagining he would settle in my studio, sleep in my bed and wear my clothes.

Far from it! Upon my return I found everything was clean and in order, and not a pin was missing. I heard from Beppa he had come every day to dust and open the windows: he had done so with so much dedication that she had not raised any objections. A few months later, the war swept him away, together with so many others.

Chapter 7

Italian Neutrality

Giacometti often invited me to his studio in order to show me his work or else he came to mine to see what I was doing and chat for a while. He trusted my taste, and would often bring sketches along whenever he worked on a decoration. These sketches were always quite small and invariably done in pastel: using the same motif he would make fifteen or twenty samples, and then he would choose.

One afternoon –I knew he was working on a project to decorate a church in Stampa, his native village– he rang the doorbell to my studio with one of his middle fingers, or so I believe, for he couldn´t have rung the bell any other way, given how he was standing when I opened the door: he had his elbows perpendicular to his sides. He carried four pastels in each one of his huge palms, measuring 4 centimeters by 4 centimeters apiece. He wished to know my opinion: after discussing the matter for some time, he decided on the one I had chosen, and I eventually I saw the photograph of the finished work.

Once in a while, I also visited the studio of young Italian painters. The ones I considered interesting at the time were Guido Ferroni, Francisco Dani, Rosai and Gino Sensani, though I preferred Lega and Garbari. None of them had any thing to do with Futurism.

I used to go to the Delle Giubbe Rosse café together with Sensani and Garbari, both of them friends of Soffici´s. Being the most advanced students, they defended Futurism, and discussions arose nightly regarding modern and traditional art, in order to condemn the official action that imposed an obsolete education in an academy in ruins.

Soffici was a writer and a painter (in my opinion, more of a writer than a painter); he had lived in Paris for many years and become acquainted with the most renowned artists and men of letters. Braque, Picasso, Modigliani, Derain, Apollinaire, Max Jacob and other important figures were among his friends. He was thus the only one who could speak with authority on the new artistic tendencies, whereas the brilliant one in philosophy was Papini. The young painters greatly benefited from Soffici's incisive observations on contemporary art, besides becoming familiar with names that later became illustrious. At times, the heated arguments unleashed harsh responses from those who participated in the discussions.

I came to realize that there were many things that prevented me from working smoothly, and that I wouldn't progress if I didn't moderate some of my activities, distractions or worries. It seemed unthinkably hard to give up my habits, for they contributed to my satisfaction and sense of well–being, enriching both my knowledge and fortifying the inherent romanticism of youth, from the impassioned reunions at the café, to bathing in moonlight on the Ponte Vecchio.

It wasn't Nella that robbed me of my time, for she accompanied me to places where I would have gone alone in order to become more enlightened. There were other things besides art that sidetracked me, at times, as I have already mentioned, in agreeably annoying ways.

As Curatella was about to leave Florence and head for Paris, I suddenly felt I had to follow his example: perhaps Paris was the right place for my art. Soffici agreed, whereas Sensani doubted. I finally made up my mind to leave, but fate decided otherwise: my grant money was delayed. When it reached Florence at the end of August, war had already been declared. Though Italy maintained its neutrality, men were drafted and the borders closed down. To cross them was dangerous for me, for Italian law requires sons of Italians to adopt their parents' nationality.

Lamanna, frightened to death, had only one thing in mind: to flee from Italy. I had just met the wife of a shipowner from Liorna and exposed my friend's wish to her. Very kindly, she arranged, through her husband who owned a fleet of cargo ships traveling along the coast of the Mediterranean basin, for Lamanna to embark. This is how he reached Barcelona, and eventually Buenos Aires.

In order to know exactly where I was standing before the Italian laws, I took a rapid trip to Rome to see the Argentine Ambassador. Then, I took another trip to Genoa to speak to the consul general. Both told me there was nothing they could do to prevent a draft.

Facing a dilemma, I decided to take my chances and remain in Italy. Now that my mind was set, and since my time was precious, I pondered on the best way to use it. Searching for a way to keep temptations at bay, I thought of something radical that would oblige me to remain confined, and decided to have my hair cropped. Immediately I went to see my barber on Via Masaccio, who resisted as long as possible. However, upon seeing how determined I was, and not wishing to lose a client, he finally accepted. Nothing better than a bald head to oblige someone to stay home. In those days things were different: had I gone out onto the streets like that, the whole of Florence would have run after me. I looked so ugly I felt like playing a joke on my mother: I had my picture taken and sent her the photograph for her to see my new look.

I thus shut myself in, removed from the world in order to work, without opening the door to anyone except Codegoni, my faithful friend, who proved to be ever so solicitous. He did all the necessary shopping and took care of every detail. Gemmina brought me food from the restaurant at set hours, knocking at the door the way Beppa had taught her to.

At least two months went by like this, working without respite. Codegoni would go to see Gonnelli, and bring me the «Lacerba» magazine and the books I had ordered. The magazine was now completely focused on war, filled with opinionated articles, especially those written by Soffici and Papini, yet stained throughout with the grimness of censorship. The writers harshly criticized the Government, reminding them of Italy's duty to fight on the side of France against Nordic barbarity, so as to safeguard the rich heritage of Latin culture and civilization. From the moment the conflict was declared, to Italy's giving in to the pressures of public opinion favorable to the allied cause, the «Lacerba» magazine remained exclusively political. It was sold for 10 cents instead of 20, in order to reach every home. When embarking on its brave campaign in favor of the war [12], it announced it would return to its regular activities as soon as it was over; yet, when the war ended, the magazine no longer existed.

When my hair finally grew a little, that is to say, when I considered myself «presentable», the first thing I did was to stop by the University to see Nella. As I didn't find her, I had someone send her a note telling her I had returned from a long journey. If I hadn't written, the message said, it was due to my stay in the jungle. Naturally, she was angry, but came to the meeting anyway. When I removed my hat to greet her, she almost screamed, probably imagining a dreadful illness. I told her the truth and she understood, so that our relationship was renewed without a shadow. I needed her company: she was a home bird, just like my sisters, and the few times I visited her family, I felt comforted. I now think this friendship counterbalanced my disorderly life.

I'd like to remark that the joke I played on my mother when sending her the photograph ended up being counterproductive: instead of making her laugh it made her cry bitter tears, for she believed a terrible disease had affected me. As soon as my hair grew, I sent her another one.

---

12   This campaign began on August 15, 1914.

My reappearance at the Caffè delle Giubbe Rosse went unnoticed. The atmosphere was strained and so were the people. I saw strange faces and war was on everyone's lips: the Germans carried on with their triumphant march, there was little the Allies could do and the neutral attitude adopted by Italy was an offense to anyone possessing some sense. The habitués of the Giubbe Rosse café never disagreed on this issue; both Futurists and sympathizers supported interventionism, on the side of France.

The Fine Arts Society of Florence was organizing its First Tuscan Winter Exhibition opening in December 1914. Reserved for the region, as its name indicated, it was easy to imagine it would not only involve academic art. My interest lay elsewhere, which explains why I didn't present myself, so certain was I to be rejected.

I had not counted on chance, and as chance would have it, one of the many painters who had their studio on 6 Via degli Artisti, was a member of the Admissions Committee. He was a genial little old man, who dedicated himself principally to commercial art, but this did not prevent him in any way from appreciating the work of young painters. As my studio was on his way, he often asked me whether he would be allowed to see what I was doing, showing great enthusiasm for the problems I was tackling.

One day he came to ask me if I knew about the forthcoming exhibition and the role he played in it. He recommended sending work to the Salon, and to tell the other young painters to do the same, as he would defend us in order to at least obtain the acceptance of one painting from each one of us. I told Dani, Sensani, Ferroni and Garbari; they in turn informed their companions and thus a group of fourteen painters was created. All of us were admitted, with a handful of works each. As for myself, they received all of my four paintings. Two of them were drawings focusing on movement. Since they were abstract, and I couldn't find a name for them, I called the two belonging to the same series, «Harmony (abstract design)». This is how they figure in the First Tuscan Winter Exhibition catalogue.

Probably, so as not to be at odds with either the Admissions Committee or the public, the organizers of the show lumped us all together as if we had been lepers in a small room on the first floor, which no one ever entered. But it so happened that this room, transformed into the cornerstone of scandal, attracted the largest crowd.

Chapter 8

Towards an Expression

It doesn't bore me to speak alone. I've gotten into the habit of doing so every morning, confined in a small room where my paintings line up: in keeping with an old habit of mine, I always get up early, while my home and neighborhood, Saint–Germain–des–Prés, still sleep.

There are mornings, like these, when I doubt the usefulness of these talks. Who are they aimed at? And I tell myself: once these words are typed, put in order, cleansed of everything superfluous and perhaps published, will they prove interesting, will there be anyone taking his time to read them? Without a doubt, what spurs me on is the deep necessity to liberate myself from so many memories.

I have described my artistic beginnings with the utmost care, and perhaps time has come to take shortcuts. If I insisted on the early periods it is because I believe the first steps in a man's education are the ones that count most, especially if this man, who is at once an artist, did not have any teachers to guide him when starting off. Granted; I had my grandfather, who helped me as much as he could, who gave me beautiful art books in which I saw, without any preconception, paintings belonging to all periods of history and read theories by a handful of aesthetes; but my grandfather was not a painter and could not direct me insofar as my artistic vocation was concerned.

I educated myself by the light of nature, working desperately hard to improve myself. At one point I realized that the only way to tackle art in a serious way was to pay no heed to the gift bestowed upon me at birth: the ability to paint. Many an artist who had taken advantage of this skill had been led to destruction. I believe I mentioned that in my adolescence, when living in La Plata, I could paint a picture in only one attempt, as can be seen in the 1908 drape studies depicting a candelabra, and which my brothers own.

To combat this talent, in Florence I prepared burlap, which I first coated with glue in order to smooth the hairs, and then again with plaster to slow the movement of the paintbrush down, preventing it from gliding upon the surface as it was used to doing. To finish each work I had to therefore insist heavily. As can be inferred, I also had to use another type of paintbrush.

This experience opened my eyes to the importance of technique in a work of art, besides correcting the «bravura» defect, responsible of killing so many promising and impatient painters; the same impatience that had me paint a large canvas in a day.

Gradually I became more experienced and I felt I was slowly treading firmer ground; I began trying out different media, varnishes, paintbrushes, adjusting them to the needs of my new procedures.

All this concerns method. As regards a work's beauty or spiritual content, or however one wishes to call it, fortunately for me I had arrived in Europe with eyes devoid of prejudice. I had seen nothing and my spirit, in a state of receptivity, embraced at once the newest and the oldest, allowing it to follow the path that best suited its ideals. A man of my time, I could not conceive expressing myself in another language that was not contemporary, the way every artist had done in his age, reflecting it or anticipating the near future.

I began thus unburdened, thanks to the fact that all I had drawn and painted in my native city had completely erased itself from my mind and did not influence my education at all. So much so, that it obliged me to modify my way of painting, because it wasn't working.

The only masters that guided my artistic career, begun at the age of 21, were the great Italian artists of the Quattrocento and the Etruscans. Another powerful impact was the Futurist art exhibition, which revealed new horizons to me. The rest I learned from living in such an exciting environment. To conciliate the old and the new, to create quality painting expressing the new times through fresh and solid forms was a tempting proposal. But, how was I to reach that goal? Learning the pictorial language in depth. Painting was my passion, and my faith in the creation of a personal universe, boundless. It was a question of getting down to work. Without losing sight of the study of construction of form and color —these being the essence of painting— I followed the path I had first taken, developing on the one hand the idea of movement, and on the other, experimenting with the overlapping of forms in a way I considered novel and original. My conversations with Soffici came in handy, for at times they affirmed a concept or unraveled a mystery, yet I was completely in the dark regarding the artistic preoccupations of other European avant–garde artists.

Soffici spoke about Cubist forms and wrote on Cubism in the «Lacerba» magazine, but his magnificent articles were never illustrated with reproductions; the art magazines were also going through a difficult moment and the plates, just like today, were extremely expensive; this is the reason why the Italian youth of 1914 and later years lived in total ignorance of what was happening in the rest of the world. In those days, news did not travel fast: cinema and television did not exist, and there was only a limited edition of tricolor impressions. Besides, there was a shortage of art books and monographs, especially if it entailed modern artists: only the elite and the connoisseurs knew about Klee and Kandinsky.

In short: I set to work decomposing and recomposing common forms taken from nature, and did so in the most constructive and serene of ways. This alone set me apart from the Futurists, for they were after a sensory effect and attained it –at times– juxtaposing, say, the most common elements of a landscape as seen from a window of a moving train: at times they superimposed telephone poles, trees, houses and meadows, whereas my more reserved nature sought something else, represented I believe, in some of my collages and drawings, and in my first oil versions of Vallombrosa.

The first page of the «Lacerba» magazine that came out on October 1, 1914 –I had just turned 22– invited all «intelligent Italians» to rebel against a «vile and treacherous» government that did not side with its ally and sister, France. To illustrate the publication, I made a collage named «Il sifone». This is my anecdote on the matter:

I had bought the whole «Lacerba» collection from Gonnelli, and kept it carefully. Months later, going through it, I realized the October 1 issue was missing; annoyed, I remembered I had used it to make a collage, and that I had not made the effort to buy another copy when it was still possible. I ran to Gonnelli's only to find out that that number was no longer available. Knowing full well he kept complete collections for privileged clients under the counter, I did not insist.

One morning, as Gonnelli was absent, I seized the coveted copy. Unfortunately for me, he realized the magazine was missing, and since he was smart, it did not take long for him to find out who the culprit was. When I stopped by his bookstore, some days later, he exclaimed, point–blank: «You stole that copy you needed!» As you might remember, he was a large and corpulent man and when I realized he was leaping the counter in order to catch me, I ran off as fast as I could.

I stopped going to the bookstore for a while, and whenever I neared his store on Via Cavour, I would walk on the opposite sidewalk. I once called out his name from there: he came to the door and I understood by the look on his face his anger had subsided. In effect, he beckoned me over, and though I felt somewhat uneasy, I crossed the street. He came towards me, and tapping me on my shoulder with a fraternal gesture, led me into his store: «Come, with me» he said, «everything is fine; you're a good rascal…»

One day, someone knocked at my studio door and I found myself facing a young man short of stature, with an angelical smile. His round face was illuminated by two very blue and limpid eyes, which revealed the transparence of his soul. He told me his name was Antonio Sibellino and that he studied sculpture. He had come from Paris, he said, where he had heard of me and had obtained my address; at this moment he was touring his beloved Italy, but once the journey was over, he would embark for Argentina, his home country.

The first thing I asked him was whether he wasn't afraid to be drafted, being the son of Italians. He was flabbergasted. He truly believed that since Italy was not yet at war, no-one would be interested in him as a soldier. We immediately became friends and that same evening we held extensive conversations on art that lasted forty some years in all: thirty-nine years of regular tête-à-têtes and six years of correspondence.

He was a studious young man, curious and highly motivated to work. When he had to leave Europe after having studied there for five years, he was almost in tears. The grant the National Congress had awarded him had expired two years ago; it was only because he had been thrifty that he had been able to continue living in Paris and travel about.

On his second visit he brought me photographs of his work; it was very seriously done and confirmed my first impressions. He was annoyed with his patron Ernesto de la Cárcova, for the latter had made him study two years at the Royal Academy of Turin, where he believed he had been losing his time. He considered that being very methodical in his studies, and having attended the Buenos Aires Academy, he did not need any further study; in his eyes, European academies were conceived, like everywhere else, for those who are unable to study or aspire to get a degree. My new friend traveled through Italy for two months, after which time he returned to Florence.

The eventuality of war was on everyone's lips and in everyone's heart, but peace reigned in Florence where my life continued its normal course, concentrating on work. I reduced my number of acquaintances, keeping only the most precious. My care in choosing friendships, or if you wish, my prudent distribution of time, dates back to those days, for I was completely committed to consolidating and developing my art. I have had very few friends ever since, and all of them have been constructive in the sense that they helped me complete my knowledge, leading me to live a more or less orderly life. This doesn't mean that, as all youths do, I never let off steam from time to time. But the flurry never lasted long.

One evening, I found Marinetti at the Delle Giubbe Rosse café, passing through Florence. He asked me if I was already a Futurist, and I said no, though I had been working in a similar direction, and offered to show him my paintings. He couldn't promise, though, for he was leaving for Milan the following day; however, he would be back soon. In effect, a few days later I received a note telling me he would stop over in Florence on his way to Rome, and that he would meet me at my studio at a certain time. As regular as clockwork, he arrived that afternoon accompanied by a Milanese writer.

I showed him drawings, collages and paintings that could interest him; among the ones I had created last, he showed a definite preference for a series I had named «Luci nel paesaggio», forms in movement whipped by light. As far as the drawings were concerned, he did not favor those I believed to be the best, but rather, those that most approached what he understood to be Futurism.

He suggested I adhere to the Movement and sign the new manifestos in preparation. Instinctively I said no, adding that not even I was able to perceive where my work was heading for. What I did not say then, for I didn't think it appropriate, was that regarding his Movement, I totally shared Soffici and Pappini's points of view: I did not agree with most of its methods, as for instance the constant need for innovation, the uninterrupted proclamations (manifestos were launched for no reason at all) and the indiscriminate recruitment, that not only increased the number of ill–prepared and often incompetent adherents, but harmed the cause of Futurism.

Marinetti kept on insisting: in his opinion I was ready. Probably I was, compared to most of the new members that clang to the letter but not to the spirit of a tendency that had to justify itself through the value of the created work. He seemed to believe that by launching manifestos young people became artists, whereas my common sense told me that manifestos did not contribute to the making of art at all. I wasn't mistaken. Other important movements in the development of modern art, such as Impressionism, Fauvism and Cubism have not needed any manifesto, and yet have left us their legacy.

That day Marinetti, visibly annoyed, puffing out his large chest, called out these words as though he had let out a prophecy: «The day will come in which you will be sorry...»

I never regretted anything, though he was right; a large amount of painters have become famous after having accidentally signed proclamations.

Towards the European Spring of 1915, I finished off several self–portraits and two more mosaic pieces that completed the series of three: I also tried my hand at sculpture, an art which I can say has taught me to paint and have always enjoyed as much as painting. I made a few sculptures and some polychromatic bas–reliefs, that I lost track of. Gonnelli closely followed my work, encouraging me in my new endeavor.

Chapter 9
War. Trip to Sicily

Several problems arose in the course of the period preceding Italy's decision to take part in the war. I still found myself in a neutral land, but since crossing the Atlantic was not devoid of dangers, ships were delayed. As censorship was enforced, letters and money orders, foundation of all sustenance, were also belated. Seven months went by before Miguel Angel Negri received his grant money: in my case, it wasn't more than three.

I had saved some money; but in the face of uncertainty I decided not to spend it as a precaution against what might come. In order to live, I pawned, just like Negri did, everything I felt I could do without. Negri, who had not been far-sighted enough, and had other obligations, ended up wearing the same clothes every day, and since he was small and thin, my clothes were of no use to him.

When the situation became critical, I went to see the restaurant owner where we used to eat and asked him to give both Negri and me a loan (Codegoni and the others had already left). He accepted willingly, demonstrating his affection towards me in such a way, that on Sundays and holidays Gemmina brought me five liras in an envelope on behalf of her uncle and employer. What a magnificent man! Fortunately, both my friend I paid back all of our debts.

I did not visit the café as much, where the discussions on art had subsided to give place to those on politicians and the military. On the world's chessboard several changes had taken place. After months of benevolent neutrality towards Austria and Germany, the Government became worried as trouble drew closer: Italy's participation in the conflict. The whole country clamored for it, and finally, in the month of May, war was declared. On the

22nd, eve of the official declaration of war against the Austrian Empire, the «Lacerba» magazine published its last number, and it was both a cry of triumph and agony. «Evviva la guerra!» celebrated Palazzeschi, while Papini exclaimed: «Abbiamo vinto!» The magazine died the way heroes do, after having fought a ferocious hand–to–hand battle against the established powers.

As the situation became critical, Negri looked for work and found it: he sewed bags meant to carry biscuits to the front. They paid him by unit and he managed to produce a great quantity of them, thanks to a special awl that he himself had made remembering those used by the Argentine gauchos. They were small and quite curved, allowing him to work rapidly. He made one for me and many a night we worked together.

While we were giving these matters all our attention, I received a letter from Paris signed by the Viscount of Lascano Tegui, journalist whom I knew by name. He told me he was organizing an exhibition of works by Argentines living in Europe, which eventually would be shown in Buenos Aires. His intention was to raise a sum of money through the sale of paintings in order to help our compatriots forsaken by their government. He offered to dispatch a couple or more paintings, if I so wished.

Those students that depended on grants could not afford the packing and shipping expenses, especially if the recompense was unlikely, and we were obliged to wait for more clement times. I would have sent two paintings in one single shipment, but to make a special container and face the expenses was too much to ask. I exposed the situation to my correspondent, thanking him for his kind attention. The Viscount of Lascano Tegui transcribed part of this letter in an article published on 14 October 1915 in the «La Gaceta de Buenos Aires» newspaper, article with which he naively intended to call the attention of the Argentine government about the predicament of art students in Europe.

I have never had the temperament of a hero, something I thought was an inherent deficiency, and was certain other people were. However days went by, and weeks, and months, and I noticed that very few of my friends and acquaintances marched towards the firing line. Although everyone had the word «victory» on their lips, I didn´t feel people had the desire, so often expressed, to rush to the front and share the glorious life of the trenches with their companions. Most of them were enlisted, but they served in the civil defense and were glad to find themselves protected. In general, Florence´s calm atmosphere did not convey the feeling of conflict. It was only at the train station, upon the departure of the Tuscan soldiers who had been called to increase the civil ranks, that the air was imbued with a war–like mood.

At the end of August 1915, I went on my first long study tour through the South of Italy. So far, I only knew the neighboring towns, such as Sienna, Pisa, Luca and Arezzo; my longest journey had taken me to Venice. I could no longer ignore works as considerable as the ones preserved at the Vatican or in Naples, town in which the art of Pompeii beckoned to me. I also passionately wished to learn something more about the Etruscans, whose art I had studied in Florence and considered pure and grandiose.

I stopped over in Perusa and Asisi en route for Rome, where I remained only five days, visiting the city and its surroundings. From there, I departed to Naples, which I had thoroughly explored only two years ago with my friend, the mathematician. Nothing had changed, everything was just as dirty and good–natured, but I myself was different. I went to Pompeii, and immediately thereafter visited the National Museum of Naples. It dazzled me, and found it similar to the art of the Impressionists. Soon, I was boarding the train, and heading towards Polla, my mother's native town.

I followed the instructions she and my grandfather had given me. Indeed, as soon as I got off at the station, I saw a hotel standing across it. The sky was overcast, and rain fell relentlessly. I had scarcely mentioned my mother's name to the landlady, and who I was and where I came from, that she welcomed me with open arms: she had been a fellow student of my mother's and she was thrilled to meet her son. People standing around her smiled at me with deference, and I felt happy to have made such a good impression.

I went to the presbytery, with the hope of getting to know the priest who had been my grandfather's companion, but he had passed away. His successor, a friend of both men, received me with open arms and told me succulent anecdotes about José Casaburi's youth. «This is between us, from man to man», he said. He remembered him as a regular devil, but with great affection. I promised him I would return the following day to continue the conversation, and in effect, that was my intention. But unexpected events upset my plans.

Arriving at the hotel, after a walk in the rain through the peaceful city, I realized my presence had moved quite a few people; they looked at me in a friendly manner, almost with patriotic pride. It was time for dinner: the landlady told me she had especially prepared a table I was to share with a cultivated traveling salesman. The truth is I never found out whether my interlocutor was enlightened or not, for when we were just about to eat our minestrone, he declared how happy he was, as an Italian, to see a young artist who had crossed the oceans in order to fight for the land of his forefathers. I almost choked! I realized at once I had fallen into a deadly trap, and thinking only about fleeing, my minestrone lost its appeal. The man ranted on: I told him I was no longer hungry on account of tiredness. As soon as possible, I ran to the station to check the train schedules. Little did I care where the trains would take me, the point was leaving. But they ran infrequently. The only train I could catch that night headed towards Naples and arrived at two in the morning. If, according to my plans, I wanted to travel to Reggio Calabria, I could do little else but get off in Battipaglia and wait there for several hours. Back at the hotel, I told the owner that I had a habit of paying my room every night before going to bed, to which she formally opposed herself. In distress, I looked around to evaluate which door would best suit my purpose: there was the main entrance, which gave onto a large room with tables alongside the walls and a bar at the rear, yet I discarded it as it was too conspicuous. The bar led to the dining room, whose door also gave onto a street. Fortunately, there was a staircase at the end of this hall that led to the first floor, where I had my room. Therefore, I only had to walk down the stairs and cross the dining room in order to reach the door. For the moment it was open, but an iron crosspiece told me it would at one point be closed.

I raced upstairs. In a state of frenzy, I wrote the good woman a letter, thanking her for her warm reception and telling her how sorry I was to have to leave, but that I had suddenly remembered I had an appointment in Rome. I assured her I would return in a few days to remain at least a week in this beloved town. I placed my letter and a ten–lira bill on my bedside table.

Those few hours seemed to last forever. When I thought an hour had gone by, the hand of the clock had barely moved. Worst of all, I wasn't able to read nor concentrate on anything. At long last the moment came: with my shoes, my raincoat and my umbrella in one hand and my suitcase in the other, I silently crept down the stairs. It creaked with each step and I held my breath, so as to become lighter. Every step was a moment of suspense. I finally reached the dining room, submerged in darkness.

The main entrance was closed, as I had guessed it would be. However, the door giving onto the bar was not, and there, beside the large closed door in the corner, someone was sleeping: the night watchman. What if he woke up? I felt relieved to think that having left more than enough money to pay off both my room and food, no one could take me for a thief, and so, if the man did wake up, I would tell him the same thing I had written in my letter. I crossed the dining room on tiptoes. The key was on the lock and I turned it, ever so slowly; then I pushed the crosspiece aside. Like a ghost I opened the door and slipped out, luggage in hand.

It was still drizzling. I put on my shoes, sprinted across the railroad tracks and got into the station. The train arrived a few minutes later. My adventure, akin to a heroic deed, had not lasted more than a quarter of an hour.

What a provincial train station looks like in times of war is no secret to a European, but it is to an American. When I got off in Battipaglia the only thing I saw were trains that were evidently heading north, loaded with merchandise and provisions.

They slowly changed tracks a hundred times before finally departing. Not one passenger train could be spotted, and I waited in the station all day long, or so it seemed. Finally, mine pulled in: it was a stopping train changing tracks at every station.

I arrived in Reggio Calabria, a war zone, at midnight. I saw the passengers showing a safe-conduct when getting off and then continue their way. For want of it, I let them see my passport, but two police officers caught me by the arm and locked me up in a small room. I heard someone talking on the phone, saying: «It's a foreigner, an Argentine». They finally let me go at two in the morning.

When leaving the station everything was pitch dark. Suddenly, someone snatched my suitcase and another hand tried to seize my umbrella. I attempted to fend my attackers off, but two young voices calmed me down, telling me almost in unison they would take me to a hotel: I understood they had been waiting over two hours for a tip.

Searching for a hotel through the wet, solitary and dark streets was an odyssey I can't possibly begin to describe. I only know I was so exhausted, that those two strangers could have easily killed me without no-one realizing it. There were no available rooms anywhere and our nocturnal pilgrimage continued. At long last, a voice coming from a dingy little room answered affirmatively. I only wanted to rest, and giving five liras to the shadows walking behind me, I followed my guide.

Before leading me to my room, the man asked me to pay him an exorbitant sum, which far exceeded the price of even the most luxurious hotel. He then took me to my den where the bedstead barely fit in. A very thin partition separated this poky little room from the one next door, and the ongoing buzz coming from it was such that I didn't sleep a wink all night.

As soon as it was daylight, I headed for the harbor where I boarded the ferryboat that would take me to Mesina.

Upon arriving, I dropped off my luggage at the station and went to a tobacco store with the sole purpose of buying stamps. The two men that had been following me since I had disembarked and whom I reckoned were investigators, also halted. There was no doubt this concerned me. The situation was beginning to amuse me and the devil did the rest: my weariness vanished and the fun began.

The huge 1908 earthquake had wrecked the city. Some buildings had been rebuilt but work was slow: for every construction standing, there were at least three demolished houses. My investigators followed me from a distance, always in single file, slowing down or quickening their pace, in keeping with what I was doing. At times I walked slowly, at times I ran, disappearing and reappearing from behind a wall, in the most carefree of ways, and shaking the dust off my lapels whenever they drew closer. It was grand! I saw them flying towards me whenever I turned the corners, and then slowing down, feigning indifference. Rarely have I enjoyed myself so much in my life, and it is difficult for me to say how many times I ran around the block, hiding from the pair of investigators. The game lasted until I saw them as worn out as I was. Once at the station, I had lunch, and took the train to Taormina.

Upon my arrival, I looked for the hotel that had been recommended to me. I lay down, and for the first time in my life slept at a stretch until morning. As there were no investigators following me around in that city, and having already surmised that no warrant had been issued to arrest me, I felt perfectly free. The telephone conversation, held by the police officers in Reggio Calabria, was proof enough I was considered a foreigner.

One of the most interesting features regarding this tour was the Greek Theatre situated on the hills overlooking this beautiful city, and the volcano Etna, whose imposing outline I had glimpsed from a distance. However, since the theatre was considered a war zone, as was the whole of the Straits of Mesina, I wasn´t allowed in. From the theatre, I had been told, one could see the fortifications built in the area some thirty years ago. A permit turned out to be the solution. It was given to me, thanks to my admission card to museums and national monuments. Yet, I was not allowed to visit the theatre on my own: I was flanked by two soldiers almost as young as I was, who loaded old guns with bayonets. While we walked together I offered them cookies, becoming friendly with both, and on the following day they argued among themselves as to who was going to show me the fortifications.

From Taormina I went directly to Palermo, and stopped over in Mesina once again. I wished to better see the magnificent Straits I had only furtively glimpsed on my way up, on account of my weariness. I visited the Diocesan museum, the palaces of the Normandi and Solafoni, the San Giovani and Degli Ermite churches; in Monrreale I saw the magnificent mosaics. Not once did I eat in a restaurant, for in that city, I discovered truly exquisite desserts and ice creams. I also very much enjoyed the Palermitan coastline, and in order to continue beholding the sea, I decided against taking the train: instead, I set sail for Naples. Unfortunately, on my way to Rome, I lost a folder that contained all of my pictures drawn in Naples, Taormina and Monrreale. I´m certain I still had it in Palermo, but when arriving at the hotel in Rome, it was gone.

Chapter 10

Meeting Balla

I remained in the City of the Caesars from September 16 to October 15. After two or three days in which I visited Tívoli and other places, including the catacombs, I went to see Giacomo Balla, whom I considered to be the only painter among the Futurists. At the time he was about forty–five, yet a thick and reddish beard made him seem older. In effect, when he shaved it off some time later, he seemed rejuvenated.

He received me warmly, and was full of optimism regarding his work. He didn't hide, however, that times were hard. Poverty stalked him and he had to display all of his ingenuity to deal with this predicament. His studio was provided with a small and assorted arsenal of tools, wood that he sawed up, adhesives to glue the pieces together, paper and cardboard with which he made toys and numerous practical objects that he sold whenever he had a chance, like lamps and folding screens. Though he was going through hard times, he told me that the secret of happiness consisted in «facing adversity with courage».

He showed me the paintings he had in his studio, some of them quite different from those seen in Florence during the Futurist exhibition. In these, the motif did not exist: they were simple iridescent planes, or vortexes of color that expressed the dynamism of force in movement, similar to how I understood and practiced movement in many drawings and in some paintings, as for instance, «Luci nel paesaggio».

The works that Balla showed me, achieved in 1912 and subsequent years, seemed to reveal a new conception of Futurism: they were geometric forms in tension, extending from one edge of the canvas to the other, or vortexes, whose lines converged at the center of the canvas. His painting was far removed from the superimposition of wheels and feet, so offensive to my taste. I told him so sincerely, and that made him happy: his very light blue eyes lightened up with joy, the way a child shows his pleasure when his effort is rewarded. Like all great artists who abandon themselves to their work with generosity, Balla was far from imagining that he had paved the way for the era of Abstract Painting in Italy.

I'd like to state that among the Italian painters, the first one to create what today is called Abstract painting using only his intuition was Giacomo Balla. The second painter was me, as from 1914 and also intuitively. This is documented in official catalogues and articles of that period that fortunately have been preserved. As a protagonist of a particularly interesting time and having witnessed quite a few events, I can assure you there was no artist in Florence between the years 1914 and 1917, except myself, that painted or at least showed a picture in which the motifs were not manifest. I did not lose contact with Florence and my friends up until 1924; afterwards, I remained in touch by writing articles on the painters that had evolved the most: it would have given me great pleasure to commend an abstract artist coming from the city where I had been trained. Yet without the shadow of a doubt there was no such painter. Abstract art, as everyone knows, is no–one's privilege, but merely a logical consequence of a revolutionary mental state born with the daguerreotype, culminating in a rebellion against decadent formulas that paralyzed the arts. But once the spell was broken, art liberated itself, and nature was recreated in a completely new fashion, until it reached an unmistakable non–figurative character in the works of many artists. To claim the privilege of being the first is an arrogance in itself, for many arrived at abstraction through ways of their own and moved by different reasons. Some were influenced by Futurist theories that spread like wildfire through the artistic centers in Europe, thanks to the enterprising Marinetti and his power of communication. Others, like Balla, because they actually practiced Futurism or, like Mondrian, as a result of reaching the essence of Cubism.

At any rate, Abstract art, practiced since 1910 and probably before that, (there is an abstract work by Picabia signed in 1909, named «Caoutchouc») wasn't always named as such. Many painters who followed it in its very first period identified it with other names: Kandinsky, in Munich, called it «art without object», Laroniov and Gontcharova, in Moscow, «Rayonism», Delaunay, in Paris, «Orfism», Balla, in Rome, «Futurism», Malevitch named it «Synchronism» and Mondrian «Neo–plasticism». If I, in Florence, termed it «Abstract», it was because it seemed natural to think that abstraction was something people did not consider intelligible when contemplating it.

I return to Balla as I wish to emphasize he was no apprentice when he engaged in Futurism: on the contrary, he was in every way an accomplished artist. He had studied in Paris and was one of the first to introduce Impressionism and Pointillism in Italy. Restless, he searched for technical perfection, a certain light, a certain mood that enveloped the subjects and the objects of his choice.

He had taught Boccioni and Severini at the turn of the century, when chance was on his side and his reputation seemed consolidated. His thematic works sold well and the Roman bourgeoisie raved about his portraits. Famous politicians as well as friends were depicted in an original, unpretentious way, and though he lived comfortably, deep down he was searching for something else, a unique form of expression that would embody the times in which he lived.

Balla felt he had found this unique form of expression in Futurism. It will be remembered that the foundations of Futurism were first set on paper, after a painstaking effort by Boccioni, Carrà and Russolo, with the help of Marinetti and Decio Conti, the group's secretary. Balla backed them up, just as Severini had. The latter was living in Paris as from 1906, but had not previously seen the text of the proclamation. Anyhow, the point for the artists was to find a new way to translate words into form and color, thus creating a new language, articulating it, and this with the sole help of intuition.

Giacomo Balla's case cannot be compared to those of the other Futurists who embraced the cause when still young, at the beginning of their careers; they had nothing to lose when embarking on the adventure, whereas Balla took the biggest chance of his life: not only was he already enjoying a considerable standing, but he had a home to keep up. Deeds like his, so seldom performed in the life of men, cannot be explained if it weren't for folly or heroism. His circle called him foolish: I judge him brave. Never have his relatives and admirers been able to understand why he relinquished luxury and blandishments, nor why he renewed his faith even in the face of poverty, that also threatened his small family, his mother, his wife and two daughters.

The wealthy clientele ostensibly turned their back against him, no longer giving him any commissions, while critics recommended exorcizing the bad spirits in order to redeem himself. He had no alternative but to break with the past once and for all. So as to indicate to his family there was no going back, he auctioned his previous production. A placard, scattered with black crosses, read: «The works of the late Balla are sold here».

He paid dearly for his caustic sense of humor, for he was ostracized for twenty–five years, and reduced to penury. When I saw Balla in Rome he was living with his family in great want, painting Futurist pictures in the day –to make things worse, these were not figurative– that were laughed at by the experts, and at night making objects in order to earn a living. To make matters worse, his family harassed him, blaming him of their misfortunes: they believed that by harrying him he would return to the «right path».

Balla's resolution when defending his convictions, his unfaltering dedication, his sincere enthusiasm, truly impressed me. I saw he had been hurt, yet he was cheerful and optimistic, as though feeling fulfilled for having created something new and profoundly his.

That night I wondered if I would have to battle against life's vicissitudes, and I reached the conclusion that it would be more tolerable if I were alone to confront them.

As I had not visited Rome properly on my outward journey, I did so this time, and while I was at it, I also returned to Asisi, Perusa and Arezzo. I was mainly interested in studying the frescoes by Giotto and Piero della Francesca.

During my brief stay, one of the first Roman avant–garde men I met was Anton Giulio Bragaglia, director of the Experimental Theater, the «Cronica d'Attualità» magazine and the Casa d'Arte that was named after him. We liked each other from the start. At nightfall, the most prestigious Roman artists and intellectuals met at the magazine's editorial office: together with the «La Voce» and the «Lacerba» publications, they were Italy's vibrant voices. There I made the acquaintance of Pannaggi, Bandinelli, and Paladini, three Futurist painters who became my friends. Though the three were very intelligent, as painters they left no trace. I also got to know Enrico Prampolini, a Futurist at the time and Vittorio Orazzi, his brother, a good writer, whom I'm still friends with today and who wrote many articles on my work.

As days went by, I got to know many people. Among these was Sproveri, director of a Roman gallery, the Futurist Gallery, if I remember properly. This gallery, in 1914, had mounted the same exhibition I had seen in Florence and which had so stunned me. I also met Spadini, a Florentine painter, who after having been awarded a grant allowing him to study in Rome had remained there; they called him the «Italian Renoir». Compared to what other Italian traditionalist painters were doing at that time, Spadini was by far the best. I took to him for he was intelligent and kind; sadly, he was ill, and died some time later.

Among the first people I met in Rome was Emiliano Gómez Clara, a painter from Córdoba [13]. He lived a few steps away from Piazza del Popolo, in a studio built on a roof, to which he had added, on the other end of the terrace, a small room that he used as a darkroom. He earned his living as a photographer, but the profession was ungrateful and he was finding it difficult to get by. He was sentimental and cried about everything. As a picturesque detail of his life in the city, he told me that since he had begun developing the pictures that he took during the day at night, he had to cross the terrace with a lamp in order to walk from his studio to the darkroom, and people had taken him for a spy, something that caused him quite an inconvenience.

Commissioned by an advertising company, I believe, he'd been asked to

---

13   Córdoba is a province in Argentina, located in the center of the country

take some nocturnal pictures in the vicinity of the Temple of Vesta, and invited me along. I gladly accepted. To keep me amused, he gave me a camera to take pictures with, while he took his: he had to leave the shutter open, and placed his camera on a tripod. For a while I watched his work with interest, observing how he closed the shutter every time a streetcar came by, and then opened it again. After a while, I walked away to take my own pictures.

I was doing just that when I noticed a crowd surrounding him. People brandished their fists threateningly. My small camera in my hand, I hastened to help him, realizing soon enough it had been an imprudence; the mob turned against me, yelling out in anger: «He is a spy too!» Blows were dealt and they would have probably lynched us if two police officers had not arrived. They took our cameras and tripods, leading us to a police station whose main entrance gave on to a street and the back door on to the Tiber. Meanwhile, the mob had followed us, screaming abuses. Since some loyal patriots were patiently waiting to take the law into their own hands, the police officers had us leave through the back door, which gave on to the Tiber.

I ran across Marinetti while holding a conversation with Bragaglia in the editorial office of the «Cronaca d´Attualità» newspaper. Once again, he brought up Futurism, but in a pleasant way, and I managed to shift the topic of conversation. In my Roman days I had seen too many Futurist works for him to be able to tempt me, and many felt the Movement was heading towards banality. Its main pillar was Balla, who identified with it without having any ulterior motive. Rather, he had an authentic vocation towards everything modern. Unfortunately, one or two artists do not make up the masses, and the masses, thinking perhaps that method can substitute for essence, turned Futurism into some sort of trademark.

On the other hand, the following words were engraved in my memory: «Great artists have never needed to sign a proclamation or a theory in order to make art. A painter of genius creates and imposes himself, with neither theories nor declaration of rights. Theories can be dangerous, for groups weaken spiritually, prompting some sort of unilateral quarrel».

This maxim was signed by Giovanni Papini and had been published in the «Lacerba» magazine in January 1913, when the publication, created by Prezzolini, Palazzeschi and Tavolato, was not yet linked to Futurism; on the contrary, it attacked it. At the time, the magazine was pure pure poetry in the revolutionary sense and independent of all schools or groups, according to what Soffici and Papini later disclosed in their writing. The men explained that if they had accompanied the Futurists part of the way it was because they had wanted to «give this valorous avant–garde Movement the substance it seemed to lack, liberating it from an attitude that to many seemed mere charlatanism or clownish theatricality». The partnership lasted only for a year, though both groups remained friends.

Chapter 11

First Solo Exhibition

Back in Florence, one noon I went to a café that stood on the corner of Piazza del Duomo and Via dè Martelli in order to get a cold drink. Tables were placed on the sidewalk, even in winter. Many people frequented it, for not only was it near to the Cathedral but it was also the terminus of the streetcar line that ran from Florence to Fiesole and Settignano.

I didn't usually go to cafés during the day and I was sitting alone, letting my mind wander freely, when suddenly, looking towards Via Calzaioli, I noticed a tall young man crossing the square, between the Baptistery and the Duomo, with a very small suitcase dangling from his hand, striding purposefully towards me.

He planted himself in front of me, akin to one who has finally reached his goal, and asked me in Spanish whether I was Pettoruti. I nodded, and he introduced himself: Alejandro Schulz Solari. His name didn't produce any effect on me, but not so his figure and face: upon the very tall body was a well–formed head, with a pair of intelligent kind eyes. His first words uttered were funny and witty.

I asked him, startled, how he had managed to recognize me amid so many people, to which he calmly replied that having guided his steps, I could not be someone else. They had spoken of me in Paris and given him my address, just as they had given it to Sibellino; first he had tried my studio and as he hadn't found me there, had headed towards the Cathedral. I asked him, concerned, if I could help him in any way, to which he answered that he would very much appreciate it if I could find him a small room, albeit the smallest one in Florence. Upon inquiring about his luggage, he showed me his suitcase: that was all he carried.

After walking around for a while, we found a room to his liking, though it did not agree with his stature. That evening we had dinner together: he came to my studio, saw what I was doing and we endlessly chatted till two in the morning. I realized he was keenly interested in the world around him; art, linguistics, philosophy, religion, esotericism, everything attracted him to the same degree. Our conversation followed no specific trail: astronomy and oceanography, the pictorial techniques and the musical ones, all subjects were broached. He was a charming young man, slightly extravagant, as limpid as a child.

Three days after his arrival, he told me he wanted to buy himself antique rings, yet the ones he bought were so large he couldn´t fold his fingers. He also developed a mania for walking sticks, yet some of the ones he bought were so long that when he went out for a stroll, everybody turned round to look at him, for in his solemnity he resembled a master of ceremonies.

We became close friends and this encouraged him to remain in Florence; he therefore wrote to his mother in Zoagli for her to send him his trunks. As soon as these had arrived, he showed me his paintings, most of them watercolors. I must confess that I didn´t like the oils he had painted so far, whereas his watercolors were extremely beautiful and original, with a fresh compositional approach and extraordinary colors.

His watercolor technique was already polished, and he handled the transparent and opaque colors to perfection. He knew how to apply them, when not to and which papers to use in each case. Xul so mastered this technique he remains unmatched. In this respect, I believe his work will be valued as time goes by, once the public´s taste is educated, for his painting is not common and cannot be pigeonholed. The images are personal, and just like him, ethereal: that is why they aren´t easily understood and enjoyed.

While I examined his work, my new friend told me my name was appropriate for a painter but that he didn´t like his. I suggested he change it and we became absorbed in finding him a pleasant and sonorous name that would bear some relation to his own. After having imagined a thousand combinations, we came up with the name he is known by today: Xul Solar.

I told Xul about the pleasant atmosphere that reigned in Gino Sensani´s studio, and I took him along to a meeting. As usual, there were all kinds of people: intelligent, schooled or snobbish, as is usually the case in this type of social gathering. Xul was delighted; at times he would speak to someone about the signs of the Zodiac, at times about Egyptian mummies. One guest asked him something about the tango; very matter–of–factly he replied that his friend Pettoruti was an expert dancer. Whoever has met Xul knows how much people took to him. A polyglot –he spoke five languages: Spanish, Italian, English, French and German– it did not take long for him to make acquaintances and familiarize himself with his environment, especially one so attractive to foreigners. He had barely arrived that already he knew everyone; that is, every original human being, strange or eccentric, and if enigmatic, occupied with esoteric problems or three–legged tables, even more so.

He always caught people unaware, and like a magician, could perform any trick. One day, he invited me to a reunion at the home of two rather peculiar ladies of ancient lineage. I can still remember the parlor filled with antique furniture, lace–covered pillows, screens, small tables and knick–knacks. He had them believe, as he had others, that I was a wonderful tango dancer, though I assured them of the contrary. In the twinkling of an eye, all obstacles, including the rug, were stacked up in the corners, as one of these ladies sat by the piano and started to play a tango on the piano. And what a tango, good grief! She practically ruined it! The other lady offered me her arm and I had no other choice than to dance. As one can imagine, I limited myself to doing pirouettes, hoping for the right moves, remembering what I had seen. The funny part of the story is that, on our way out, Xul stopped in the middle of the sidewalk to tell me: «you danced that very well!»

During the first months of 1916, Xul Solar posed for me several times. I kept on working intensively, especially as I was projecting to mount a solo show at the «Gonnelli» gallery at the end of spring. Both the owner and my friend encouraged me enthusiastically.

It was inaugurated at the beginning of July, and consisted of thirty–five works, nine of which were drawings achieved between 1914 and 1916. I exhibited fifteen paintings –temperas and oils– and among these there was a portrait of Codegoni and a study of Xul Solar´s portrait, which I had called «Luce–Elevazione». It did not represent his features objectively, but rather, depicted him the way I saw him, as an otherworldly being, all light and spirit. There also were two studies inspired by Etruscan art, named «Costruzione antica» and «Forme statique». Among the landscapes, one of San Giminiano and two of Vallombrosa, that I called «La foresta» and «Paesaggio verde». There was yet another one, that belonged to the dynamic series «Luci nel paesaggio»

These paintings, representative to me, were considered Futurist at the time, though most of them were static; then, people branded them as Cubist; today they are called abstract and tomorrow they will probably belong to a new category. Only valid works survive labels.

At the exhibition, there were also still–lifes and interiors, a collage and a mono–copy. In an adjacent room, I had assembled eight mosaics on cardboard, including «Spring»: in the middle of the room I had placed one of the two mosaics achieved in the course of the year 1915, named «Meditazione». Gonnelli loved this mosaic. While the exhibition was still on, he told me one day that if I gave it to him, he would carry it on his shoulders from his gallery to the Duomo, some two hundred meters away.

The mosaic, measuring 91 cm by 78 cm, made of solid iron, cement and glass, needed the strength of two men to be moved, and though the singular proposition tempted me, I refused. Although Gonnelli meant well, it was too risky. The exhibition was well received by everyone, yet one of my biggest satisfactions was to see Nella again. I was growing increasingly fond of her, and had especially asked her to come. She did, on the morning following the opening, accompanied by her mother and one of her sisters. I took to them both and I believe it was reciprocal; at noon we had vermouth in a bourgeois tearoom and all of us chatted like old friends.

Chapter 12

Rome

I realized that life in Florence would prove to be impossible for me, not only because it was a city where paintings were hard to sell, making it difficult for me to imagine living off my art, but also because it did not possess any art–related industry that would allow me to exercise all that I had learned on the subject of decoration. Moreover, it did not have large publishing houses where I could find work, and the few available jobs had already been monopolized by local artists.

I could not count on my grant, which was irregular and about to expire, nor did I want to return home before having produced some work. The solution, if I wanted to stay, was to try my luck in Milan, the only wealthy city in Italy, where, as far I knew, one could make a living from painting, decoration or illustration of books.

Milan thus became my aspiration. But before leaving, I wished to probe into the artistic and intellectual atmosphere of Rome, undoubtedly the most interesting and vital city of Italy, as much for its avant–garde publications as for its theatre, its concerts at the Augusteum and the artists and intellectuals who worked in it.

I made preparations to leave everything in order behind, so that the crates with my paintings and my trunk with my clothes could be sent to me whenever I needed them. I separated the work I was not going to take with me, and Nella selected several drawings, collages and paintings. Many people did the same: Celestino Celestini, my former engraving teacher, and some friends of mine, Lega and Gino Sensani. Gonnelli told me the paintings and drawings he had chosen could eventually be exhibited. I also shipped a large tempera (160cm by140cm) to Buenos Aires, achieved at the end of 1914. It was bound for the 1916 National Salon; more specifically, the Decorative Arts Section, the only department that accepted abstract work. The painting represented the four seasons, symbolized by different colors. As I did not wish to give this work a logical title, so as to discourage people from searching for form, I named it «Harmonies», already used on other occasions. The art critics of the «La Nación» newspaper (September 22, 1916) gave it a lot of attention, describing it as «something novel as well as beautiful». I still cannot understand this miracle.

In order to understand how many objects a person can accumulate in the course of three years, one has to go through the experience of moving oneself. The task of putting books in crates was endless. I had begun to enjoy reading at fifteen and have never stopped since: my first book, «The Arabian Nights», given to me by my grandfather, accompanied me until 1924. When I first moved to Florence I had been under the impression I wouldn't have had enough time to time to read, yet the volumes that now sprung from all corners proved the contrary. I only selected those books that had annotations in the margins; the others I gave to Nella.

I have always had the habit of jotting down reflections, whether they agreed with the thesis that was proposed in the book or not. Every time these reflections required elaboration, I wrote them down in thick red notebooks that accompanied me for years and that subsequently remained in Italy, at the bottom of a large trunk or in some of the crates that are presently in Florence. Many things that I now miss and need I left behind.

My life has always been rather agitated, moving from one place to the next, from one city to another. Living in three different countries, means getting rid of hundreds of objects: in the hustle and bustle of moving, these are judged unnecessary or are ill–appreciated. How many things I discarded in order to lighten my baggage, every time I had to move! Innumerable studies and paintings, sketches and drawings!

Europeans are quite different, however, for they generally live and die in the same place, often in the same home they were born in. They therefore keep all of their belongings, from the first to the last, though what they hold on to has often little value, excluding the sentimental one. That was not my case. For one reason or another, throughout my life I have damaged at least one third of the work I have achieved. My thirst of destruction has always been unquenchable, yet I wouldn't recommend it, except if the art is insignificant. I recall having ruined many beautiful works that either exasperated me at the time, or took up too much space. When I think about it, my blood runs cold.

At the end of September 1916 I left for Rome, some days before Xul traveled to Zoagli, where his mother and his aunt lived. We were so intimately attached, that he could not conceive of Florence without me, nor I conceive of the Eternal City without him. Yet circumstances didn't allow him to live in Rome, though he was about to do so on several occasions. Henceforth, the long walks along the Arno and the conversations that made it so pleasant were resumed in Lungo il Tevere, in the company of new friends and framed by other sceneries.

The first thing I did in Rome was to keep the appointment with Guillermo Laborde, a Uruguayan painter whom the government had awarded a grant to, and who had visited my studio when in Florence. I wanted to find out whether there was a room available where he was living. Though the landlady had none, she gave me an address that I immediately considered, after fixing another appointment with my friend.

As I was crossing Piazza Barberini, I ran into an old acquaintance of mine from Florence, accompanied by the painter and sculptor Roberto Melli. Upon telling them why I was in such as hurry, Melli exclaimed: «Why, I've just moved out of my studio. It's right here, on the square; you can have it!» It was in that Piazza Barberini studio that overlooked Via Veneto that I spent the eight months of my stay in Rome, spending very little and perfectly comfortable.

Melli had asked me out of the blue what I thought of Michelangelo. The question was so unexpected it left me speechless. Without batting an eye, he added: «Michelangelo is a cretin». Immediately he proceeded to expose a series of clever reflections, to prove his point of view. Such was the intellectual climate that reigned in Rome at the time, in the avant–garde circles.

We immediately became friends, and our friendship lasted until his death: no shadows darkened it, in spite of our frequent and even violent arguments when discussing art. He was one of the best and most intelligent men I have ever met.

I also became close friends with Guillermo Laborde, so much so that when I left for Nemi for a fortnight, he stayed at my studio. According to him, he achieved his best paintings there. We often met in the city, and then in Milan, where he took up residence after having lived for a while in Madrid and Paris. In Milan he felt at ease because he loved the opera. Many of the singers were his friends, and he himself enjoyed warbling; his voice was not particularly full, but I remember it harmonious. Just as he had painted the portrait of his friends the singers, he painted mine. I saw it again in Montevideo, but in spite of his promise, he never gave it to me.

In Rome I quickly became active. The editing office of the «Cronaca d'Attualità» magazine continued to be one of the meeting points of those academics and artists most considered for their modernism. There I got to know the Roman intellectual circles, unexpectedly discovering I enjoyed controversy.

Either because I had gotten used to listening to those who knew more than I did on all subjects, from the humanistic to the artistic, or because I feared not being able to express myself clearly in a language that wasn't mine, the truth is that in Florence, and particularly at the Caffè delle Giubbe Rosse, where Papini, Palazzeschi and Soffici handled the philosophical, poetical and artistic languages to perfection, I had never become involved in heated discussions. I only argued with Soffici, Garbari or Lega perhaps because we were alone.

This taste was revealed to me without warning on an afternoon in which a fiery discussion was being held at the Aragno café. I passionately took part, broaching a particularly contentious subject. It was only after I had won the battle that I realized how much I had learned in my adored Florence and with my beloved Nella. From then on, I participated in all conversations that touched on topics I knew about, in practice or in theory, without paying any heed to my learned opponents. Without training there is no practice, without practice there is no proficiency; this is what I believe.

As I have always attempted to do, I worked in Rome every morning up until one o'clock. In the afternoons I visited museums and churches and explored the city alone or accompanied; at nightfall, I met with a friend to walk and chat, or went to the café. At times I headed for Bragaglia's editing office, and together we had dinner at his theater. Bandinelli, Pannaggi or Prampolini would sometimes join us.

One afternoon I met Serge Diaghilev, animator of the Russian Ballets that became so popular in Paris and in the whole of Europe, at the editing office. He was mounting the ballet «Parade», with music by Eric Satie. While I was there, Bragaglia showed him a portfolio I had left with him, filled with costume designs, settings, and a hundred other things of the same order that Diaghilev just loved. In a fit of enthusiasm, he told me he would perhaps entrust the decorations and the costumes for a ballet in preparation to me. As I never saw him again, the project fell through.

Giorgio de Chirico and I became friends. He was working on a painting I considered rather poor and heard him say that he was going to the Villa Borghese museum to copy the old masters, for he wanted to learn to paint like them. He lived, just as he does today, preoccupied with painting techniques, though it is fair to say that in those days, given the radical change his art was going through, he absolutely needed to tackle them. He told me he had gone from a metaphysical painting, flat and literary, to a realistic one: the latter had been suddenly revealed to him in a dazzling way. The situation was not easy for him, since the new manner required chiaroscuro, impasto, nuances and «sfumato»: in a nutshell, all that he had not practiced.

Given his temperament and his eminently literary inclinations –he loved the mythological painting by the Swiss Arnold Bröecklin, which amounts to saying it all– leads me to believe that Realism was not his field.

However, it took root in him, and probably because he was very intelligent he understood that his metaphysical work would not lead him very far. When I saw him in Rome he was working on a completely objective self–portrait. I visited him a few times at his home, where I met his mother, a woman of penetrating intelligence, lucidity and unusual discretion. I chatted a great deal with her, and she took on to me. She said she was happy to know we were friends.

My conversations with De Chirico, often held at the café, invariably turned to the subject of technique; he selected the topic deliberately and this flattered but also intrigued me: none of the painters that belonged to my circle were obsessed by technique. Balla, who mastered it, spoke about painting in general, regardless of its era and tendency, and mused on its spirituality, as did Soffici, Garbari or Melli. Prampolini, on the other hand, fanatical about Futurism, spoke only about dynamic impulse, simultaneity, lines of force and plane interpenetration.

As regards Prampolini, here goes a short anecdote:

I had taken a few cardboards with me to Rome to show everyone what I was doing, and among these was the initial version of «La grotta azurra di Capri», achieved in Florence in 1915 upon my return from my trip to Sicily. On that occasion, I hadn´t been able to visit Capri and the cavern extensively, but nonetheless, had felt delighted by its strange submarine luminosity. I had made sketches of it, which I later used to tackle the problem of the transposition of light. This entailed the light of the painting itself, rather than the fleeting brightness that penetrated into the cavern. Prampolini, who stayed for long periods of time on the Island, had never thought of painting this fabulous cave, similar to a cathedral. Only when he saw my painting did he decide to make a watercolor, which right away was reproduced in several magazines.

I don´t believe this work enhanced his reputation nor do I think anyone remembers it: this story could have taken place thousands of years ago, for throughout time there have always been artists craving to steal the limelight, when in fact one should remain true to oneself. It goes without saying that this incident did not disturb my friendship with Prampolini. Throughout life we have always chatted a lot, and have always respected one another. Always eager to learn, he was a very active and talented artist and a man of great imagination. No–one told better tall tales than he did: he made up adventures his fantasy adorned with the most unbelievable and exciting details.

It was through Prampolini that I first learned about the Dada Movement, generated in Zurich. He corresponded with half the world, and had just received a set of reproductions that he showed to me, asking me for my opinion. Schwitters' collages amused him because they were smaller than the photographs we held in our hands, though the size indicated on the back of the reproductions stated the contrary. I recall having told him that I approved of the rejection of morality, religion, the State and all other conventions. This was a sign of health, but if seen through the eyes of painting, I deemed it to be too literary. I still believe this today, though many great artists participated in this movement: Hans Arp, Marcel Duchamp and Prampolini himself.

Bragaglia was certainly a unique man in this lively and eclectic world in which I moved; he was remarkable for his infinite goodness and his multiple activities: he directed a theater, the magazine, his gallery, he wrote books and journalistic articles and did all he could to help youth out, being himself still a young man. Everybody loved him and he deserved it. Our deep friendship lasted until his death, and I recall him fondly.

During my Roman period, I also became friends with Mario Broglio, a youth very well versed in the arts. As a painter he lacked imagination and he knew it. He had therefore always refused to exhibit his work, in spite of having been pressed to do so by flatterers. His large fortune enabled him to publish, two years later, and from 1919 to1922, the «Valori Plastici» magazine. As far as I know, it was the best one in Italy at the time, as far as modern arts were concerned. I received it in Milan, where I was living, thanks to his generosity; it was profusely illustrated, leaving no doubt as to his prosperity. Through the black and white reproductions, I got to know what many Cubists were doing: Archipenko, Marie Blanchard, Metzinger, Gleizes, Herbin. The magazine also reproduced still–lifes achieved earlier, signed by Braque, Picasso, Juan Gris. The most renowned pens of the European avant–garde contributed in «Valori Plastici». I remember articles by Maurice Reynal, André Salmon, André Breton, Jean Cocteau, Max Jacob, Soffici, de Chirico, Savinio and others. Some of these authors also wrote in the «Cronaca d´Attualità» newspaper.

From the years 1915 to 1925, these intellectuals and some members of the political spheres frequented the Aragno and Il Greco cafés (the latter being today a national monument), discussing public and artistic questions with a great deal of inspiration and talent.

I would lie if I said that the atmosphere of war was felt in Rome; at least not in my circles. Some of my colleagues and friends had to abide by a schedule in barracks and ministries; they wore uniforms, but apparently their lives went on, as usual. The harrowing news came from the countryside, where the cannons rumbled.

If I had to assess the eight months I lived in Rome, extraordinarily active in retrospect, I would say they made me a better judge of characters, or at least of certain characters, which perhaps explains many things. I spent the month of July 1917 in Florence; an absolutely peaceful month. I had just sold the paintings I had created when staying at the Lago de Nemi for a few days: Sproveri, the director of the Futurist gallery, bought them at a very convenient price for him... and also for me.

In Florence I saw Nella almost daily. We visited the places we knew and explored new ones. At times, her sister accompanied us; I went to her house for dinner, invited by her parents who approved of our relationship. Were we friends? Did we love each other? It was true I adored her, yet a formal relationship was simply impossible. Painting was a jealous lover that demanded total independence and I didn't want to see it disturbed by responsibilities of any kind. Mind you, we were happy that way, and didn't ask for more. After having visited my old friends in Florence, I boarded the train for Milan. I was twenty–four and leaping into the unknown.

Chapter 13
Milan

It is curious that when living in Rome or Florence, where I had so many friends and acquaintances connected to the Milanese society, it did not occur to me to find out the address of a hotel or ask someone for a letter of presentation. I was facing the new city that I knew to be harsh, totally alone; as a result, I was neither too optimistic nor too cautious.

On the train, a traveler with whom I engaged in conversation indicated a hotel to me, and that was all. From there, I went to look for a room and found it not too far away from the Duomo. I had enough money to resist modestly for four or five months. I paid my rent two months in advance and began to meditate on what to do.

That morning, in the large gallery that faced the Duomo, very well known by both the Milanese and foreigners, I had run into Tulio Garbari, whom I knew had taken up residence in the capital of Lombardy some months before. We had a coffee and talked. Though we were very good friends, I didn´t dare to reveal my critical situation to him, thinking perhaps that his situation wasn´t brilliant, either.

The first thing I did in Milan was to write Xul a letter, as we had agreed upon. He came immediately. I arranged with the landlady for her to put a pair of couches in my bedroom in place of a bed. Xul, as usual, akin to a juggler who throws balls in the air and catches them all at the same time, revealed some brand new ideas to me: the quarter tone on the piano and a universal language, «Esperanto».

Though we were cheerful, neither one of us knew what to do; Xul wasn´t doing very well economically either, for the income his mother received from Argentina arrived extremely irregularly.

In those days, postcards that came in series were at the height of fashion; either they portrayed Love, Maternity, Spring or the Life of the Soldier, and each series was composed of six cards. Using gouache, I began painting cardboards and completed two series, in the hope that some editor might show some interest in them. The task accomplished, Xul and I went out to find someone who might want them. It was extremely hot. All of our possible editors told us the same thing: too modern, too refined, they would not please the run–of–the–mill customer.

My disappointment was great. After having conducted a survey among the salesmen, I bought some postcards that people most liked in order to become inspired and created another series, as ordinary as could be. The result was the same. In spite of all my imagination and Xul's fantasy, we didn't succeed, everything was a loss of time.

We began to economize more, limiting ourselves to one nightly meal. At noon, when Xul came back from work (that is, attempting to find someone interested in my work), he would whistle «Bicho feo» [14] from the sidewalk. I would then lean out of our window on the fifth floor to tell him whether «it» would be «yellow» or «white». «It» referred to either the polenta or the fresh bread that made up our lunch.

Neither he nor I enjoyed hardships, but we were young and carefree, waiting for better times. No–one noticed how difficult things were for us, not even the landlady. More than once, after having finished our polenta or bread, we left to «walk the meal», telling the landlady: «Arrivederci, ce ne andiamo a pranzo», and she wished us the best of appetites. At times Xul stayed home, exhausted of walking about and I would tell the landlady that I was having lunch alone, because my friend wasn't hungry. In the meanwhile, Xul, who knew how much I detested cold polenta, lingered on the stairs so as to hand it to me frozen. He would then gobble it up amid peals of laughter.

I had my baggage sent from Florence. A portfolio filled with sketches destined for stained glass gave me the idea to present them to a factory. I looked through the telephone directory and immediately headed for the one nearest by. A friendly gentleman received me and he observed my drawings with a great deal of attention, one by one. Then he kindly asked me to look at those designs that were used as samples. They were in the worst of taste and we understood each other without needing to speak. Nonetheless, the gentleman looked at my drawings once again, and told me they were beautiful, alas, too beautiful.

I was about to leave when, mysteriously, an Argentine expression slipped into my speech; actually, I do know why, for it had already been for over two months that Xul and I spoke to each other only in our mother tongue. The gentleman, intrigued, asked if I was Spanish; when he learned I was Argentine he was overjoyed and wished to know whether I knew the Barolo

---

14 Translator's footnote: In Argentina, " Bicho feo" is the popular name for the mokingbird. It produces a cry similar to that of its name, which literally means "ugly creature

Palace in Buenos Aires. I answered that of course I did, and delighted, told me it had been his brother, the architect Ugo Palanti, who had designed it.

The conversation, on the brink of petering out, suddenly picked up. Mr. Palanti wished to know when I had arrived to the city, what I did for a living, how I lived and if I was well–connected. I thought it best to tell him the truth, and he offered to introduce me as soon as possible to the best art critic in Milan, a friend of his, who worked in a publishing house, besides being the director of a magazine and responsible of a Fine Arts section in the Milanese newspaper, «La Sera», very important at the time. Without losing a second, this generous and helpful man spoke on the telephone with Rafaello Giolli, the person in question, and arranged a meeting for the following morning.

Happy as can be, I ran to give Xul the news. I had every reason to be exhilarated! At nine o'clock the following morning I met the most enchanting and humane man in the world and one of my most beloved future friends. After a while, Giolli asked me if I wished to illustrate books intended for children. He immediately gave me the first one, which I illustrated at once. Then came the other books.

Rafaello Giolli was the key figure who opened up the doors of the artistic Milan to me, introducing me to many well–known artists, among them his close friend Aldo Carpi, Arturo Tosi, Mario Sironi, Adolfo Wildt, Achille Funi and so many others who very soon incorporated me into the «Famiglia Artistica» they belonged to. I joined this association as a «member painter» in 1918.

Almost immediately I met painter Piero Marussig, who became a great friend of mine; the sculptor Arturo Martini, and the writers and poets Dino Campana, Giuseppe Ungaretti, Mario Buggelli, Paolo Buzzi, Emilio Settimelli, Luigi Pirandello, Massimo Bontempelli, Ada Negri, Enrico Somaré, Umberto Notari, Ugo Martelli and so many other people. It was Ugo who introduced his good and dear friend to me, Mrs. Palmer, owner and director of the Palmer House of Fashion.

While I illustrated the books, something that came to me naturally, I returned to my painting. In fact, I had never abandoned it, if one considers that a painter does not only paint when holding a brush in his hand; he paints when he speaks, eats, walks, rests, for his art exists within him. Although I had less time, I was at ease economically and soon I learned a new skill: that of the distribution of time.

Xul returned to Zoagli and I first rented a large room, then a small apartment in an alley, composed of five rooms, most of them small. Two of these had an independent entrance and a kitchen. An old couple took care of my things and cleaned up the place for me. There I lived and worked until I returned to my home country.

During my first months in Milan I neither visited Marinetti, nor Carrà nor Rissole. I mentioned that I saw Garbari quite by chance. I had wanted to solve things on my own, without sharing or revealing my difficulties, for I have always believed that personal tribulations interest very few men. I was conscious that mine could only interest those people that were very close to me, or those who were very sensitive. On the other hand, I have always trusted time, the greatest of healers. I have never sunk into despair when going through rough spells; I never lost my head when going through good ones. Moreover, the advice that marked my life was the one given to me by my grandfather, product of his own disenchantment: «Never ask anybody anything; it is the only way to keep friends». Personally I wasn't disillusioned, but just in case...

One afternoon, after the critical phase had subsided and already settled in my room, I went to see Marinetti at his house, the famous Casa Rosse, where he lived with his charming wife. The last time we had seen each other was when he had passed through Rome (Marinetti was always passing through, except when in Milan), at Bragaglia's publishing office, so that when he saw me and I told him I was living in Milan, he could neither believe his eyes nor ears. We talked about this and that and for the first time he didn't ask me whether I was a Futurist; I wished he had, for now I had enough experience to answer back. Instead, he introduced me to Gabriel d'Annunzio, with whom he had an appointment at the Cova café, on the Piazza della Scala. This great man that I had imagined immense, was actually small and thin and wore a jacket that seemed to be too tight at the waist. His ardent eyes shone as though he had a fever. He was the only one speaking, and always about Trieste.

More at ease now, I also visited Carrà. As he didn't remember me well, I gave him details of our first meeting. He lived with his young wife in two tiny rooms and in squalor. They were good friends of Medardo Rosso, whom Carrà had met in Paris. I became acquainted with this great sculptor at the couple's home, where he was often invited to dinner. He would then arrive by car, which he filled to the brim with provisions.

Whenever he and I met, it was at the «Famiglia Artistica». I liked to contradict him, as his reactions and arguments had a rustic quality to them; in general he was self–assertive and brusque. One day, we argued more than what prudence allowed and he left irately. When we met anew, some weeks later, we greeted each other coldly. When I told Marinetti we were on bad terms, he shrugged his shoulders: «¡Beh! lui è come tanti altri; ha approfittato del Futurismo per farsi un nome, poi è tornato ad essere quel che è stato sempre: un vero pasticcione...» [15]

And then he changed the subject.

As I have already mentioned, the war did not make itself feel either in Florence or Rome. This was also true of Milan, in spite of being so closely sit-

---

[15] Translator's Footnote: "Bah, he is like the rest; he took advantage of Futurism to make a name for himself, now he is back to what he has always been: a true impersonator..."

uated to the battlefields and exhibiting so many uniforms. One day, however, panic spread in the laborious city: the day of the Caporetto disaster. These were moments of great tension, for the Austrian invasion seemed imminent. Yet, the news that the enemy had been detained lightened up the gloomy expressions; the knitted brows smoothed out as if by enchantment and all returned to a certain order.

I attended two exhibitions in 1918, held at the Famiglia Artistica, and exhibited at the Secessione of Rome; I also participated with my painting «L'istitutrice», which I had recently finished, at a collective show organized by Bragaglia in his Casa d'Arte. I had almost adapted myself to the Milanese environment, in which my life evolved in a rather agreeable manner. At night, I went to the cafés frequented by painters and poets, or dined at Marussig's, with whom I had become close friends.

Piero Marussig was a talented and intelligent painter. He came from Trieste, from a wealthy family and had lived in Paris for many years; he found it hard to get used to Milan, which he considered dry and inhumane, and where Mammon ruled. His general culture was very vast; as far as art was concerned, he went no further than Van Gogh, Gauguin and Cézanne: he fervently admired them. Of Cubism, of which I so wanted to have his firsthand opinion, he knew nothing: like so many others, he had lived surrounded by it, but had failed to see it. Carrà was the only one who at times spoke to me about Cubism, but since he was against it, his biased opinion wasn't very helpful. As he had traveled to Paris, he knew the Cubists personally, as well as their works, which he did not care for. After having been a Futurist and experimented with metaphysics and primitivism, he was immersed in the naturalistic Lombard painting, which deep down he had always felt his. Mine bothered him for he considered it too rational and excessively modern; to him, and as he left behind in writing, I was losing myself in «abstract fantasies».

Whenever I visited Marinetti, always at his Casa Rosse, we spoke about the Futurist movement. He continued to think I had to join it, and found it odd that somehow influenced by the movement –he felt its effect to be present in some of my works– I wasn't totally involved in something he believed to be the most extraordinary pictorial adventure of the century.

There was no doubt I sympathized with the Futurists and he knew it; but if I sided with them it was because the traditional arts in Italy, of such a low standard, needed that healthy jolt and because I did not identify with the «Pompiers», something my actions and my beliefs demonstrated. To accompany them did not mean to accept their conceptions, for I wanted to achieve art that was solid, the way Cézanne wanted it, and present too in the works of the 14th century Florentines. I did not feel Futurism fulfilled my aspirations.

To me, once Boccioni had died —who, besides being one of the key figures, in the artistic sense of the term, proved to be an agitator, almost as vehement as Marinetti— and Carrà, Severini and Sofici estranged from the Movement, for they were already into another kind of painting, there remained no other pillar of pictorial Futurism than Balla, and only up to a point; Russolo did not count as a painter, in spite of having signed proclamations. I therefore did not believe that the Movement had a brilliant future.

It goes without saying that the manifestos were still advocating the most unbelievable issues. Exhibits were mounted attracting newcomers, but this harmed, rather than favored, the few serious artists that later joined the group. Moreover, my painting, eminently constructive from its beginnings, adapted itself poorly to the lineaments of Futurism.

During my last months in Florence I had achieved some paintings —of which I name only those that are well known— such as «Light–Elevation», «Ancient Construction», «Static Figure» «Vallombrosa», as well as the first version of «The blue cave of Capri». All of them were very measured and still. During my Roman months I had painted, among others, pictures such as «The friend», «Woman at a café», «Friend at the window», «Maiden in the garden», all of them far from embodying Futurist conceptions. In Milan, among my first works «The philosopher», «The teacher», the definitive version of «The blue cave of Capri», my first studies on traveling musicians and a series of self–portraits that I have lost track of, after the manner of the «Self–portrait» owned by the Di Tella Institute in Buenos Aires. The only painting with a Futurist touch is «The dancers», achieved in 1918 and based upon an old drawing in which I searched for movement. In order to convey it, I resorted to the confrontation of perspectives. The idea came to me in 1916, while Xul Solar danced the tango in one of those New Empire–style mansions that we used to frequent. Having reflected about Futurism, it's understandable that when Marinetti insisted on me joining the Movement, I was able to refute him in the most reasonable of ways. Never again was the point brought up, though I know he was upset.

I never stopped going to his house because deep down we liked each other and I knew through Benedetta that he appreciated me. Sometimes, when we ran into each other at the entrance of the Casa Rosse, I would tell him that I was not visiting him, but Benedetta. In effect, it was she I wanted to see and I did so gladly; we often became engrossed in long conversations, often bringing up the theme of Futurism. On one occasion I told her that I failed to see why some artists insisted on painting velocity, dynamism and the like in the old Impressionistic style, for that was a contradiction. Unperturbed, Benedetta remained pensive; this was her attitude when something interested her.

One afternoon in October —it was the year 1918 and I had just received a catalogue of Giacomo Balla's exhibition at the Casa d'Arte Bragaglia– I received a letter from Nella, mailed from Venice, in which she told me she was planning on visiting Milan with her mother, where she hoped to stay for a couple of days. It was a surprise, and indeed a very pleasant one! No adventure erased her from my heart, and it was always she I wanted to have by my side. I went to fetch them at the station, accompanied them to the hotel and waited for them to get ready. It was a beautiful day and I proposed eating in Como, where we spent the day by the lake. The following morning we all went to see Leonardo's «Cenacle» and the ancient basilica Di Santo Ambroggio that I often visited myself. I never ceased to be impressed by the serenity of this architectural monument, so purely and clearly designed. Nella commented that it reflected a complete absence of religious sentiments and as usual, her opinion coincided with mine. Then we headed for the Duomo, gothic art of reason, and she immediately recited Michelet: «Art of the buttresses, of the eternal scaffolds forgotten by the mason». Her mother listened to us in delight, absolutely convinced that she had seen Milan's most beautiful sights, and proud to have had such a knowledgeable cicerone. As for me, that visit was like a ray of light shining upon my solitary existence, for all that surrounded me was harsh and my struggle intense.

CHAPTER 14

Artistic life and struggles

The war ended, at last, and as joy overwhelmed us, I understood how much it had weighed on each and every one of us. It was some sort of collective resurrection, as though the tombs had released every dead man. The people Milan, leaving their doors unlocked, ran to the Piazza del Duomo to shout, to laugh, to cry, to embrace one another.

I too was extremely moved, standing amid the frenzied crowd. For a moment I thought they would trample me, and cautiously crept round the porticos. Finally I got into the building that housed the Famiglia Artistica, where my companions hugged me.

By then I had adopted my colleagues´ habits; they had their own tailors, shoemakers, hatters and physicians, whose services were paid with paintings. This allowed me to be always well dressed and shod, the way my grandfather had taught me. Unfortunately, I fell gravely ill, in the most severe of ways, and I called one of my two doctors, for strange as it might seem, I had two physicians. He told me he believed I had contracted «la spagnuola», the flu that affected all of Europe; in Italy it was creating havoc.

I was running such a high temperature that not even the physicians that most solicitously came to visit me, believed I would survive. However, here you have me remembering the sad episode. The news that my good friend Aroldo Bonzagni had passed away, swept away by the same disease, broke my heart. Together with Romolo Romano, he had signed the first Futurist manifesto (a leaflet inserted in the «Poesía» magazine, directed by Marinetti) in 1910. Both men quit the Movement a few days after having put their signature to the proclamation, and it is obviously a matter of circumstance that

Bonzagni and Romano have remained unknown.

Besides illustrating books and designing posters I started to contribute to the following magazines: «Satana», «Il Mondo» and the «Giornalino della Domenica». Almost simultaneously, I began to work for the Palmer House of Fashion, which paid me generously whenever I designed clothes and accessories, as well as pillows, folding screens, and all that rich clients desire for their homes. What I did with the greatest of pleasures were the shop windows; more than once did they hold up traffic in the narrow Corso Vittorio Emmanuele, attracting the attention of the press. This benefited me as much as it did the Palmer House, though the latter certainly did not need it, considering its reputation amid the elegant Italians. Palanti too asked for stained glass projects to present at an exhibition; though these were considered as works of the house, I signed them. Around that time, I worked for a puppet theater, designing the costumes and the sets for the Teatro Sperimentale of Bragaglia, as well as for a ballet that was shown in Rome, at the Apollo variety theater.

My lack of precision concerning dates should surprise no one: just like the portraits or posters that I achieved effortlessly, the jobs I landed either helped me earn a living or please a young artist, composer or stage director. What really mattered to me was my painting, the art that I created. Yet, these paintings that could galvanize sensitive people like Rafaelo Giolli, Piero Marussig or Mario Sironi, did not sell.

During the war and the postwar period, an enriched bourgeoisie known as the «i pescicani» imposed its taste on the market; the artistic production had to please their narrow mentality if one wanted to survive. That is why painters as lucid as Marussig or Carrà could not make a living from their art. Marussig was well off and led a comfortable life, whereas Carrà who wasn't, led a miserable one. His situation improved towards 1922, when the newspaper «L'Ambrosiano» was founded and its director, Umberto Notari, who was also his friend, appointed him art critic.

Paintings such as «La signorina del cappello verde», «La signorina del ventaglio verde», «Dintorni di Milano» or «Quartetto», painted in 1919 [16], could practically not be sold. I even had difficulty in exhibiting them, except at private shows or exhibitions organized by friends. The paintings that I did manage to sell, albeit with effort for they were considered too modern, were abstract landscapes.

In order to display my work I decided to mount a solo show in Milan, at the Lyceum. It was held in June 1919, and was well received by the press. Moreover, it served as a pretext to decline Marinetti's invitation to participate in the «grande mostra», the large Futurist exhibition to be held at the Gran Caffè Cova. The show was as huge as a monster, and to be fair, just as atro-

---

16 I mention only those paintings whose destination I know; in fact I produced many more, not only the year in question, but before and after that period.

cious. At the same café, I cannot recall whether it was before or after this event, a pitiful retrospective was held of Umberto Boccioni's work; the show displayed every piece Boccioni had ever produced, including what he would have preferred to lose or burn had he been alive. By the way, this doesn't surprise me, as lack of criteria is common in most parts of the world. When will it be understood that a retrospective is not an exhibition that displays a hodgepodge of works, obliging the spectator to choose the better ones and thus tiring him in the process: its function is to present the most relevant production of each period, revealing the artist's creative vigor. Apart from the frescoes, not too many paintings created by the Great Masters remain, and yet such is their significance, that only ten paintings by Vermeer would suffice to underscore their importance.

One afternoon, the Argentine poet Oliverio Girondo, whom I didn't know, visited me unexpectedly at my studio. We went out for a coffee and he told me all that was happening in Argentina, the land of abundance, the marvelous El Dorado that fascinated everyone. He told me he was a correspondent for the «Caras y Caretas» magazine and that he had just finished writing an article on the Lago di Como that he wished to read to me. As he had to return to his pension for dinner, we agreed that I would stop by later. It was a luxurious pension, reserved for people of the theater: singers, dancers and actors. The noise and the large quantity of women talking and arguing frightened me: a veritable parrots' cage.

I saw Oliverio at the same pension once or twice during his convalescence, for he had undergone an urgent appendicitis operation. Incidentally, Oliverio later became my friend; moreover, he was one of the three or four Argentines who, when passing through Milan, came to visit me while I lived there.

In Trent, once again a part of Italy after the war, a national exhibition was being organized: the «1^a Esposizione Cispadana», and the Famiglia Artistica had chosen me to represent the halls of Lombardy. I had often curated shows in Milan and my impartiality was being trusted.

I traveled to Trent, where I met with Tulio Garbari, a native of that city, and through him I learned that the delegates of several Italian regions were at odds for always the same reasons: they all wanted the best halls to themselves. With respect to Garbari, he had been invited to participate like any other ordinary artist and not as a special guest whose excellent work deserved to be exclusively displayed.

Giving my colleagues time to reach an agreement, and above all, trying not to interfere, which is always uncomfortable, I accompanied Garbari to Milan for him to fetch his paintings. When we returned, the discussions had reached their peak. As I wanted things to remain harmonious, I spoke to the delegates individually. As a result, we held a plenary session, and someone proposed that the delegate of Lombardy, the region most amply represented at the exhibition, should be in charge of its organization. This implied distributing more than a thousand paintings in a space as large as a block.

A heavy burden was placed on my shoulders. I told them I accepted if the assembly so desired, on condition that no–one enter the area until it was time for the «vernissage». Most delegates were on my side, perhaps because there was little time left. Everyone worked day and night without respite: a tour de force. But the exhibition was ready three hours before the official opening.

It had been the first time ever I had organized a large show. As far as I remember, there were no complaints, and even fairness was mentioned. In the Social Bulletin of the Famiglia Artistica, (August–November 1919), my contribution was highly praised. During that year, I took part in four open exhibitions in the city: «Milano Vecchia e Nuova», «8º Salone di Acquerellisti Lombardi», «Esposizione Regionale Lombarda d'Arte Decorativa», and another organized at our center. Moreover, I also participated in the «Francesco Francia» show held in Bologna, the «1ª Esposizioni Le Arti», held in Brescia, and once again, in the Roman»Secessione».

I attended the weekly reunions that the Sarfatti's organized for their friends; it was a salon frequented by both the Italian and the foreign elite. Margherita was in her forties and beautiful; she knew how to liven up the soirée and make her guests feel comfortable, and her gatherings were always a roaring success. There I met both new people and saw my old friends again; Ada Negri, Ungaretti, Folgore, Malerba, Buzzi, Marussig; Funi, Bontempelli, Sironi, Arturo Martini, Buggelli, Buci are some of the names that come to mind, and last but not least, the unparalleled humorist Sinopico. He was witty and had a flair for telling jokes; his company was very much sought after and time went by most pleasantly. At time he walked about with a blank expression on his face, while people doubled up with laughter.

Towards midnight, a waiter would tell some of us (we were about ten) that Donna Margherita invited us to stay over for dinner. One could never leave the Sarfatti's home before three in the morning.

Once in a while, I also went to the Sunday reunions held by writer Umberto Notari and his wife at his Piazza Cavour residence, and many were the writers, poets, musicians and artists that gathered there. Besides listening to excellent music, chatting about a thousand things and listening to interesting points of view, one could also try his hand at billiard. There were other entertainments as well and the buffet was truly memorable.

At a collective exhibition, mounted at the Famiglia Artistica, I once ran into my dear friend and hostess Margherita Sarfatti, who at the time also exercised her talents as art critic in the «Il popolo d'Italia», a Milanese newspaper. Walking through the halls, we stopped before two paintings by artist Arturo Tossi. Margherita turned towards me, and vehemently said: «See how this rich chap wastes his time and ours!» In those days she defended Achille Funi's Neoclassicism, and therefore, I could not expect a more moderate opinion. Without exerting any pressure, in a «kind» manner, I asked her to carefully look at the other paintings on display and to compare them to Tossi's, inviting her then to tell me whether she believed Tossi's importance had been overrated. She complied, and realized that what I had said was fair. However, being such an opinionated woman, any contradiction irked her; we walked on, without touching the subject again.

To my greatest surprise, in her review of the show, she, who never mentioned Tossi's name in her numerous articles, cited him with admiration. And even more surprisingly, I saw Tossi the week after at her home, at the Thursday reunions. The ice had been broken.

Tossi was a great friend of mine, and I considered him a typical Lombard artist. I liked his work because he followed tradition. One night, while we chatted, alone in his studio, he spoke to me about his dissipated youth... He had once been fond of drinking, and very keen on beautiful women; he had had a lover that had driven him crazy: «Dio, cuanto mi piaceva!» Around that time, many years ago, in 1895, he had painted a series of nudes that he had never shown to anyone, and since he had left his beloved and gotten married, he had led an orderly life. He wished to show me those nudes in the secret of intimacy, if I promised not to say anything to anyone.

Like a child revealing his treasures, he let me see them, and I told him frankly that they were his best paintings ever. He was reluctant to believe me, and torn between amazement and confusion, stroke his chin in the manner of Augusto Giacometti, seized with an emotion so Latin that I though he was about to burst into tears. My sincerity, which he could not doubt, and his reliance on my judgment, led him to the happy conviction of having created lasting work. So much so, that the paintings never returned to the corner where he had kept them rolled up for years; on the contrary, he cleaned and framed them. He then showed them to the astounded Milanese artistic milieu, and a new painter was discovered.

The night I am referring to, Tosi asked me to choose one of his nudes, the one I most liked; I did not want to rob him of an important moment of his youth, for those paintings reminded him of unforgettable bohemian times, of rich bohemian times to tell the truth, for he had always been wealthy. As from the following day, he told everyone who cared to listen about my discovering his old paintings and the opinion I had expressed.

He even mentioned this moment to a reporter of the «L'Europeo» weekly who interviewed him on the occasion of his eightieth birthday in 1951, and the journalist faithfully transcribed all that Tosi said: «If those paintings exist, it is because Pettoruti discovered them». This clipping is in my possession thanks to Dr. Augusto Palanza.

One Thursday night, the Sarfatti's had invited an industrialist who happened to be a multimillionaire, and who was reportedly fond of artists. Donna Margherita, who loved them too, perhaps taking advantage of a previous conversation or a psychological moment, asked her guests for a moment of silence; she then spoke, very much surprising everyone, including the industrialist, judging by his face: «Ladies and gentlemen, I wish to disclose the happy news that Mr. So and So (I forgot his name), has decided to award the sculptor Arturo Martini and the painter Achille Funi a scholarship. This will enable them to work for a year at the Lago di Como, in a villa that will be at their disposal; at the end of the year, the artists will exhibit their work. I must add that our generous patron will open an art gallery in a property he owns on Via Dante and that the writer Mario Buggelli has been appointed director». The applause was deafening, and the embarrassed industrialist had to keep his promise... in honor of Donna Margherita.

This is how Martini and Funi worked for a year in perfect agreement, and how the «Arte» gallery, directed by Buggelli, opened on 10 Via Dante. The first exhibition gathered some of the most interesting painters of Milan, and the sculptor Arturo Martini displayed two of his works. Anselmo Buci, Aldo Carpi, Carlo Carrà, Giorgio de Chirico, Leonardo Dudreville, Achille Funi, Piero Marussig, Luigi Rissole and Mario Sironi also exhibited, including myself.

It is curious that Carrà and Russolo, who had signed the first Manifesto of Futurist painting, and who acted, at least for a while, in keeping with the spirit of the Movement, exhibited paintings so contrary to that spirit. Carrà displayed two metaphysical paintings named «The son of the constructor» and «The daughter of the west», whereas Rissole exhibited an objective picture, «Portrait», harsh and devoid of color.

I occupied the first hall with ten works. Tough the show was acclaimed by the press, some journalists criticized it: the truth is that not a painting was sold. Anyway, on the day of the opening, a large crowd and all of the artists were present: at least we saw each other. There I ran into Russolo, whom I hadn't seen since Florence; he was a surly person and lived like a hermit. When living in Milan, I only saw him once or twice.

In Stockholm they were preparing an exhibition on Italian Art. As head of a commission, the Swedish painter Maja Sjostrmö came especially to select work from local artists, and she chose a handful of my paintings, certainly more than five. According to what was said, the exhibition was a success. To the exhibitors' enormous satisfaction, many works were purchased; mine were all sold.

The year 1920 proved to be prosperous, brimming with activity. I painted, or redid, a series of itinerant musicians: «The guitar player», «The accordion player», «The blind flutist», «The singer» and «The cellist».

Moreover, I completed other paintings, such as «Lost in thought», «Portrait of Xul Solar», and produced a limited edition of engravings, using the press that had once belonged to Boccioni; a Swiss commission agent, who came to see me in Milan with a letter of presentation written by my former engraving teacher, bought a great number of them.

As far as the exhibitions are concerned, I was invited to a large show, the «Esposizione Nazionale della Città di Vicenza» and to the «Esposizione Francesco Francia», held annually in Bologna; I also participated in the II° «Esposizione Le Arti in Brescia», and was given a hall of my own at the exhibition in Gardone. At the «Famiglia Artistica» my paintings were displayed twice.

For artists my age –I was already 27– especially those immersed in the avant–garde, there existed in Italy only one official and unassailable venue: the Biennale Internazionale di Venezia. It had been suspended while Italy was at war but was now functioning again; so far it had ignored the existence of avant–garde art. The Biennale was preparing its 12th edition, and a group of painters got together to plan the assault of the citadel, which we would ram into with our works. We all attacked in unison. Among the ten conspirators, seven of us got in, Marussig and myself included. Bravo! For the first time, the Biennale opened up its respectable doors to young Italian painters.

Let us recall that when I was young, not only in Italy, but all over the world, people weren't that open minded. Yet youthful clamors have always existed; for instance, after having manifested its spirit of revolt with a great deal of bonhomie devoid of pretension, the Dada movement vanished from the scene without anyone paying any attention to it, and another movement took its place: Breton's Surrealism, Freudian par excellence and led by men of letters that denied intelligence and calculation in painting. Valid or not, these movements sought a niche for themselves, but the prevailing ideology ignored them.

I attended the Venetian exhibition. In the French pavilion there hung a magnificent set of works by Cézanne that thrilled me, as well as works by Seurat, Signac, Valloton, Odilon Redon, and Maillol. The most modern were Bonnard, Cézanne and Matisse. The Russian pavilion, on the other hand, displayed numerous paintings, and surpassed all in audacity; works by Archipenko occupied an entire hall and there were also paintings by Larionov and Goncharova. Even in the Italian pavilion a breath of fresh air flowed, something that had been absent at the previous Biennials; I was surprised that the paintings, including mine, were so well placed.

The «Biennale di Brera» was held that same year. To our surprise, all those who had been accepted in Venice were rejected in Brera. Though there existed no ultimatums nor pitched battles, we, the young artists, Futurists and others, lived at war with the academics that persecuted us. Considering the flagrant injustice, those of us that had been affected by the measure decided to mount a retaliatory exhibition, naming it «The rejected artists of Brera». It provoked quite a scandal. The evidence of the injustice gave the critics a chance to formally denounce the abuses perpetrated by the jury. Rafaello Giolli and Margherita Sarfatti defended our cause through an ardent and sustained press campaign, backed by other critics. However, I must admit the rejection particularly favored me.

I haven't yet described Rafaello Giolli. Of medium height, always soberly dressed, his face, or rather the expression of his face –he would half–close his eyes when smiling– reminded one of a young Chinese; he did not have high cheekbones nor almond–shaped eyes. Rather, it was a movement of particular muscles that created the resemblance.

He was morally upright, introverted, perhaps because he had led a lonely childhood; his shyness could only be compared to mine, and this was perhaps why we understood each other tacitly. We knew, without having to speak, that we were identical in that respect, and that we could trust each other fully.

However, this quiet man was a lion underneath, ready to defend the good causes and to attack the unjust ones, and always prepared to put a noble design into action. He lit up when speaking and his eyes shone ardently, and knew many things of which he never boasted, revealing them with the modesty of scholars. He was full of ideas and always wished to carry out projects in the field of the arts. Loved by everyone, for he was sincere, he was feared at the same time, due to his righteous severity.

This exceptional being, whom I stopped seeing in 1924 and whose memory lives on as though he were still with us, died in the Second World War, savagely massacred in his own country by the Nazis. Rabidly antifascist, he collaborated with the «partigiani» in the Resistance, with the courage that characterized all of his actions. We were so fond of each other, and we trusted each other so completely, that there existed no other reservations other than the temperamental ones. I was his confidant and best man at his weddings, and we worked together on innumerable occasions.

Responding to my wish to know more about the painting of Lombardy, one night we had a tête–à–tête in which he gave me a lecture on it. As he believed I would get to know it even better through the old living artists, we undertook a pilgrimage into the past visiting the studios of people such as count Gola, a charming gentleman who received us with open arms showing us all he was doing, or Previati or Corconi, honored by Gioli's visit. I realized that the greater the artist, the more naturally he behaves: it is only men without grandeur that are unbearably vain.

In August I received a letter from Xul transmitting an invitation from his mother for me to spend my holidays in Zoagli. I remember it as one of my most enjoyable ever. Neither his mother nor his aunt, both delightful, treated

Xul any differently than they did me. I imagine that to them it must have been like having two overgrown boys at home. An aside: on the day of my arrival, while Xul and I placed the contents of my suitcase in the closet, I heard them call out: «Kiddo! Kiddo!» Unaware there was a child in the house, I turned around: imagine my surprise when I heard Xul answering their call.

Xul was given to sleeping and all I could obtain was, once in a while and with great effort, for him to get up at 8.30 in the morning. Our long walks along the Ligurian coast would be sprinkled with lengthy conversations, or we would head towards Chiavari where Milanese artists friends of ours were spending the summer. As usual, the attention centered on Xul and his eclectic habits: now he was interested in Hinduism and Sinology, and preoccupied by acupuncture and other Asian medical sciences.

Moved by curiosity, friends expressed their wish to visit us, and Xul invited them for tea in the Chinese fashion. For this purpose we entirely decorated the large living–room with strips of colored paper that hung from the ceiling, approximately one meter apart from each other; on these strips black signs were painted vertically. Xul gave such measured and yet far–fetched details of these signs, that it left everyone mystified.

Speaking with Buggelli in his art gallery, I found out he wanted to mount a personal exhibition of works by Arturo Martini; however, he was running into a difficulty, for Martini had made very few sculptures and had no drawings to cover the walls. I therefore proposed a joint exhibition with Xul, explaining to him what he was doing and he took my word for it. I immediately wrote Xul a letter, announcing him the good news: he would exhibit in the best of companies, in an important gallery and without having to spend a cent. Together with the letter I sent him a small chart with the measurements, in order for him to select his paintings. As soon as he replied, the catalogues would be printed.

Bugggelli couldn´t agree more, and Xul arrived with his works; on 27 November his paintings were seen hanging next to the works of one of the most important sculptors of Italy. Arturo Martini, whose catalogue had been prefaced by Carrà, exhibited eight sculptures, and Xul, prefaced by me, exhibited forty–six watercolors, four temperas and twenty oils. There were works of incomparable beauty among them, such as his «San Francisco», and his «Annunciation». Both artists were given rave reviews.

Martini and Xul were made to understand each other and they became friends at once. Like Xul, Martini possessed a vivacious temperament and was quite entertaining. His mind was open to all artistic movements and philosophies. He enjoyed conversation and told interesting stories that had taken place in Paris, Berlin or Munich, cities that he had never visited, describing their promenades, avenues, squares, streets, cafés, night–clubs and characters with such a profusion of details, that whomever did not know him intimately, believed him right away. He was a dreamer who fantasized about all the places he would have wanted to visit.

And now something that describes one of Xul's extravagant ideas: some hours before the opening of the show, I had invited an art collector who had bought me some paintings and trusted my judgment. I had told him he would see extraordinary works by an artist unknown in Milan, and that his paintings weren't therefore too expensive. The man felt rather disconcerted upon seeing Xul's work, but while he chatted, and looking at them with renewed attention, he ended up buying two watercolors.

Xul appeared right at the moment in which the gallery director was about to tell the collector the price of the paintings. Happy with my doing, I introduced them, telling Xul that the gentleman, and important art dealer, had just bought two watercolors. Xul looked at his buyer with the gesture of one who cannot accept contradictions, and exclaimed: «Why! You are a collector and you buy such trash?» The man froze, and Buggelli and I got tongue–tied. As a result, the collector bought nothing at all. Naturally, Xul's «boutade» spread like wild fire across the artistic milieu and every one interpreted it his own way. The fact is that his show, praised, successful and visited by so many people, closed without him selling one single work. And Xul returned to Zoagli.

Chapter 15

1921: In Munich

Speaking with Marussig one day, I told him how worried I was. I considered that those artists living in Milan, those that worked seriously of course, were, for one reason or another, scattered. Many lived far away from the center of town; it was difficult for them to attend reunions, and they never frequented cafés, either because of the fog, snow or cold. I suggested forming a group that he would direct, considering his authority and the ampleness of his studio.

We studied the benefits and disadvantages, yet the idea did not quite convince him. I must admit that the reason for my proposal was to lessen Marussig's isolation. Like Giolli, he was an introvert, and the exaggerated reserve he displayed in his painting prevented him from improving. I insisted once and again; as I often had dinner at his home and his wife approved of my idea, he ended up accepting it.

He invited a large group to his studio, some fifteen painters, of which only half came. In principle, they all agreed. After much talking and arguing, a new meeting was arranged, only to realize that I wouldn't be in Milan at that time. In effect I wasn't, for I had projected a trip to Munich where I had to meet Xul.

I sent my friend a telegram, telling him I would be arriving to Munich on the following day; in other words, on Sunday at midnight. I didn't speak a word of German, but I took the train without apprehension, certain Xul would be there upon my arrival. Yet no–one was at the station, and after waiting for an hour, I left the station to look for a hotel. The following morning, after breakfast, I went out; everything was snowed under and I hailed an open sleigh. I showed the driver the slip of paper on which I had written down Xul's address, and very politely, he got off, helped me to sit down, wrapped me up in a thick blanket and returned to his place. The sleigh departed, and the trip seemed never–ending; it was one street after another, at times a bridge, or a square. I was overjoyed, for it was the first time I was riding a sleigh; my hands were protected and ice–cold wind blew on my face. So happy was I that I became disoriented, in spite of having studied the plan of the city beforehand. At once I had the impression I was crossing the same bridge, the same streets, the same square, and the situation rather upset me. «What an odd city, everything is so similar!» I thought to myself.

Finally, the vehicle dropped me off at the requested address, and I realized it was a school of decorative arts; Xul attended it and I saw my telegram lying about on a table. Luckily I managed to find out where Xul was staying, and headed for the boarding house. When he saw me, he was dumbfounded. I gave him details of my long sleigh trip, and how I had finally found the school, and Xul burst out laughing: the hotel was situated in front of the station, and on the same block, on the opposite side, stood the school. Only then did I understand why we had crossed the bridge and the square over and over again. Yet, I bore the driver no grudge.

Immediately I set out to visit the important museums in Munich, its galleries and art libraries, where I bought splendid books; it was the time of the devaluation of the mark. In Munich I also saw the first Expressionist works, and other works of art, and I felt overwhelmed.

Xul and I dined together that night but he told me he couldn't accompany me to the café for he had an important date. However, he walked with me to the entrance of a very large and crowded coffee house, in which a violinist was performing. The place was like a theater: there were stalls and two rows of boxes, and tables everywhere. Xul advised me to only ask for a «machine–kaffé» in order to avoid language complications.

There was only one empty place left: a chair on the first row of the first box, and I climbed the few steps that led me there. As soon as the waiter came, I asked for my «machine–kaffé». Yet something horrible happened: the waiter left it on the table, without telling me how this wondrous device worked. A small flame burnt beneath the pot, and as I waited for the coffee to warm up, I began to sketch. The violinist started playing and I suspended my work, lulled by the melody of the «crescendo». At once my «machine» began to whistle stridently: it was a penetrating sound that pierced the eardrums. I didn't know what to do, nor where to hide. People screamed: «Ausländer, Ausländer», words that remain engraved on my memory. Chaos ensued: the public shook their fat fists at me, the coffee pot kept on shrieking and the violinist brandished his instrument in my direction. The waiter, tray in hand, came running to help me, but lost his balance on the steps, and a «machine–kaffé» and several cups rolled onto the floor. Yet he rose as quickly as lightning, and removed the small container of burning alcohol from beneath the coffee pot. It was the simplest thing in the world, if only one knew what to do. What to think of those people sitting next to me, who didn't lift a finger to help me? I was afraid to leave lest they kill me and there I remained, making myself as unobtrusive as possible until everyone calmed down and no–one looked at me in a sullen way any longer. I then made a dash for the entrance.

Xul was having a love affair with the landlady's daughter, a beauty of a girl, as tall and slender as he was. He therefore spent less time with me and often I ate on my own. One night, as I was about to have dinner, and looking at the long list of dishes whose names were unintelligible to me, I decided to guide myself according to the prices, with the idea that the most expensive dish had to be the best one. When I showed the waiter what I wished to eat, he opened his eyes wide. He seemed reluctant yet I insisted, waiting for a long time in the crowded restaurant, where people ate frugally.

The waiter appeared unexpectedly, carrying an immense tray. The entire head of a calf was placed in the center, garnished with different kinds of vegetables. What I had chosen was a dish serving six people! I felt everyone was looking at me in a hostile way; their eyes were full of reproach, scorn and resentment. In the midst of my confusion, I hastily set a larger sum of money on the table than the one indicated on the menu, and almost ran out of the restaurant.

When in Munich, I witnessed a military parade quite by chance, and the spectacle created a strong impression on me. I was standing in the atrium of the Old Gallery waiting for the rain to stop, when on the sidewalk, in rows of eight or ten, perfectly symmetrical, expressionless platoons untiringly marched beneath the rain, their necks tense, the chins rigid. They were divided into precise rectangles, as if drawn with a ruler, and never will I know where those troops came from or where they were heading. The uniforms these men were wearing, originally designed for parades, were old, discolored, incomplete and even tattered. It was as though they had been worn on a battlefield, yet the soldiers were so martial and stoic they seemed to belong to triumphant armies. Their boots were old, and many wore espadrilles or shoes that resembled accordions. Caps had been placed beneath the gray helmets so as to protect them from the rain. Indifferent to the gaze of the citizens that respectfully contemplated them marching by, they advanced, deaf and blind to anything that wasn't the rhythm of their step, like automatons that never wind down, imagining perhaps they were still wearing their beautiful uniform. I shall never forget that parade, for it revealed the spirit of discipline that overcomes any disaster; it symbolized the capacity to start anew no matter where, no matter when.

In a bookshop in Munich, I saw an exhibition of works by Klee. I wasn't too impressed, comparing it to Xul's. Both of them followed the same direction, yet I found the work of the latter to be more organic. The owner of the bookshop, from whom I had bought beautiful books, spoke Italian; he introduced me to Klee, who also spoke some Italian and who momentarily lived on the bookshop's upper floor. At one point he mentioned the international word «musik», to which I replied I enjoyed «musik» very much. Klee, delighted, took me to his room, where we talked for a long while. Then, he grabbed his violin and gave me a concert. This I remember as one of the sweetest moments in Munich, and owe it to this great artist.

The subsequent Expressionist shows I visited caused the same disagreeable impression on me as when I saw their work for the first time; I found the impasto in their painting vulgar, and there hovered an eroticism verging on decadence. I attributed this to the excesses generated by the war. I also saw paintings by Arnold Böecklin, Von Marees and others. The first one, of whom De Chirico had spoken so favorably, I did not like at all; I found him to be a mediocre painter, a hackneyed Romantic. On the other hand, Hans von Marees caught my attention. I found out that he had painted some frescoes at the Aquarium of Naples, and the first time I traveled to the Gulf I went to see them: his painting was discreet.

Sometimes, Xul and I went to the Latin neighborhood, to some of those small crowded cafés. On one occasion, a young man with a leporine lip and a peculiar voice asked us in Portuguese where we came from. I told him and he introduced himself: Alberto Da Veiga Guignard, Brazilian, attending the Munich Academy. As I had visited it, and considered it to be much better than the Italian ones, on account of the order that prevailed and the way students benefited from practical teaching, I told him my impression; he disclosed he had studied in Paris and had decided on Munich, precisely for that reason.

We saw each other often, and we became friends. From that day, and up to 1929, year in which we met again in Rio de Janeiro, never a month went by without me receiving a letter or a postcard from him. He was an incomparable loyal friend, ever so generous and good! When I saw him again in Rio, he had become a renowned painter, one of the best. Yet he is one of those artists, just like Xul Solar, that will only be appreciated in the course of time.

Chapter 16

Meeting with Mariátegui

Back in Milan I realized events had precipitated themselves during my absence. In the artistic milieu the news spread that a group had been formed with the best Milanese painters. Pesaro, the director of one of the most important galleries at the time, contacted the painters, letting them know that he wished to mount a show. The exhibit was greatly praised, and many painters sold their work. This group became the «900 Italiano», headed by Margherita Sarfatti.

I requested from the «Famiglia Artistica» to use the great hall to set up a solo exhibition, and my wish was granted. The news got to the ears of Carrà. One morning, to my great surprise, he burst into my studio. Point-blank he told me, in his raucous voice, dubbed «the voice of the socialist deputy»: «I know you are about to exhibit at the «Famiglia Artistica»; well, I will take care of the preface, and it will be involved».

He did indeed, and his gesture describes the integrity true artists possess. Don't think for an instant that this circumstance modified our relations. Not in the least. After so much cordiality, our friendship adopted the same ritual. However, most importantly, we knew we could count on each other.

Nella surprised me the day of the opening, and to see her made me indescribably happy. I was alone, I have always felt alone, since I was born, even when surrounded by people. Yet I am also very sensitive, and the disinterested love my family had always shown me soothed my childhood and part of my youth, providing solace to my constant exile. Thrust into life when barely a man, in Florence my solitude took on disproportionate dimensions, until I met Nella. Deprived of her company, I felt ever so lonesome in Milan, in spite of my deep friendship with Giolli and Marussig, whom I dearly loved.

But they could not substitute for that serene warmth so sweetly feminine that Nella embodied and irradiated.

All that takes place within an artistic milieu, no matter the place, is no mystery, and we each have an idea of what sort of life a young successful artist might lead in such a mundane and snobbish environment. The mad euphoria, or rather, the licentiousness, present while the country was at war, anaesthetized any romantic consideration. Promiscuity, indifference, liberal thinking, nymphomania and the unbridled search for pleasure were present everywhere.

Man among men, the opportunities abounded, and in general, I did not reject them; but they gave me nothing, except when living the fleeting moment of abandon. Rather, they even aggravated my malaise; so true is this that all that surrounded me seemed foul and corrupt, and I myself felt soiled without any possible refuge other than my work and without any other consolation than the image of a young woman who represented all the virtues of the Eternal Woman.

Taking the train to see Nella was like traveling towards a source of light that cleansed me of all impurity. Others see their confessors. Instead, I went towards silence. Yet, she, who knew so many things about my spirit, was never aware of its other facets; Nella never even learned about my serious illness that almost killed me. Perhaps it is question of temperament. At times, when thinking about the way people perceive me, I smile.

My exhibition at the «Famiglia Artistica», like all the other artistic events, served to strengthen my reputation. Little by little I was gaining ground, leaving the boundaries of Lombardy behind. No longer did I send work on my own initiative to the salons; they invited me now from all over Italy to exhibit at the most important shows (Oddly, in Buenos Aires I was systematically rejected from the National Salon. The last time this happened was in 1921).

That year I exhibited at the «1ª Mostra del Paesaggio Italiano», celebrated in Gardona, where I was given a hall of my own, and at the Esposizione Nazionale della Città di Roma. The painter Cipriano Oppo had been assigned to personally invite artists residing in Milan. He had come to my studio and selected three paintings, yet I only delivered one. The reason remains unclear, but I suspect I had forgotten to get them framed.

While the last show was being held, the writer Ricardo Sáenz Hayes came to Milan. He had been sent as a special correspondent by the «La Prensa» newspaper of Buenos Aires to interview a few European presidents and important politicians, Mussolini among them. Upon returning from Rome, we met again; he reproached me for not having told him that I exhibited at the «Esposizione Nazionale»; he had seen a painting of mine there, and had sent a cable to his newspaper about it (in effect I read the news some time later); yet of all that he told me, what most excited my imagination was his interview with Mussolini. Sáenz Hayez told me that he had asked him whether it was true he was born in Argentina, considering that he was called Benito and that he had relatives in the province of Buenos Aires. Mussolini, who neither affirmed nor denied, apparently answered: «Let things from the past rest». The story is told exactly the way Sáenz Hayez disclosed it to me.

Marussig asked me to travel with him to Rome, the Eternal City, as much to visit some museums again, as to attend a series of concerts programmed by the Augusteum. The proposal tempted me, for on the way back, I could stay some days in Florence. At times I had taken a trip in order to see Nella, but they had been very short.

I didn´t have much time to see my friends in Rome. Of course I saw Bragaglia, who invited me to exhibit at his «Casa d´Arte» the following spring. Quite by chance, I met the Peruvian writer and rebel José Carlos Mariátegui. He was very young, and looked like a boy, a boy who had just gotten married. We took to each other from the start and so strong was this emotion it seemed we had been friends from childhood. We promised to write; he was planning a trip to Milan soon.

Nella was waiting for me at the station with her sister and I introduced Marussig to them. This time around I remained in Florence for five days, and they seemed to fly by. I also saw Gonnelli and other beloved friends that belonged to my old circle. Augusto Giacometti had already left for Stampa, his native town a long time ago, and though we used to write one another, I never saw him again. Our correspondence continued up to 1926 or 1927, from across the ocean.

One day, without any previous notice, Giannetto Bisi, director of the Milanese «Il Mondo» magazine, and who had always showered me with affection, sadly revealed to me one afternoon that the directorate had appointed Zacchetti to write in my place. On the one hand the news vexed me, for it meant less earnings, and on the other I felt relieved. If in the «Satana» magazine my responsibility was to illustrate current events in color, in the «Il Mondo» it focused on the political caricature. Since I had no talent as a caricaturist, the task was labored, and Bisi, invariably, explained the most relevant political events of the week to me.

As can be understood, I had good enough reasons not to feel bad about having lost my place, and besides, it pleased me to think that Zacchetti, a born caricaturist, and whom I very much appreciated, had replaced me. I told Bisi this, assuring him it would be beneficial for the magazine.

Zacchetti adored Buenos Aires, city in which he had lived for some time and where he had met his wife, the only love of his life; this was another reason I felt attracted to him. What I did not approve of was that he had offered his services asking for a lower remuneration than mine. The gesture was absurd; given his talent, he could have easily have asked for more.

Mariátegui came to Milan and I spent as much time with him as I could. He invited me to Frascati for a couple of days. He lived in a beautiful villa and I accepted with the idea of staying a week, but ended up staying almost a month. I must admit my stay was pleasant and instructive for both. Mariátegui kept abreast of the current artistic movements, and I learned about the struggles of our oppressed and beloved America.

One thing is certain: we lost no time. In the mornings, he wrote for his newspapers, which he was paid for in pounds, and I drew; in the afternoons and at night we spoke about all kinds of things. He posed for a portrait I did not complete, and which finds itself in Lima in the hands of his relatives. We lived together in Berlin the following year, and then he returned to his home country. In 1925 he wrote a review on my art in «Variedades», a magazine from Lima and added another article, signed by Baldomero Sanín Cano, in «Amauta», a publication that he directed. We stayed in touch by letter regularly up until his early death, a great loss to Peru.

At the end of 1921, I left for Vienna to visit its museums. They were all closed and there was nothing left for me to do other than visit the city. From there I traveled to Munich, where I spent a wonderful New Year's Eve in the company of both German and foreign friends. I got to know Dresden and Hamburg, as well as their museums. In Dresden I recall having seen a Venus by Giorgione, and a wonderful Van Gogh, whereas in Hamburg, an immense and pleasant surprise awaited me: on the brink of leaving, and tired of looking at uninteresting paintings, I unexpectedly stumbled upon a salon, brimming with works by the Impressionists. This discovery thrilled me beyond words: it was the first time I was looking at such an important selection of paintings.

Chapter 17

Exhibition at «Der Sturm» art gallery, Berlin

I had worked hard in Milan during the course of the winter, and I kept up the same rhythm all throughout the first months of the year 1922. I needed to save in order to work without tension in Tegernsee, a lake next to Munich, during the summer. I knew some fellow countrymen there, in whose home I could live peacefully. I only saw my friends once in a while, except for Giolli and Marussig, and practically stopped going to the cafés and reunions.

I was fortunate to meet Herward Walden, the owner of the «Der Sturm» art gallery of Berlin, for it proved to be beneficial for my art. Moreover, I made the acquaintance of Alberto Sartoris, a young man in whom I saw myself reflected; he was as serious as I was, and as tenacious and enthusiastic, and meeting him influenced my life significantly. He was from Turin, but spent as much time in Switzerland as he did in Italy. Both a lover and student of art and architecture, he worked, did research and was crazy about all that was modern. Fours years back, when still an adolescent, he had presented his work, a prelude to the new architecture, at the Academy of Fine Arts, and wanted me to see it as soon as possible for me to grasp his line of thought, so similar to mine. It consisted of drawings that exalted pure geometry. He was Marinetti's friend and knew the particulars of the Futurist Movement; he had been part of it since 1920, yet conditionally, for he wished to maintain his independence. We both admired Marinetti and his work. With so many ideas and feelings in common, we could only but be friends. Though he was still quite young, Sartoris had a penchant for matters of the spirit, implicitly renouncing to material pleasures, devoting his entire life to the renovation of the arts.

One afternoon, Herward Walden unexpectedly showed up in my studio.

He told me he had especially come to Italy to contact the young avant–garde artists of Italy, and that as much in Milan as in Rome, people had spoken well of me. There he was, then, waiting to see my work, and I gladly showed it to him, even more so upon noticing that we corresponded in our tastes. Without hesitation he chose my most modern work and proposed to exhibit my paintings at his gallery in Berlin, something I agreed to, providing there would be no costs involved; I would take charge of the transportation of the paintings, but the catalogue and other expenses would be on him. We decided the exhibition would be held in the spring of 1923.

At the end of July, just as I had planned, I left for Tegernsee, and headed for a place named Adwinkel. I took with me my painting tools and some cardboards and pictures I had already finished so as to get more frames and stretchers made in Munich: I wished to exhibit them in Berlin.

In Adwinkel the weather wasn't on my side; the end of the summer was rainy and the beginning of fall even rainier. This made painting in the open air difficult, though by no means did I lose my time: in spite of the inclement weather, I never interrupted work while traveling. All that had to do with the illustration of books, magazines or design for Palmer, I punctually accomplished, no matter where I found myself at the time. Since my work involved working on cardboard or paper in watercolor, tempera or India ink, I sent them from wherever I happened to be. I also drew a great deal to please myself those long days in Atwinkel, a habit I never got out of: some of these drawings have become paintings.

One of my objectives was to have an eminent physician check my eyes in Germany. I had already consulted one of the greatest oculists in Genoa, named Müller. Though he predicted my left eye was doomed, he recommended an operation just in case. I did not want it performed at the time and returned to Milan disheartened. Now, without any reason in particular, a new hope surged: the hope of a miracle.

In Munich I had two genial friends: the Paraguayan brothers Ricardo and Víctor Boetner. One studied chemistry and the other medicine, and I asked the latter to find me the best oculist in the country. He recommended Dr. Herz to me, and it so happened that this renowned ophthalmologist, who taught at the University of Munich, also had his consulting room there.

On the day of the visit, the two brothers came along, and Víctor became my interpreter.

In defeated Germany there was a certain resistance towards all foreigners, and I acutely sensed this latent aggression. The doctor remained stern while listening to my friend, which made me quite nervous. At one point the word «painter» was mentioned, bringing about a change of attitude that reassured me; at once the doctor showed interest in what I was doing. In the waiting room, I had left a portfolio full of watercolors that I was meaning to leave at a publishing house as soon as the consultation was over. The oculist requested to see them and became so enthusiastic when browsing through them that he seemed to have forgotten all of his other patients.

After an exhaustive examination, Dr. Herz repeated almost exactly what his colleague in Genoa had said. This time around, however, I accepted the operation and we agreed that it would be performed after my return from Berlin: I wished to fix the exact date of the exhibition and leave Walden some of the paintings that had traveled with me and that had been framed in Munich.

Yet, I was barely back from Berlin that I received a letter from Victor telling me Dr. Herz had died all of a sudden. Another preoccupying news would arrive a bit later: that of the March of the black shirts advancing on Rome.

A room awaited me at the Berliner pension where José Carlos Mariátegui was staying. It was a real pleasure to see him again and to resume our conversations. We spent some very pleasant days together and I especially recall introducing him to a poet from Cologne, whose name I unfortunately forgot, a charming and brilliant man that spoke many languages fluently, including Russian. They became great friends.

A journalist came to visit me, sent by the «Atlántida» magazine of Buenos Aires. His name was Julio de la Paz and his mission in Europe, he said, was to interview a few Argentines. I showed him some of the paintings that I had with me, not before warning him about the bewildering sight he was about to witness. The shock was violent, and he cringed. How to make him understand my art? He listened to me speak without taking down any notes; then we went to a café where I introduced him to Mariátegui, his compatriot. To tell the truth, I believed he was going to write a nonsensical article, yet I must admit he wrote an articulate piece, very satisfying, in fact.

I was lucky to see many things in Berlin: among these, the «Exhibition of Russian Art»: painting, sculpture, drawing and engraving. It seemed rather chaotic; all sorts of paintings made up the six hundred works, from the most pedestrian to the most elaborate, though talented painters such as Gabo, Archipenko and Pevsner in sculpture, and Malevitch, Rodschenko and Kandinsky in painting, were also present at the show.

I forgot to mention that I had found the «Der Sturm» gallery very beautiful, and Herward Walden to be a highly receptive being. Upon handing him the first paintings, we set the date of the exhibition: the whole month of May 1923.

Before proceeding with my account, let me say that around that time I started to feel homesick. Ten years had passed since I had last seen my mother and I knew my grandfather, who was getting old, complained about me not visiting them. As ships were swifter now, my uninterrupted stay abroad was interpreted as indifference. I quite understood my family's reasoning, but I was absorbed by so many things, my life was organized in such a way, that interrupting the rhythm of my work, even for a couple of months, was not only problematic but risky. However, the idea was taking form, especially as I was thinking of exhibiting in Buenos Aires. In my letters I wrote that I might travel: I was only waiting for the right moment to break off my exhibition engagements in Berlin and take a trip to Paris.

About my solo show at «Der Sturm» in Berlin I can only say, without being extremely presumptuous, that it was an enormous success. I had exhibited thirty–five works, all of them displayed in the main hall, while a reduced number of works by Archipenko, Klee, Marcoussis, Jacques Villon, Zadkine, Schwitters, Moholy–Nagy, Gleizes and others hung in the adjacent ones. Walden was delighted; to him, I was «his» find.

Thanks to this exhibit I got to know many German and foreign artists. The majority did not speak a word of German, and I have forgotten most of their names. If I remember those of Marc Chagall and Alexander Archipenko it is because I kept on seeing them, especially the latter. In effect, I became a good friend of Archipenko, who became, in the course of the days, one of my staunchest supporters. One afternoon he challenged a critic opposed to modern art who disapproved of my work, and a huge quarrel arose; Walden let them argue and translated the discussion to me. The review turned out to be favorable, and I never got to know whether it was because Archipenko alarmed the critic or because the latter ended up liking my work. I sent Nella a few clippings of those articles as soon as they were published.

Archipenko, like Kandinsky and Chagall, had left Russia disappointed. Their action had been thwarted, after having been provided with all the facilities to work there and attempting to show the West that the arts in the Soviet Union were on a par with contemporary culture. This could have been the case, if history had only changed its course. One has to bear in mind that the new artistic forms had admirers that exceeded the October Revolution. Lenin himself defended them, as his reply to Clara Zetkin's criticism discloses. He believed their impetuous rhythm was «natural and convenient», only to add, facetiously: «Yes, my dear Clara, there is no doubt that we are old: the new art has beaten us, and we can only but limp behind».

I visited Chagall, who literally lived amid rugs and pillows; he painted thus, and to the surprise of those who believe me so neat and tidy, I enjoyed being there. He told me that every day it was becoming more difficult for him to communicate with his young daughter, for she was attending a German boarding school where she no longer needed her mother tongue. Chagall's painting at the time was exactly like the one people know today; he was an illustrative painter whose art did not modify itself much over the course of the years. From the very beginning he was inspired by the Judeo–Russian folklore, not very popular in the West; this is why his flying characters are thought to be a manifestation of modern art.

Life, as usual, kept on providing me with opportunities to meet interesting people; I thus became acquainted with Sem Roam, a writer specializing on art, who published an interesting article on my work in the «Der Sturm» magazine. I greatly took to him, and his nature reminded me of my dear friend Giolli´s, timid in his dealings with people and intrepid whenever he had to expose truths. He was young, charming and cultured, and I often wonder where he ended up. He was about to write both the prologue to the catalogue of my Berlin exhibition and the monograph the International Publishing House of Berlin decided to publish as a result of the successful show, but reasons beyond our control prevented him from doing so. Both texts ended up being written by Alberto M. Candiotti, the Argentine consul in Berlin. If Sem Roam, rather mortified, decided to publish one of his two texts in Walden´s magazine (named after his gallery), it was because he liked me and respected the German art lover.

In Berlin I also made the acquaintance of Ruggero Vassari, an intelligent colossus and an eternal student of the law, maintained by his wealthy Sicilian parents. He would drink a bottle of whisky every night, and it was impossible to find him in his right mind until the following morning. He was a great lover of painting, on which he had written several articles. He wrote two on my exhibition, which were then published in newspapers of Rome and Milan. We often saw each other while I was staying in Berlin, and since he owned a car and was extremely rich, before long he introduced me to the city´s night life in all of its aspects, but that is another story. One only has to remember that homosexuals possessed legal existence there and that Freudian theories were «le dernier cri». Everyone wished to increase his libido.

Together with Herward Walden and his beautiful wife, a blonde and exuberant Dane, I spent lovely afternoons. We used to have tea together and I often visited his private collection, situated in the basement of the gallery. At the time it was perhaps the most important avant–garde collection in Europe. He and I looked at the collection in parts, which allowed me to appreciate Walden´s knowledge and erudition as regards modern art: and there was something else, a certain flair that guided him in the selection of the works, painting or sculpture.

He assured me that the first ones in acquiring avant–garde paintings, displaying tendencies such as Fauvism, Expressionism, Cubism, Futurism and so forth, had been the Germans, and almost simultaneously, the Russians: the other nationalities lagged behind. This refined man so versed in the arts also dedicated himself to music. He had composed several pieces of which he spoke with great enthusiasm, one of them being the «Dance of the pins»; as soon as he pronounced these words, it always put me in an excellent mood.

There were certain aspects of Walden I admired, such as his impeccable taste, his achievements and his efforts to impose avant–garde art in Germany, but at the same time I noticed he had succumbed to gaudiness, and he, who ordinarily was so discreet, elegant and simple, on occasion displayed flamboyant attitudes. For instance, I disliked his long and cheaply adorned cigarette holder with which he smoked, and perhaps also the way he took the cigarette out of his mouth.

I sold two paintings while exhibiting at «Der Sturm». Mrs. Walden bought the third one: she too was a painter. The work she purchased was burnt some years later, together with the whole collection, by Hitler´s orders.

Walden wished to manage my work in Germany and suggested I leave some paintings behind. Though this greatly pleased me, I replied I had planned a trip to Buenos Aires and that I would be away for about six months. Perhaps I would also exhibit there. The idea, in effect, had taken shape, and it seemed to me that the most sensible thing to do was to have my perfectly framed works shipped from Berlin, in order to save time and money once I found myself in Buenos Aires. And so it was done; many of my paintings began their transatlantic journey from Berlin, and I told Walden that upon my return we would calmly study the situation.

Back in Milan I received the happy news that my exhibition in Berlin had had a positive repercussion in Italy. I delivered my work to Palmer –besides the work that I had already sent– and resumed my «active life». My intention was to leave Milan for Paris at the end of the year, remain in the City of Light for a couple of months before undertaking my transatlantic voyage. Once back from my long stay, I would settle once again in Milan in one of those modern studies that the Municipality had especially built for artists. We had been asked to sign up as tenants and I had done just that; we had to estimate a year, perhaps a year and a half, before being able to live there, and I had more than time enough to visit my family and come back.

Before leaving for Paris I took a quick trip to Florence to see Nella. She knew about my desire to stay six months in Paris and six in Buenos Aires; she also knew a brand new studio awaited me in Milan. I cannot say awaited «us», for I never included her in my projects nor did she include herself; simply they were not plans in common nor could they be, for between us there existed a kind of rhythm that depended on fate. I mentioned to her that upon my return from Paris I would leave some paintings, work supplies and unnecessary clothes in Florence, and she immediately offered to look after them. Unfortunately I did not accept, for I had already arranged everything with an old friend of mine: the Argentine consul and painter Fernando Oscar Soria, who was also a native of La Plata.

Chapter 18

Paris

With only a suitcase, a traveling bag and a few paintings, I left for Paris on 31 December 1923, where surprises lay in wait. Some were so fortunate they seem to be a figment of my imagination.

My bearded and obliging friend Amadeo was expecting me at the Gare de Lyon. Together we headed for the hotel, Rue Delambre, where he had reserved a room for me. Over dinner that evening he told me all that I was burning to know; then, we went to the famous «La Rotonde» and «Le Dôme» cafés that stood on the corner. I met Argentines and Spaniards sitting in groups at different tables; so many people did I meet that night and the following, that their names are jumbled up in my memory; I only recall those of three Spaniards: the sculptor Mateo Hernández, for he was working on the bust of the poet Oliverio Girondo, and those of the painters Celso Lagar (at one point I went out with him, his wife and a few others to visit the Montparnasse cafés in a merry mood) and Manuel Ángeles Ortiz, whom I saw again in Buenos Aires.

I first visited the Louvre, then the National Museum of Modern Art, poorly situated in those days in the Jardins du Luxembourg. During the first two weeks I did little else but visit museums and I became acquainted with Paris by walking through its streets until dusk, at which point I was exhausted and rested at some café where I would always find Latin Americans, Italians or Spaniards. I only interrupted this frenzied rhythm to visit Chartres, Reims, Versailles and Fontainebleau.

I had heard so much about the «Académie de la Grande Chaumière» (it owes its name to the street on which it is situated), that I became curious; it turned out to be an academy frequented by many foreigners, especially

Nordic. The «Lungo il Mungone» academy, and I say this without any «parti pris», had nothing to be envious about.

My impression of Paris was that of a huge center, of a city unique in the world. Why? Because everything gathered in its core: it was a place where universal thought converged and radiated, and at the same time a city shaped by a hundred different sceneries.

An artist, wherever he comes from, is not a stranger in Paris, and when I asked myself why, the answer came naturally: its spiritual climate envelops the artist in an exultant protection. In short, I realized that being in Paris was like finding oneself in the heart of the world itself, where one's feelers stretch so as to correspond with other artistic centers of the world. A great freedom reigned in Paris, something that was constantly alert.

Besides, what modesty! One came across renowned figures all the time, who instead of acting aloof, dealt with people discreetly, as if they knew that it is not one man that makes up history, but many, national o foreign.

As far as the Métro was concerned, I found it simply fabulous. Like a child I continually climbed up and down the stairs, fascinated by the novelty, but I soon abandoned this activity to return to what I liked most: walking through the city, which to me was the only way to familiarize myself with it. I regularly covered the distance from my hotel to the Louvre; suffice it to say that I explored Montmartre and a million other places on foot. The only thing I didn't do, and haven't still, was to climb to the top of the Eiffel Tower.

I had Viscount of Lascagno Tegui's address with me, and went to see him. He lived in Raúl Monsegur's home, to whom I was cordially introduced. We soon became friends, and that same morning I asked him whether it was difficult to find a studio in Paris. He replied that he owned two and could give up the smallest one. I thus settled in a small studio on Rue Vendôme fifteen days after having arrived to Paris. It wasn't terribly comfortable, for light flowed through a small window and from the ceiling, and was poorly distributed at that. However, I managed to paint and draw, and produced the work for Palmer in Milan. Assuredly, the convenience of that studio lay in the neighborhood and in its low rent.

In those days, Lascano Tegui was one of the most distinguished citizens of Montparnasse. Loquacious and absolutely charming, the whole neighborhood was fond of him, starting out with the purveyors. He was street–wise and knew like no–one else where to buy the cheapest merchandise. At the time he was going out both with his ex–wife and his girlfriend. To make matters worse, he tried his hand at dentistry, and people ran after him wanting to kill him. Walking with him on the crowded streets was a real torture, for everyone stopped to greet him. He was witty, and the jokes and «boutades» poured. Often, he'd recite poems out loud. Yet he had possessed other talents as well: a born journalist, he managed to write an article off the top of his head, and was a terrific cook. His hare and chicken «à la marinière» were unrivalled. To complete the picture, one more detail: he always came up with ingenious sayings and Dadaist proposals to solve aesthetic problems.

One late afternoon I went to visit Pablo Curatella. I cannot recall the name of the street where he lived, but I do remember one entered through a large gate and that one had to follow a corridor to the end. Halfway through this corridor I found him and his wife Germaine, about to leave the house. He had no idea I was in Paris and was astounded. I was no less surprised: he had gotten married and was already going bald. I laughed heartily, reminding him that in Florence he had predicted I would lose all of my hair precociously, whereas he, with his thick mane, was certain to keep it for the rest of his life. Such was our meeting: surprise and laughter. Night had fallen; we parted on the sidewalk, arranging to meet another morning.

That day, Curatella showed me his work. It clearly indicated Bourdelle's influence, and indeed, he he had studied with him the year before. At the time his teacher was André Lhote, and we agreed that together we would go to the Academy in order to meet him. The «Lhote Academy» was famous in those days, frequented by many aspiring artists that had come from all over the world; nonetheless, this prominent theoretician of avant–garde art, who had not been able to apply the brilliant propositions for which he was famous to his art, had not managed to form disciples capable of sustaining his system. The «Lhote» students form legions, but not one of his apprentices has distinguished himself.

I think that a sharp distinction ought to be made between the terms «artist» and «art theoretician». Both are necessary, yet the artist is the one who lasts, for the simple reason that his reality is action, whereas the art thoretician remains caught in abstraction. Ozenfant, Lhote, Gleizes, Le Corbusier (whose pen name is Jeanneret), are all theoreticians: as painters they haven't gone far.

One morning, Curatella came to fetch me at my studio. I was surprised to see him carrying my bas–relief under his arm; when he told me he was taking it for his teacher to see it, my surprise turned into irritation, and I confess having felt uncomfortable. Fortunately Lhote did not attend the Academy that morning, which relieved me: I had been dreading the old scene of 1913 would repeat itself.

All along, both Curatella and his wife were very kind to me. We didn't often meet because I soon began to work in the mornings until one o'clock, and needed the rest of the day for other things. Moreover, I had made the acquaintance of a young Turk who adored music, and who often surprised me with the pleasant news of having obtained some tickets for one concert or another. As music has always been a passion of mine, I was in heaven. I had also become friends with a very beautiful girl called Hélène, and my friends from Italy continually came to Paris, Massimo Bontempelli among others. Anton Giulio Bragaglia arrived around March, and stayed fifteen days at a small hotel in the Quartier Latin, where he received journalists and wrote his articles. I saw him almost every night; we had dinner in Montparnasse and then headed for the «Closerie de Lilas», where Parisian poets, led by Paul Fort, received him with open arms.

The Rue de la Boétie, flourishing with the most important art galleries, became familiar to me; there also were a few galleries on the Rue de la Seine. I was looking for some Cubist works to better understand this art movement, but practically these were neither found on the market nor in museums. What abounded, either in the shop–windows and galleries, were works by the Fauves, Impressionists and Post–impressionists. There also were paintings devoid of any personality, which isn't surprising, for few artists truly egage in aesthetic exploration.

To see something out of the ordinary, I sent Gino Severini (whom I did not know personally) a few lines, requesting an interview. He replied at once that he was at my disposal and received me with great cordiality. At the time he was working on a large objective painting, measuring at least 1.20 meters, in which two «pierrots» were playing cards. He was annoyed with his art dealer, for the latter wanted the curtain he had painted next to a window, instead of in the background, and that posed a technically insolvable problem to him.

Several topics were discussed while chatting all afternoon, including Futurism, and he expressed his disagreement on several of its aspects. We often agreed, and when we parted, we promised to see one another soon.

In Paris I met a group of Argentine artists, among them the architect Alberto Prebisch, whom I often got together with. He was a studious man; he read a lot and was interested in the world around him. He told me that upon returning to Argentina he would deal with architecture practically, but that for the moment he wanted to spend his time studying and investigating all he could. It seemed a very sensible determination, especially when observing that some artists, after having attended the Buenos Aires Academy, wasted their Parisian afternoons idly drawing nudes at the «Grande Chaumière» academy or others like it.

A friend of mine told me about the interesting weekly gatherings organized by the painter Van Donghen. More than interesting, they were picturesque, for many actresses, dancers and wealthy American women –Van Donghen's clientele– frequented the artist's home. There I ran into Juan Gris quite by chance, for he told me he seldom left his home after sunset. This painter, whose work I had seen at Herward Walden's collection in Berlin, caused an excellent impression on me. He didn't look Spanish at all and was such a gentleman in the way he dressed and in his measured word. We took to each other to such an extent, that while the gathering was at its height, we left together to continue our conversation in a café. He was extremely pleasant and tackled with clarity all problems related to painting.

He spoke to me about the Parisian environment and I hastened to ask him a few questions, especially on Cubism. All he told me was absolutely contrary to what Carrà had mentioned. So satisfying was our conversation that time went by without us noticing it, and when we parted, we arranged to meet at his studio.

Zadkine was one of the renowned artists that frequented «La Rotonde». We became good friends, and sometimes I visited him at his studio for him to play some pieces of Russian folklore on his accordion.

Those were hard times for young artists who swam against the tide. In order to live, Zadkine sold pictures or watercolors for a few francs. The client was so important to him, that he studied his gestures with great care. Whenever he sat down to play his instrument, he did so strategically: he would leave the door of his studio ajar, and I would sit quietly in the room. At the height of the concert, someone would push the door wide open, at which point he'd drop the accordion, and show the visitor his «jungle», which included sculpture carved in the finest of woods.

Zadkine was quite a good psychologist; upon noticing that his visitor, because of his taste or wallet was not going to buy any sculpture, he would show him his portfolio filled with drawings and washes. Rarely did a client escape him; with his bright eyes beneath his thick eyebrows and his red hair, he was a typical «Montparnassien», and everyone was in awe of him. Zadkine, you great man! How you fought throughout your life to stir people's interest in your art! And yet, though admitting its interesting qualities, it never caught my fancy.

One morning I went to visit Juan Gris; he lived in the outskirts. I found him very disheartened and it wasn't long before he told me the reason: Picasso had visited him the day before and contemplating a painting on an easel –a portrait of his wife with a basket under her arm– had told him: «A good piece for a museum».

This could have been a compliment, but in those days, to say that a painting was a «museum piece» was like declaring it was a dead piece of work. He was most distressed by the words of his compatriot and I had the impression that because he felt close to me, it made it easier for him to relieve his pain. I tried to console Gris, and told him how futile censorship was when the artist knows where he is heading.

All that he showed me that day –some thirty–odd small paintings– did not follow the Cubist path; rather, they were figurative, with slight distortions. I asked him why he no longer displayed his usual rigor, to which he replied that he only listened to his intuition.

As far as technique was concerned, his paintings seemed rather strained, and I attributed it to health problems, for it was evident Gris was suffering from a physical impairment. Yet later, after having seen more of his work, I understood it had always been a real effort for him to paint; he was too eager to probe into the consistency of the represented object. He confirmed my impression telling me that painting was hard work, and that it took him at least eight days to finish off one of his small paintings.

All of Gris′ pictures, seen either in his studio or elsewhere possessed quality. Beneath the geometric rigor, the objects found their contours, and there hovered a rational light brimming with poetry. Measure and lyricism. His work was the result of reflection and refined sensitivity; a spectrum of gray of extreme delicacy. In fact, his artistic name derives from the characteristic hues of his painting: his real name was José Victoriano González.

My visit lasted a couple of hours. We decided that one morning he would come to see my work. I wished him well, feeling that he was a painter without any spirit of adventure, but of exceptional sincerity.

An exhibition of works by Picasso was being held Rue de la Boétie, at the gallery owned by his art dealer, Paul Rosenberg (Léonce′s brother), located in the same building in which the painter worked and lived. I was heading towards the gallery with a Spanish friend when we ran into Picasso, who, if I remember correctly, was wearing a derby. My friend introduced me and they greeted each other cordially, after which Picasso told us a rather coarse incident that had just happened to him, and that I will not repeat.

My friend told him I was a painter, and I saw fit to ask him whether I could visit his studio. Since I was staying in Paris for another couple of months, I proposed leaving him my address in order to meet whenever it proved convenient to him. Without hesitation he replied he expected me the following day at five o′clock in the afternoon.

We visited the exhibition at Rosenberg′s; the work displayed was objective, and among the paintings hung several portraits of his wife Olga. The following day I arrived on time; Picasso himself opened the door and our conversation touched on many subjects. I told him I had seen his series of brick–red pastel nudes in Berlin, achieved after his trip to Rome. What had greatly interested me, I said, were his paintings owned by Herward Walden. While we chatted, he showed me his most audacious paintings. Actually, I was the one who spoke, and he listened to my comments without interruption. I asked him questions about Cubism, yet did not obtain any concrete information; like all the rest of the avant–garde artists, Futurists included, he was into something else. At any rate, after having observed his work, I noticed a taste for adventure predominating in his work, something I had not sensed in the paintings of Juan Gris. I was shocked, however, by a certain callousness, a certain declamatory vehemence, a certain rudeness, totally opposed to that secret equilibrium present in the painting of his compatriot.

One morning, Juan Gris showed up at my studio around eleven o'clock. I knew he would come, but not that soon. I said I had visited Picasso's studio, describing the paintings I had seen, what I thought of them, and the way the artist used color, as an auxiliary and even a complementary element. He seemed surprised, almost taken aback; though he had visited Picasso a few days before, the latter had not shown him most of the paintings I was referring to.

I showed Gris some of the pictures I had brought with me, and those I was working on. His praise seemed sincere for it was measured and sensible; these were the words of both an expert and an artist, something rare to find: there are artists who neither value their work nor that of others, or who lack the vocabulary to express a fair analysis. «The blue cave of Capri» Gris particularly fascinated Gris. Whenever he stopped by, and he did so often, he would ask me to show him that particular painting. A few times we had lunch together and our friendship lasted up to my departure. I never saw him again. He died in 1927.

Severini, whom I was in touch with, told me that he had read in the newspapers that Marinetti was coming to Paris to give a lecture at the Sorbonne. He felt uncomfortable, without knowing quite which attitude to adopt, given that his relations with the apostle of Futurism had turned sour. Furthermore, he knew my relations weren't brilliant either, and wondered whether I would see him in spite of it all. I replied that we had to side with him, and that listening to Marinetti was always interesting. I myself was planning on giving him a hug, and offered to greet him on behalf of Severini, if the latter decided not to do so personally.

Fortunately, we arrived early, for the large hall filled itself to the brim in order to listen to the sacred monster and prepare for a debate. The spectacle was beautiful: it began with a musical number, a singer with such a beautiful voice she enraptured the audience; I have never heard something quite like it again.

When Marinetti appeared on the proscenium, the whole house vibrated in unison and thundering applause broke out. Then, silence ensued; everyone seemed captivated by the spell of the wizard. His topic was Futurism across the globe, and his voice rose, ardent and intense. Suddenly, Severini and I gave a start: we had just heard our names, exultantly pronounced by Marinetti. He had no idea we were in the auditorium, and even if he had thought Severini was present, for the latter lived in Paris, he could not have guessed I was, considering I had not even said goodbye when he had left.

An agitated debate arose once the lecture was over, [17] of which Marinetti came out triumphantly, refuting the opponents' arguments in such a fluent

---

17 This lecture was published in the "L'Impero de Roma" (20 May 1924) under the heading "Il futurismo mondiale".

French –so Gino said– he must have been the envy of many Frenchmen. As you might know, Marinetti was born in Egypt to Italian parents and studied in Paris; that's why his first poetry books were written in French, and only later translated into Italian.

I held Severini by the arm, and together we went to embrace the great man. Marinetti was thrilled, and I understood more than ever how incapable he was of bearing a grudge against people. Gino had to leave, and I stayed behind. From the Sorbonne, in a «petit comité», we headed for the Café de la Paix. Marinetti arranged to meet me the following day at the hotel, where we chatted for hours, finally discovering that we had more things in common than we had expected.

Since everything came easily to him, he asked me whether I had an art dealer in Paris and what his name was. Upon realizing I had not even considered the subject, he declared it was essential for me to have a truly magnificent «marchand». Immediately he decided I should meet Léonce Rosenberg, the owner of a «non plus ultra» gallery as far as avant–garde art was concerned. Rosenberg himself called it the «Temple of Cubism», and only select people were allowed in, providing they had a special pass. Concomitantly, the «marchand» also edited the «L'Effort Moderne» magazine.

My old friend phoned from the hotel and we left at once. Rosenberg received him affectionately, and Marinetti greeted the art dealer with the enthusiasm typical of his nature. Marinetti then introduced me, telling him I had just held a successful exhibition at the «Der Sturm» gallery in Berlin. For the first time Rosenberg noticed me, as if associating me to the name of the gallery. I then realized that mentioning «Der Sturm» in certain European centers was akin to showing a safe conduct: it always led to success.

I discreetly stood aside so as to allow them to speak in private and meanwhile I looked at the work that was hanging; they were of the highest quality. When we said goodbye, Léonce Rosenberg asked me for my studio address; as I was very poor, I lied to him, telling him I was staying in a rather dark hotel room, and that I would bring him the work. An appointment was arranged for the following afternoon.

In one of those Parisian taxis as big as removal vans, I headed for the Rue de la Beaume at three o'clock in the afternoon. Rosenberg led me into a beautiful gray room with matching carpets, into which my feet sunk most agreeably. Three easels stood in the back of the room, and facing them, some three meters away, two comfortable armchairs and a coffee table covered with ashtrays and different brands of cigars and cigarettes. He told me to take a seat, sat down himself, and told his employee to place two paintings on the lateral easels, and one of my pictures on the easel that stood in the middle. Rosenberg gazed at the three paintings in silent curiosity, as if waiting for them to speak. He had the two works on the side switch places, and kept on scrutinizing; then, he changed the painting in the center, substituting it for another work of mine.

I believe this ritual lasted at least two hours, and time seemed to have stopped. Rosenberg never addressed a word to me, and as he communicated with his employee from a distance through the means of signs, it seemed as though they had lost their tongues. Trying not to feel uncomfortable, I began to make my own comparative analysis, astounded at times that my work harmonized so well with the other ones. They were new to me, and not always identifiable. However, there existed a parallelism in the diversity; the same conception, a similarity of ideas synchronically parallel or a same quality uniting them in certain cases; in others, the only common link was the mood of the period impregnating the work.

Never like that afternoon did I have the opportunity to see and judge my own paintings with such objectivity. I noticed, for example, that works such as «La Gruta Azul de Capri», «Self–portrait» or «Pensierosa» resisted examination effortlessly, whereas «The blind flutist» or «The soloist» was saved only by color, my strongest point.

Among Rosenberg´s Cubist works, there were some that belonged to the analytical period, which I consider the best. I had only seen them in reproductions, and upon noticing that they were painted almost wholly black and white, or brown and white, I realized the copies had been faithful. Though I appreciated their quality, I deplored the absence of color. Don´t forget that having studied the great Renaissance masters, I consider color to be essential, as it always has to agree with the idea it attempts to express.

Painting is made up of color. Those who state not being interested in color and in its great expressive power cannot truly be called painters, for they aren´t capable of conveying the broad spectrum of feelings: from the simplest to those possessing the greatest dramatic intensity. The truth is that he who does not feel color will not resort to it, and it goes without saying that whomever does not feel it is not a true painter; in the best of cases he might be a good drawer. If to this we add that the handling of color is not an easy task, that it requires a great deal of effort in order to master it, and that feeling attracted to color is in the blood, it is not difficult to understand that there are so many artists that shun it, finding easy excuses for their lack of interest.

I think Rosenberg felt the same way, for when he had at last finished his inspection, he told me he was indeed very pleased with my paintings and that if I wished, he would represent me.

The proposition bewildered me, for at the most I was only expecting kind words. Pulling myself together, I thanked him and explained I was planning a trip to Buenos Aires, where I would be exhibiting. He was taken aback upon learning I was Argentine and not Italian. He gave me his opinion regarding the show, telling me it was a mistake to hold it; it implied costs and unnecessary worries. To prove his point, he told me that in 1923 he had exhibited a magnificent selection of modern works in New York, none of which he had been able to sell. As far as the critics were concerned, they obliterated his effort at the stroke of a pen. If this could happen in New York, what would await me in Buenos Aires? However, my mind was set, and we agreed that upon my return I would settle in Paris, where he would see to my every need. He asked me to leave him biographical data and photographs for his magazine, for people to get to know me in the meanwhile. I had no paintings with me in Paris, and since I felt reluctant to tell him I was on a tight budget, I promised to send him my work from Milan.

In Italy, I had very little time left to move out of my Milanese studio, and realized, in the frenzy of the last days, that six months would fly by. I therefore decided to not to send Rosenberg any paintings from Italy.

One evening, together with Marinetti and a group of friends, we went to the «Magic–City» dance hall, where a costume party was being held. Dressing up and wearing a mask was optional. We arrived just at the moment André Derain was being tossed like a large ball from a box. He had drunk too much and those around him, just as inebriated, thought the stunt to be hilarious. Fortunately, those who occupied the box below had had the opportunity to protect themselves. Fortunately Derain came out unharmed, confirming the popular belief that nothing ever happens to children or drunkards.

The hall overflowed with artists, and I shook hands with all those that Marinetti and my other friends greeted. The public was highly original: I have never seen so many full and beautiful necklines than those belonging to men dressed up as Salomé or Marie–Antoinette. The Surrealist group was complete: among them was Tristan Tzara, wearing a monocle and with an air of conqueror, quite unbearable. Mind you, I wasn't the only one who felt this way: it was a generalized opinion. Because that night we were in the mood to play pranks, we left early, around two in the morning.

In 1956 Tristan Tzara and I became friends, for he no longer wore a monocle nor flaunted that unbearable air of his youth. Besides, he was a close friend of a friend of mine: Sandro Volta. However, one night at my Rue de Mabillon home, we had an argument that stamped itself in my memory. Alberto Sartoris, Carlos Prina, his wife María Rosa and I, had been in his apartment in the afternoon, looking at his collection of paintings, collages and African art objects, some of them very beautiful. He showed us the originals of the book he was working on, dedicated to François Villon: it was full of erasures, corrections and annotations between the lines and in the margin, indicating a conscientious process of elaboration.

When night fell, we all had dinner at my studio, and the conversation turned to painting. Nothing could have been more explosive. Tzara vigorously sustained (faithful to the capricious theories of the Surrealists, who do not understand art at all) that painting was an instinctive language, and that it sufficed to choose colors at random and apply them onto the canvas, with or without brushes, in order to produce a work of art. He should have kept quiet! Those at the table jumped down his throat like tigers, with such convincing arguments that all Tzara said to defend himself was futile. He was asked to justify why he painstakingly worked on every line of his text, seeking the right expression and the melody of the sentence, and yet found it logical for a painter to articulate his thought coarsely.

I left Paris and arrived in Milan at the end of June 1924, with time only to move out of my studio and dispatch my belongings to Florence, where they would be kept in storage until I returned. As I was packing, Mario Sironi showed up. He told me that he and his family were poorly lodged in Milan, and that he hadn't had a chance to sign up for one of those studios with an annexed apartment built by the Municipality; he had come to ask me, if I agreed to it, whether I would transfer my lease to him. Being on my own, finding a studio was relatively easy, whereas for him, renting a studio and a home at a reasonable price was difficult business. As I had decided that upon my return I would live in Paris, I happily handed my studio over to him.

I gave quite a few paintings to my friends in Florence: to Gonnelli, to my companions, to Nella, just as I had done in Milan. There, however, I had torn my cardboards up, in spite of Marussig's objections. Besides preparing a trunk with my clothes, I had two crates packed with paintings I wasn't taking along, as well as drawings and things that might come in handy in Paris. I wrote my name on the three pieces of luggage, and on the bottom, «Paris», as place of destination. My friend Soria, the Argentine consul, took charge of them, eventually entrusting the baggage to someone else. Some time later, Soria was transferred to Lyon, where he unexpectedly passed away. I still wonder today where these crates have ended up.

I said goodbye to Nella and her family, and left Florence with a heavy heart, consoling myself by thinking I would soon be back. We didn't speak about the future. However, it's possible that she felt I had my hopes set on Paris, expecting a solid base on which to build a new life.

I stopped over for a day in Milan to greet Giolli and Marussig, and tell some other good friends I would soon be back. I joined Xul Solar in Hamburg; it was decided that we would travel together. At the German harbor, Bacerque, an old friend of mine from La Plata, awaited us tickets in hand. We would be sleeping in a six–bed cabin, that only we two would occupy. Thanks to Bacerque, I didn't have to pay for my trip, and Xul paid only a small amount, due to the fact that Cacho Oyhanarte, a childhood acquaintance of mine, had been posted to Hamburg as Consul General.

The crossing was superb, and the sea was as smooth as oil. We traveled like kings and the cook had received orders to prepare us wonderful «asados» and «pucheros a la criolla» [18] every day. Needless to say I traveled in perfect solitude, while Xul made friends right and left. He wasn't even on high seas, that he already knew everyone, from the captain to all the sailors. At night he would tell me about his adventures in the lounge. He really made me laugh one night with his tale of a tall stout lady who had accidentally sat on his hand, languidly placed on the couch. He had attempted to gently remove it, but to no avail; unsuccessfully, he then tried stirring his arm, then his shoulder; the lady, unperturbed, didn't budge. There was nothing else left for him to do than leave his hand on the sofa.

Montevideo was our first port of call. There we visited our excellent friend Guillermo Laborde at the school where he was teaching, but he was absent. Instead, the sculptor Luis Falconi received us, who after greeting us asked me: «So, you're involved in Futurism, eh? We all know what that means!» And as if that hadn't been enough stupidity, he added: «Darn! You really know how to make yourself popular, don't you! Telegrams are sent from all ports, announcing your arrival!»

There are people who travel throughout the world locked up in trunk. This man, who had lived so may years in Paris, surrounded by creative minds, had been unable to sense the revolution that was taking place in the arts.

On 31 July, my parents and some close friends were anxiously waiting for me at the Buenos Aires harbor; leaning on the deck railing, I saw them waving their handkerchiefs. Alberto Prebisch, one of my new friends, was also present. I was the last one to leave the ship, unable to move: it was as though my feet had grown roots in the wooden boards of the deck.

---

18 "Asado" and " puchero a la criolla" are typical Argentine dishes. The former is roasted meat, the latter is a stew consisting of meat and vegetables.

Part Two

Chapter 19

In Buenos Aires

To confide in this impersonal secretary, the tape that silently registers my voice, reminds me of my childhood, when I talked to myself and said so many things, knowing I was the only one listening,

The moment has come to reflect on my return to Argentina and ask myself which frame of mind I was in when I arrived, what my expectations were, or what I was planning on doing while I was there. Above all, and I say this with no hesitation, was my excitement to reunite with my family. Moreover, I wanted to show my compatriots the work I had achieved during those long ten years of absence.

I was indebted to my country, above all to my Province that had granted me a scholarship for three years and a half and I felt it my duty to show the work I had accomplished, demonstrating thus it had not been a waste of money.

We all know that imagination magnifies beloved or absent beings, and how the home country is exalted in exile. From Europe, I saw my country as a power, imbued with the cultural and spiritual attributes inherent in the most advanced lands.

Many intellectuals, scientists and artists in general had spent years living in the Old World, bringing back knowledge that reinforced the wisdom accumulated by those that had come before them. A young country in the youngest of continents, open to immigration and European culture, I truly imagined it absolutely permeable to all that was novel and vital, precisely because of its own youth and vitality.

From Buenos Aires, the large capital with major newspapers such as «La Nación» and «La Prensa» circulating throughout the whole of America and

Europe, I received news continuously and knew about its enormous material and educational progress; moreover, the finest Argentine minds congregated there. Already in 1921, young intellectuals such as Jorge Luis Borges and Eduardo González Lanuza had launched «Prismas», a «mural» publication, whose issues divulged the ideas of the Ultraist poets from walls and city trees; those same writers, together with others, eventually published another magazine, «Proa», in which the most renowned figures contributed. What the short or long–lived publications revealed was the seditious and eager spirit it brought about in the world of letters. I suppose the same revolutionary spirit reigned in other disciplines; that is why, when Léonce Rosenberg warned me that it would be nonsensical to exhibit my art here, I felt it offended our capacity to evolve. However, I did not take his words seriously; like all Europeans, he hadn´t a clue about the realities of our America.

As far as my colleagues were concerned, I went to them candidly, imagining that, like everywhere else in the world, they would be more or less cordial, more or less experienced, that some could become friends of mine and some not, depending always on spiritual or simply spontaneous attractions.

This is the reason why, no sooner had the emotions generated by the family reunion subsided, and after having contacted some of the young poets and writers grouped around the «Martín Fierro» magazine (publication which had seen the light months before in Buenos Aires under the direction of Evar Méndez), I visited the National Academy of Fine Arts, as well as a couple of studios, driven by both professional and personal motives.

Back in Buenos Aires, Xul and I had arranged to meet three days later at the Richmond café on Florida Street with Alberto Prebisch (member of the «Martin Fierro» literary group), so as to establish our first contact with the group; this gave me time to be with my family, and especially with my grandfather, whom I found as strong as an ox and still reading his favorite newspaper without the need of glasses.

On the day of the meeting, Xul and I went to visit Evar Méndez, who worked at the House of Government. If I remember correctly, he held a temporary post at the Teatro Colón, but mainly, I recall he was always full of ideas and projects. His newspaper had come out just in time to respond to the needs of the literary circles.

In his company we headed for the «Richmond» teahouse, where I got acquainted with the first «Martinfierristas», most of them very young writers and poets. A spiritual and restless spirit defined them, a desire to subvert the reigning aesthetic taste, focused on Rubén Darío and Leopoldo Lugones. Their greetings were effusive, their companionship, loyal. The circle became larger in the course of the weeks, and Xul and I were welcomed; I felt curiosity was stirred wherever I went.

A great fuss had been made over my name since Julio de la Paz had interviewed me in Berlin for the «Atlántida» magazine. The news of my return had been publicized by the press and the journalists, not possessing any concrete information, digressed or invented. Without more ado, they presented me as a Futurist painter; the comment wasn't flattering in the least, for to be called a «Futurist» in Argentina in 1924 –where the European avant–garde movements, in existence for about fifteen years, were barely known– meant one was mad, deceitful, extravagant, a fake or a liar.

That explained the irony heard in Montevideo: «So you're into Futurism, eh? We all know what *that* means!» In truth, they didn't, but many smart alecks, thinking themselves enlightened, felt it was understood that «that» meant being a charlatan «pour épater le bourgeois».

Not only artists, but also the public interested in fine arts believed this to be true. Considering I was the only one who was bringing «that» to the country, I suddenly became the protagonist of a strange spectacle that took place some days later. Journalists stopped me on the streets of Buenos Aires or traveled to La Plata, followed by their photographers. Not one wrote down my answers; instead, they invented the most extraordinary replies.

If one had believed their stories, one of my purposes upon arriving home was to destroy national art. They confused national art with folkloric expression: when Chardin paints apples, he is making French art, just like when Bonnard paints a woman in the bathtub. One finds apples, women and tubs all over the world, but motif and national essence is intertwined, preventing us from making mistakes as to the origin of a painting.

No, national art is not improvised; it is the result of an accumulation of local, material and psychological circumstances, of an immense collective feeling directed from its origins towards an aspiration or a common religion, allowing it to become fused with the spirit itself of the peoples, and it would have been impossible for me to destroy that which did not exist.

It goes without saying that I paid one of my first calls on Rodolfo Sarrat, my generous and long–time friend, whom I told I was going to hold an exhibition in La Plata. Resuming our old habits, we often got together for coffee. However, as in those days he was a Deputy, we headed for the Congress building.

I continued paying courtesy visits. I went to the National Fine Arts Commission to greet its president, Martín Noel, and was agreeably surprised to find him in the company of my former patron Ernesto de la Cárcova. Also present was the sculptor Pedro Zonza Briano, who made sarcastic comments about Futurism. I couldn't retort at the time, as I was still busy with the two gentlemen, but asked the sculptor to be patient; we would settle the matter on the way out. He didn't seem to appreciate the invitation, for after a while he politely said goodbye.

On De la Cárcova's request, I visited the Superior School of Fine Arts he had founded, and which now bears his name. He told me that due to the lack of funds they worked slowly, which didn't surprise me; in no country, no matter how small, is there any money available for culture, which everyone speaks of and enjoys.

One afternoon I went to greet Pío Collivadino, the director of the National Academy of Fine Arts, now on Alsina Street. As he wasn't in, the deputy director Carlos Ripamonte received me. I explained to him that the object of my visit was to greet them and get to know the Academy. In turn, he thanked me again for my monograph edited in Berlin; he and my former patron had been the only ones who had appreciated.

As we visited the classrooms together, I realized my presence caused quite a commotion amid the students and the personnel; as we walked by, doors opened and closed unabashedly, and through the cracks I saw angular faces peeping with curiosity: when the doorman heard my name, his eyes nearly popped out of his head.

I then held a cordial conversation with Ripamonte, as serious a man as he was reserved and prudent. On my way out, a group of students were standing on the sidewalk, as if waiting for something: I realized they wished to see the «freak». I wouldn't wish to bore anyone with details, but considering no-one knew me in Buenos Aires, my name was at once very popular.

In this vein of cordiality, I visited the studios of renowned artists, beginning with the major ones. I believe I started with the studio of Emilio Centurión, First National Prize of 1920, located in a beautiful mansion in the old quarters of Buenos Aires. On his recommendation, I went to see Jorge Larco, a young artist thrilled by the painting of Romero de Torres, who had his studio in the same stately mansion; then, I visited Raúl Mazza and others. These were pleasant meetings, which prolonged themselves in La Boca. [19]

My friend Pedro Blake accompanied me to the studio of Miguel Angel Victorica, and to those of artists living in La Boca. I recall that Victorica expected us for lunch and that we spent the whole afternoon looking at his paintings.

Later, I headed towards the other end of the city in order visit the studios of the sculptor Antonio Sibellino and the painter Ramón Gómez Cornet. Having run into Césareo Bernaldo de Quirós one afternoon, he invited me to his large studio at the Rosedal Park in Palermo. There I saw a series of large paintings that had just arrived from his province, where he had painted them.

As I went to exhibitions, which at the time were scarce, I became familiarized with what was happening in the art world. Newly founded, the «Institución Amigos del Arte» had joined the scene, making important cultural contributions that lasted for many years. I believe the painter Fray Guillermo

---

19 La Boca is a district situated in the southern part of Buenos Aires City, characterized by a large population of Italian immigrants

Butler and the sculptor Agustín Riganelli were among the first artists to exhibit in their halls, located on 900 Florida Street.

One of my major concerns was to reserve a hall in order to hold a show as soon as possible. At the beginning, Xul and I had agreed on exhibiting together, but he kept on postponing the dates and I didn't have much time. After having visited a few galleries, I decided on «Witcomb» gallery, located at the time between Corrientes and Sarmiento Streets. I walked in decisively so as to find out about the conditions, and its director, Mr. Rosendo Martínez, received me cordially. A pleased smile lit his face when I mentioned my name and he welcomed me with excitement. I clearly stated I wanted his halls as soon as possible, and that I wished to know how much it would cost me. He bit his lips, half–closed his eyes, repeatedly moved his head and answered my question with another one: «How about it, my friend, if I don't charge you anything?»

Naturally, I accepted. We agreed that the catalogue and the invitations would be on me, and decided upon 13 October as the opening date.

The weeks following our arrival proved to be very hectic for Xul and I. The people we met kept introducing new friends to us, and our commitments increased. Evar Méndez, very insightfully, for he was very well–connected to the literary milieu, invited us often for dinner at his home, so as to introduce us to intellectuals of merit that did not frequent the Richmond café.

Evar Méndez, generous and kind, gathered men of all ages around him. He had a predilection for the new ones, for his mind was young in spirit. If the «Martín Fierro» publication, brilliantly representing the voice of an anti–traditionalist generation, was able to subsist for almost four years, it was thanks to him, to his personal effort aimed at elevating and financing the publication by means of advertisements, subscriptions and contributions. It goes without saying this was no easy task. I recall seeing him running like mad from bank to bank to avoid the catastrophes that threatened his newspaper.

It was thanks to him that I met people from different circles; then again, Pedro Blake was also very well–connected, and introduced me yet to other groups. This is how I partook in the gatherings at the Tortoni café, on Avenida de Mayo. I had been told the writers and artists that met there were decidedly opposed to avant–garde movements, yet, to be perfectly frank, I did not sense this resistance at all; like everywhere else, people were at times pleasant, at times not.

I did not visit the neighborhood of Boedo, home of another intellectual group, and antagonistic towards the «Martín Fierro» members. Boedo represented the suburbs: Florida Street, the city. Those thinkers belonging to the «Martín Fierro» newspaper held their meetings on Florida Street; those from Boedo, in the working class neighborhood after which the periodical was named. They had their printing office there, their bookshops and their cafés, and these writers too wished to clarify the minds of the public; their chief concern, however, was the struggle of the classes and all that related to it. In February 1922, after having launched the rather academic literary magazine «Los Pensadores», they edited active journalistic organs, such as the «La Protesta» and the «Campana de Palo» periodicals, with which they wished to manifest their left–wing spirit and affirm their social aspirations. Whenever these two groups came in contact, they accused each other either of communism, or of political and human insensitivity.

I got to know the thinkers of Boedo and established a good relationship with them: Alvaro Yunque, at whose home I spent a lovely afternoon, César Tiempo, Roberto Mariani, Armando Cascella, but above all, Leónidas Barletta, whose friendship still honors me today.

I continued to see the «Martín Fierro» members at the Richmond café almost all afternoons; conversations became each time more vigorous, even vehement; they listened with passionate curiosity to all I could tell them about the European artistic milieu, whereas I accumulated precisions about the Argentine one. Other writers that didn't belong to the group frequented the café as well, and shared both our tables and conversations.

I started to make friends in all sectors, as usual, for I myself have always detested being pigeonholed. Besides, I am as sensitive to the gifts of intelligence as to those of the spirit, and if I happen to be drawn towards some beings because of their great talents, I am also drawn towards those who possess noble hearts. The list of friends on both sides of the ocean is therefore very large, and if I have failed to name all of them, it is because my memory fails me. It was the «Martín Fierro» supported that defended me against all difficulties: Evar Méndez, Córdova Iturburu, Pablo Rojas Paz, Ernesto Palacio, Eduardo González Lanuza, Raúl Gonzalez Tuñón, Jorge Luis Borges, Sergio Piñero, Leopoldo Marechal, Ricardo Güiraldes, Alberto Prebisch, Pedro Blake, Norah Lange, Jacobo Fijman and Roberto Ledesma.

There were others, too, that morally backed me up, men with different leanings, such as Alejandro Korn, José Ingenieros, Leonardo Estarico, Alberto Hidalgo, Leónidas Barletta, Pedro Henríquez Ureña, Pedro Juan Vignale, Sixto Pondal Ríos, Atalaya, Nicolás Olivari, Antonio Sibellino, Roberto Mariani and Ramón Gómez Cornet.

On the other hand, the personalities characterizing either one of these sectors mingled and blended, for their ideals were similar and their bond of friendship strong. Being a «Martín Fierro» supporter did not mean one belonged to a group reserved for the initiated: rather, it was a field open to those men that possessed intellectual curiosity. Since these thinkers were attractive because of their passionate views, many people drifted towards them without necessarily adhering to the movement; that is why today it is difficult to discern who a «Martín Fierro» sympathizer was and who wasn't.

At any rate, the «Martín Fierro» spirit, of which so much was said, never expressed itself in the field of the fine arts: a great deal of artists credited with being a part of the movement had actually nothing to do with it. Whenever the periodical published a reproduction of an artist's work, he systematically became a supporter.

When I returned to my homeland, the «Martín Fierro» newspaper was already the voice of a large sector of a new literary generation that felt that the incorporation of Argentine thinking and literature into the new awareness born in Europe fifteen years ago was inevitable. There was no room for the artistic in its pages. Only a few times did it touch on the subject, and definitely not to enhance that which was modern, since modernity, in the field of fine arts, did not exist in Argentina. No sign of collective unrest: in the eyes of the Argentine artists, everything was running smoothly, in the best of worlds, oscillating between a rhetorical academicism and a belated Impressionism.

The magazine turned to the arts and fought a battle in that sense as from 9 October 1924, as a result of my exhibition at «Witcomb's». An article written by Xul Solar [20] was published on my work with five reproductions, and my painting, «The dancers» appeared on the cover. These were the first modern art works that «Martín Fierro» presented. Although paintings and sculptures by both Argentine and foreign authors were included in subsequent copies, at times of a very subjective modernism, it doesn't mean that these artists were active participants in the movement: action implies confrontation, an imposition of ideas. This meant instructing a public ill–prepared to comprehend new forms, and it was therefore crucial to exhibit the new works, convincing them of the importance of an expression that saw reality differently, in keeping with the changes the world was going through.

Only two artists contributed to the «Martín Fierro» newspaper: Xul Solar and I. In order to avoid any confusion and malicious interpretations, in the number 12–13 of October–November 1924, the newspaper published an explanation under the heading «Who is Martín Fierro?» in which the names of its active members and special contributors are disclosed [21]. As far as artists were concerned, only Xul and I were mentioned, for the simple reason that there existed no others. Though some might say that other artists joined later, I emphatically deny this.

---

20 Oddly, Oliverio Girondo calls this article a "commentary", when recalling the 1949 "Martín Fierro" publication.

21 The core of the "Martín Fierro" newspaper (editors, contributors, permanent writers) consists of the following people: José B. Cairola (founding member), Leónidas Campbell (founding member of the 1919 "Martín Fierro" and of the present one), H. Carambat (editor of the former newspaper and founding member of the present one), Córdova Iturburu, Luis L. Franco (founding member), Dr. Oliverio Girondo (founding member; his task was to present the newspaper and to contact American and European youths), Luis Góngora, Ricardo Güiraldes, Ernesto Palacio (founding member), Emilio Pettoruti, Dr. Sergio Piñero, the architect Alberto Prebisch, Pablo Rojas Paz (founding member), Xul Solar, Gastón O. Talamón (founding member), Evar Méndez (editor of the former "Martín Fierro" and founding member of the present one), director of the newspaper.

The «Martín Fierro» newspaper saw the light in February 1924, and disappeared in November 1927. During this period of time, besides Norah Borges, who contributed to the publication with her exquisite work, only two artists worked in Buenos Aires in order to give the traditional forms a new accent, without abandoning them: Antonio Sibellino and Ramón Gómez Cornet. Victorica was an independent artist, who paid no heed to the renovating movements, unfamiliar to him anyway; Alfredo Guttero returned to the country in 1927, that is to say, when the «Martín Fierro» dissolved; Pablo Curatella, who resided in Paris, did not return to Argentina until 1950; Héctor Basaldúa, Aquiles Badi and Horacio Butler remained in Europe and never got involved with the periodical; Lino Spilimbergo also left for Europe in 1924, and he stayed there well after 1927. Who then were the members of the «Martín Fierro» publication, struggling to impose avant–garde artistic conceptions?

A great deal of confusion is generated at times because of negligence or convenience. This is often the case with analysts, who, not having lived in a certain era, and moreover, not having bothered to study the sources, roughly situated the artistic renovation in Argentina between 1920 and 1930, as if it were the same to determine that a historical event took place at the beginning or the end of a decade.

Much has been said as to the influence of the «Taller Libre», or Open Studio, on the Argentine artistic circles, founded in 1928 and headed by Alfredo Guttero. Even admitting this studio has somewhat contributed to encourage new artistic orientations, one should bear in mind that the Open Studio was launched in the year 1908. It is necessary to mention, however, that its principal leader, the painter Alfredo Guttero, influenced by the Viennese Secession, was more of a decorator than a painter, and that the professors who accompanied him, with the exception of the sculptor Alfredo Bigatti, who had studied in Paris with Bourdelle between 1923 and 1924, had been artistically trained at the Buenos Aires National Fine Arts Academy.

Argentine art (and what I am about to say is not an act of vanity, but rather, an urge for historical precision) began to renovate itself as of October 1924 with my exhibition at Witcomb's, where I presented my paintings; it is not that my work introduces an era in which painting is achieved in another way: rather, it is the beginning of an era in which painting can be comprehended in a different manner. Beyond a shadow of a doubt, those that had left for Europe to study came back with other eyes.

Now that this point is clarified, I wish to continue with my account as chronologically accurately as possible. I have already said that from the moment I arrived to Buenos Aires, the people I met made my cause theirs; but what I forgot to mention is that upon returning to La Plata I saw my old friend, Benito Lynch, as well as some old companions with a great deal of pleasure. Lynch, so unsociable, posed for a portrait that is still being reproduced. When he was with me, he behaved without his usual reserve, though this trait has often been exaggerated.

I also got to know Pedro Henríquez Ureña, in whose home I met writers and young poets, as well as Ramón T. García, the intelligent director of the «El Argentino» newspaper, a La Plata publication that supported me from the outset.

Among my new friends was Alejandro Korn, with whom it was a pleasure to exchange impressions, for his spirit was open to the new meaningful tendencies. We saw each other often as we both traveled back and forth from La Plata to Buenos Aires; he found the new art thrilling. There also was José Ingenieros, a brilliant and mordant spirit who could set jokes aside to speak to me about avant–garde art, and whose significance he enjoyed exploring; and there was Constancio Vigil, director of the «Atlántida» publishing press, who received me warmly and whose affection is still transmitted through his son Carlos.

And there also was my grandfather, whom I regularly visited very early in the morning. He was in perfect health, and his mind, lucid. Yet one evening, some days before the opening of my show at «Witcomb´s», I learned about his sudden death upon arriving to La Plata. At that instant, my whole childhood and adolescence vanished with him. The loss was irreparable.

The art critic Atalaya, who in some circles was disliked because of his severity, made me popular in an indirect way. I had registered at the National Salon, opening in September, with three paintings; two had been rejected in previous salons and a third one was still held up by customs. The three were listed in the catalogue, but a new bureaucratic problem had arisen and I wasn´t able to show my paintings. Yet, the critic of the «La Prensa» newspaper spoke favorably of the three, which prompted Atalaya to demonstrate in his «La Protesta» newspaper that critics of large newspapers fulfilled their task without even checking the catalogues. As a result, the «La Prensa» critic resigned.

When the Salon opened, I went to see him and some of his colleagues. A prize was awarded to the best series, and it was Lino Spilimbergo who took it; it consisted of ten thousand pesos, a considerable sum if one thinks that it was equivalent to almost four years of scholarship. When I met this painter he stubbornly insisted on hearing my opinion on his paintings. It was a descriptive work and more related to drawing than to painting, but I took great care not to tell him this, thinking that since he was leaving for Europe, he would see enough painting over there to make up his own mind.

Walking through the halls with Atalaya, we came upon two Expressionist landscapes, and this surprised me. Atalaya told me he had no idea who the author was, though he had heard that the latter lived in Lanús with his family. Eventually I understood the presence of German Expressionism in that Salon: it had circulated thanks to the painter Roberto Rossi, who had once shared a studio with a friend. One artist occupied it in the morning, the other at night. One day, Rossi´s curiosity was aroused upon seeing that one of the wooden floor boards was raised. Beneath it he discovered several numbers of the German magazine «Simplicissimus», whose covers displayed Expressionist art.

Chapter 20

The «Witcomb» Exhibition

The date of my first exhibition was nearing, and the newspapers kept on dropping bombs. I was granted an audience to personally invite the president of the Argentine Republic, Marcelo T. de Alvear, a friend of the arts. He received me cordially, stayed with me for a long while, and promised to attend the inaugural act on 13 October. As I supposed many people would show up, I suggested he come in the morning to see the exhibition in peace. It was hard for me to convince him, perhaps because he felt his presence would be more useful to me in the afternoon. In the end, the time of the visit was fixed at eleven in the morning.

By the way, the first serious article on my work published in Buenos Aires, and written by Xul Solar, appeared in the «Martín Fierro» magazine four days before the opening. Alberto Prebisch intelligently prefaced the catalogue.

The expected day was finally here: at eleven sharp, Marcelo T.de Alvear arrived at the gallery. Some friends accompanied me, but only a few knew about the presidential visit; however, when I went out to greet the head of state, I saw a mob was waiting outside. In order to prevent the crowd from barging in, we had to close the large gallery door. President Alvear chatted to all of us in the most pleasant of manners, and after having attentively observed the paintings, he wished me «bonne chance», hoping I would come out unharmed from the ordeal that was awaiting me: «Please God you won´t need the municipal health service this afternoon!» was his sole remark.

At five o´clock in the afternoon, the «Witcomb» gallery opened its doors. The crowd, which had been waiting for that moment, flocked to the large hall where Pablo Rojas Paz, one of my good friends, was to deliver his speech. People kept on interrupting him, and he hadn´t even ended his address that a loud choir of screams and protests arose, turning the gallery into a madhouse.

I never understood why my art unleashed such fury, considering that no—one even looked at the paintings in the commotion. Fortunately, the director of the gallery, foreseeing the chaos, had placed a number of guards in front of the works of art; an excellent measure, for without them, the crowd would have ruined the paintings.

The throng was so wound up, that had people wanted to punch each other, there wouldn't have been enough room: we were squashed like sardines.

Some people felt sick as a result of the jamming and the stuffiness, while others, worried, tried to leave the building. As the gallery owner didn´t want the mob to damage the floors, he turned off the spotlights that lit them, switching on a flashing light, as a warning. The public, shouting rudely, gradually left the gallery, and the doors finally closed: on Mr. Martínez´ request, I stayed behind to talk to him. According to the press, the strife continued outside on Florida Street, where people fought with their bare fists. On this memorable occasion, as well as on others, my «Martín Fierro» friends fought for my cause, which was also theirs, like true lions.

The exhibition was a success, though the evening public was ruder. Due to the constant screaming going on in the halls, one afternoon my friend Córdova Iturburu lost his voice; to his dismay and mine, for his methods of persuasions were «forceful», he was forced to return home.

At other times, the spectacle those halls offered were amusing as well as varied. I saw strait–laced gentlemen, who upon looking at my work gave a start, only to run away in terror. There were also those whose face reflected horror, and those who, overcoming their consternation, observed the paintings with curiosity. Only a few asked me to explain what the «peculiar» paintings meant.

One has to remember that the artistic education of the Argentine public was still in its infancy, for it based itself either on the poor local painting seen at the Florida Street galleries or on the European painting exported to Latin America (undoubtedly, the worst art Spain, Italy and France have ever produced this century), later sold by businessmen at exorbitant prices. As far as the local production was concerned, both the critics and buyers favored Fernando Fader and Cesáreo Bernaldo de Quirós, Pedro Zonza Briano, Antonio Alice, Américo Panozzi, Quinquela Martín, Gramajo Gutiérrez, Luis Cordiviola, Jorge Bermúdez and Rodolfo Franco.

Many people introduced themselves spontaneously. This is how I met Leonardo Estarico, who soon became one of my dearest friends. However, the first words we exchanged weren't too promising: when he told me he wrote in the «Crítica» evening newspaper, I ironically replied that I thanked him for the article published in that newspaper three or four days earlier —a ferocious article, the most caustic ever written on my work—

His candid honesty disarmed me; he replied he had never meant to offend me, and that, much to the contrary, he wished to speak to me. His office was near the gallery and I went to see him; he was a high–ranking municipal employee and at the same time, a sensitive and studious artist. He was passionately interested in the new expressive forms, and was the most learned man in the field of modern art t I have ever met in Buenos Aires. When I got to know him better he showed me his library and I understood his open–mindedness: he was completely up to date on the subject of European avant–garde artistic movements; even the latest Surrealist manifestos could be found there. Well informed, he had been the only one to realize that the painting I was bringing to the country ran parallel with the most advanced art of Europe. Finally, I had found someone with whom I could talk about the artistic tendencies of the century.

How I enriched myself in the company of so many good friends! One afternoon, a slender and swarthy young man came to see me, and handing me a book of poems, gravely told me: «Pettoruti, you are the greatest painter in America and I am its greatest poet; I will return some other time, for now there are too many people.»

This grave young man was Alberto Hidalgo. I asked him to come any day between two and four o'clock in the afternoon when there was less of a crowd; in effect, at that time I met with friends and journalists so as to speak without any interference.

One of those afternoons I arrived a bit earlier, and upon entering the large hall I saw a rather obese man laughing his head off in front of my paintings. The lady that accompanied him pulled at his sleeve, nervously whispering: «Quiet, quiet, the artist might show up.» As I wasn't wearing my painter's attire, I began to look at my paintings as if I had been the man next door. The man kept on laughing, and I asked myself whether he wouldn't collapse, for he doubled over, placing his hands upon his belly as if he had had a stitch. When I saw it fitting, I came closer and told him most seriously: «Sir, you have no idea how pleased I am that my paintings amuse you so much. An artist's major aspiration is precisely to make a man happy.»

I continued in that vein, walking next to the couple, pausing in front of every painting, adding a joke or two to my description. The man had stopped laughing and listened attentively; I even realized that he understood my comments. Before the tour was over, he pointed at a painting and said: «This one is mine. I wish to buy it.»

He and my friend Slipper were the only ones who purchased my art while the show was on. I could have sold a third one, «Pensierosa», if my ex–patron Ernesto de la Cárcova had so desired; he could have easily arranged the sale as a member of the National Fine Arts Commission. Instead, he much preferred, with his habitual courtesy, to communicate his intention to the director of the National Museum of Fine Arts, Dr. Cupertino del Campo, who categorically replied that while he presided over the museum, «not one square centimeter of a Pettoruti painting would enter the premises». And he kept his word.

The exhibition generated controversy and there was an aura of scandal about it. In those days I often saw Alejandro Korn: before taking the train back to La Plata, we used to dine together at his favorite restaurant in the province of Entre Ríos: it faced the market, and served excellent meat. Now and again we would chat until late, for time went by swiftly when we were together. This great philosopher's curiosity about the new arts was unquenchable. The same thing happened when I got together with José Ingenieros; our conversations often became monologues, for he assailed me with questions.

Though both men had been trained in rigorous disciplines and produced influential work, I found them to be a hundred time younger than most young men I met every day, for they craved to understand a branch of knowledge they were not familiar with. José Ingenieros translated the article Sem Roam had written the year before in the «Der Sturm» magazine in Berlin from German into Spanish, publishing it in his own journal, «Renovación», in October 1924.

On a certain evening, Ingenieros let me know that a banquet was being prepared in my honor to celebrate my success, and asked me whether I accepted. Although I was delighted, I could hardly call it success. Many newspapers and magazines kept on attacking me with ferocity, albeit anonymously: the public attending the exhibition ridiculed my paintings or considered them indecent, offensive, as if they had been insults directed towards the Nation; in several publications overjoyed cartoonists produced comic strips of dubious humor or acted in deliberate bad faith; every night, when the gallery closed, the scandal continued on Florida Street in the midst of insults and blows, brawls that only ended at the police headquarters. Eventually the quarrelers were released, as the police officers understood they had not been motivated by personal matters, but by different aesthetic viewpoints.

Ingenieros had a reputation as a trickster; his clever jokes played on renowned figures amused everyone, except those involved. When I told my «Martín Fierro» friends about the banquet, they warned me, alleging Ingenieros was preparing a prank to make fun of all of us, including the new tendencies. In vain I assured them he was incapable of such an action, but they had already pigeonholed him: the typical rash judgment of youth believing itself wise.

Unenthusiastically, and only because I had accepted the invitation, my «Martín Fierro» friends decided to massively attend the banquet, each one with a speech destined to invalidate anything «Pepe» [22] might say. Pablo Rojas Paz prepared the «artillery–speech», meant to defeat Ingenieros´ideas, that he believed to be obsolete. The others were in charge of the final blows and the funereal prayers.

Dinner was held at «Sumus», a restaurant on Pueyrredón Avenue, not far from the Plaza Once Square. Owners and waiters fluttered about, for so many people streamed in they never stopped laying tables. When the restaurant could no longer hold people, those that had found no table available went to have dinner elsewhere, coming back quickly so as to be present for the speeches.

In spite of my friends´ initial worries, all went very well. At last, after the desserts, Ingenieros stood up, and in the midst of a deep silence, he pronounced one of the most beautiful speeches of his career —so the press declared— not only praising the validity of the new artistic tendencies, that he said ran parallel with the freedom of man, but also commending my work.

At first the «Martín Fierro» group froze, but then expressed their joy. Loud applause broke out, after which Ernesto Palacio, Pedro Blake, Raúl González Tuñón, Córdova Iturburu and Macedonio Fernández spoke, the latter dedicating a beautiful poem to me. Everything turned out fine that historical evening, during which, as it was later said, «two generations fraternized». However, let me tell you about the outcome of that reunion: when the speeches were about to be delivered, José Ingenieros had a waiter send me some lines –he wrote them on a napkin– inviting me to stay when everybody had left, and to join his group. His group was composed of renowned figures, such as the Governor of the province of Mendoza. Unfortunately, I neither could nor wished to abandon the friends that had accompanied me in my everyday struggle. Therefore, I later went to a café with the «Martín Fierro» group, where a cluster of intellectuals holding views contrary to theirs gathered on Saturdays.

The immense café was almost full, yet we found a table. I had the feeling not everyone approved of our arrival. My hunch proved to be right: a few minutes later, the antagonistic feelings manifested themselves; angry looks, insolent smiles, ironic allusions to the hopeless decrepitude of certain ideas, to the academic superficiality, to the rusty brains, and very soon, glasses, dishes, cups, chairs and even tables were tossed about. People fled, waiters got involved, but to no avail, because everybody used their fists, gloves and walking sticks. It was an incomprehensible chaos, and the only thing that mattered was attacking.

The battle was at its best when the police burst into the café. In the blink of an eye, the participants vanished. As for myself, I was pushed towards a

---

22   In Argentina, "Pepe" is a diminutive of the name José.

door through which I escaped. I have no idea how many people got hurt: apparently, Policho Córdova Iturburu had received several blows.

The exhibition in La Plata opened in the salons of the «La Prensa» newspaper, while the one in Buenos Aires continued its course. The first one was held to homage my city and province: I wished to show everyone the way I had studied and how I had used my time during those three years and a half in Europe. I don´t believe it is far fetched to say that I'm the only one having fulfilled all the requirements of the scholarship.

On the day of the opening, besides a few of my «Martín Fierro» friends that had especially traveled from Buenos Aires to see me, many writers and poets were present, among them a dear friend passed away prematurely, the poet Francisco López Merino. In the name of the «Martín Fierro» group, Ernesto Palacio inaugurated the exhibition. Nothing exciting happened, besides the disconcerted look of some of the spectators, for in La Plata, indifference reigned. After the show, we had dinner among friends, and Alejandro Korn and Pedro Henríquez Ureña gave a small speech.

Alfredo L.Palacios and I met rather often. At the time, he was dean of the Faculty of Law of La Plata. He was planning on mounting an exhibition of my works within the University itself, so as to give the students a chance to see it; most of them were unmoved by any event that was not connected to their own disciplines. He invited me to formalize the idea, which I did, and the announcement of the show created turmoil amid the student body. The exhibition was held in mid–November. Since my arrival at La Plata, opposition groups had formed, joined by student congregations that were just as contrary. Since people in favor were present as well, madness reigned. Meanwhile, I learned that it had been Tomás M. Rojas, a representative of the student body, that had suggested the idea of the exhibition, for he had noticed that students never attended any exhibition, much less mine. Rojas believed that if a show were held on the premises, it would entice them to see it.

On the day of the opening, already marked by disorder, my intellectual friends of the River Plate, headed by the poet Pedro Blake, prepared an action plan. They knew that a man named José Gabriel and a student ringleader whose name now escapes me, had announced in unison that they would ruin the show with harsh criticism, in an attempt to demonstrate my imposture (meanwhile, none of these students had ever seen a modern work of art in their entire life...nor a classic one, at that). Blake´s intention was to have no–one attend the inaugural act until both characters had pronounced their condemnation. These chaps were looking for trouble, and would get what they deserved.

No sooner said than done. Blake sent his «scout» to the exhibition while we went to the corner café to wait for the orators to finish. The first one to speak was Pedro Henríquez Ureña, whose speech was later published in Alejandro Korn's magazine. Then came Dr. Carlos Sánchez (whose words were quite conventional), and finally José Gabriel, whose nonsensical excerpts I soon after read in the newspapers. As far as the fourth orator was concerned, believing perhaps that the third one had exhausted all insults, he did not come to the fore.

Our «scout» came to warn us that the preliminary acts were over and we headed towards the exhibition; in the garden, we ran into our «enemies», about to leave. Inside, everyone gave us a standing ovation, something that did not prevent the October–November issue of «Bases», the university magazine, from anonymously publishing such a stupid article, I still cannot believe it today.

Each day I experienced a new adventure. The one I am about to describe is just one amid thousands: on a cold morning I went to a café situated on one of our largest avenue. At the table next to mine, people were talking about me: «Pettoruti is shameless, despicable, irresponsible, conceited, an opportunist, come to exploit the candor of his countrymen. He exhibits those grotesque and unintelligible paintings of his as if they were works of art». One of them went farther; according to him, my deviousness was beyond all understanding: «One has to know him –he said– the way I know this man, in order to understand what he is capable of; he has no scruples whatsoever!»

I was upset. For a moment I believed this man's anger was the result of an unresolved quarrel and that he was provoking me. It wasn't the case: I hadn't seen him in my life and neither had he, since we were both facing each other and my face meant nothing to him.

It's true that I have always been a conventional man in dress and behavior. Therefore, the way people imagined me didn't coincide with reality. I paid for my coffee and left in a rush; I cannot say how happy I felt, for human stupidity has always saddened me.

Let me tell you another interesting episode. It involved Roberto A. Ortelli, director of the «Inicial» magazine, oriented towards aesthetics and philosophy, and which had seen the light the year before. He had published a rather vicious article against me, obviously guided either by his ignorance about artistic matters, or by his animosity against the «Martín Fierro» group. Upon entering the Richmond café one afternoon and nearing the table where my friends were gathered, one of them let me know that Ortelli, whom I had never seen before, was sitting close–by together with his friends. I walked up to his table and Ortelli rose in a defensive attitude; his friends leaned back on their chairs. I then extended my right hand and told him calmly: «Look, I'm not here to quarrel, those things lead to nothing. I have come to enlighten you, if you so wish». As they offered me a seat, I began to pick apart the entire article, paragraph by paragraph, making him feel, since I was at it, that by attacking me they were frustrating their humanistic mission: the whole table listened attentively. After an hour had gone by, I observed it was getting late and that we should leave it for another day. Ortelli and I became very good friends and he became one of my staunchest admirers.

My friendship with Constancio Vigil had deepened. From time to time, during the course of my exhibition at «Witcomb», I would go to the Atlántida publishing office, on Sarmiento and Maipú Streets, to have a cup of coffee with him. One day, he mentioned some painters had visited him: they had told him that if he got them a hall on Florida Street, they and a group of well–known artists would prepare a similar or better exhibition than the one I was holding in less than a month. They wanted to prove anyone could produce arbitrary art.

The news did not surprise me: I had learned that a large group of writers, painters and sculptors, had written a violent manifesto –never published, by the way– against the new tendencies that attempted to take root on the River Plate; it was obvious their exhibition coincided with the same initiative.

I told Constancio I found it imperative for him to clarify the truth; I therefore urged him to receive and satisfy my colleagues´ project; I would gladly participate, fearing only that my art, compared to the ultra–advanced manifestation, might be considered «pompier». At any rate, I was ready to run the risk.

A few days later, I learned that the exhibition would be held at the «Van Riel» gallery, on Florida Street, and that the artists of the city of Buenos Aires had begun their work.

By the way, the Ricordi Publishing House, whose new director was Dr. Sandro Piantanida (an old Milanese friend of mine), had published a monograph on my art with several color pictures and a beautiful preface by Ricardo Güiraldes upon my return to the country. Pleased and surprised, Piantanida told me the edition was practically out of print.

In one of my meetings with Leonardo Estarico, the latter told me he had a message for me from Natalio Botana, director of the «Crítica» newspaper, who wished to speak to me.

At the appointed time I arrived at the newspaper, in those days on Sarmiento Street. It was one of those sweltering afternoons of early spring, damp and unbearable. The stairs were full of people and I reached the first floor. There I met Negro Cipriano, the director´s ferocious custodian. Without asking me who I was and why I had come, he told me his boss wasn´t in, but when I told him my name was Pettoruti, he opened the door.

Botana, one of Buenos Aires´most popular characters, was comfortably seated in an armchair, reading. He was wearing an ample white silk shirt and carried a gun on his belt. He received me with great cordiality and struck up the conversation; ten minutes later he called Negro to tell him he wasn't in for anyone. Night fell and we kept on talking. He was a particular man, extremely interesting, full of literary and humanistic preoccupations, who had little in common with what people thought of him. He was informed about all innovations regarding literature, and asked me many questions about the European artistic milieu. He wished to know the differences between Argentine and European art, and in which way the former could be improved. When we said goodbye, he affectionately held my arm and said: «As you are well aware of, the «Crítica» newspaper is quite popular. Well, it's all yours: any of your articles will be more than welcome».

I began my contribution by presenting modern foreign artists, the way I later did in the «La Prensa» and in the «El Argentino» newspapers. I also wrote critical articles, emphasizing that a great deal of undervalued artistic talent existed in our country, and that schooling was essential.

At the end of November, the Buenos Aires press announced the imminent presentation of an «ultra–Futurist» show. The inaugural act was to start with «A new metaphysics of art», a lecture by Mr. X. The object of the manifestation, so the articles said, was to ruin the presumptuous solemnity of my exhibition, besides laughing at «those gentlemen who followed Marinetti's abstraction».

As agreed upon, I sent two small paintings to the Salon, that the «Atlántida» magazine reproduced in advance. I went to the opening with a few of my «Martín Fierro» friends; there was a crowd and we found it difficult to reach the auditorium. We sat down in front of Mr. X who was about to deliver his speech on metaphysics; he looked like a poor devil, and we took pity on him. He must have guessed our thoughts for his voice faltered; finally, he uttered a few words badly put together and the show was pronounced open.

I began to tour the halls: it is simply impossible to describe the chaos. It was stupidity at its best: no humor, no inventiveness. To top it all, the paintings were encrusted with cigarette stubs and other filth. It caused repugnance to see all this, for it reflected incurable inanity.

None of these appalling pieces of work were signed. Yet, what some of their authors didn't realize was that having visited their studios and possessing a considerable visual memory, I knew exactly who they were. Some of the painters had even cut their paintings up, believing that this represented Cubism. Artists and public surrounded me. Among the first were those who, imagining themselves clear of all suspicion, wanted to find out, standing in front of their «creations», what I thought of them; I gave them my opinion in the most courteous and cruel way; there was nothing else left for them to do than to accept my insolences.

When the exhibition closed, I realized two of my paintings had been stolen. I also found out I had new supporters. In effect, many of those that had pronounced themselves against me adopted another posture, annoyed by the cruel joke. I remember Atalaya's indignation, his slight and frail body shaking with anger; apart from having written against the expositors, whom he had called a «bunch of batrachians», he had addressed them severely: «You have assassinated Walter de Navazio and Ramón Silva, you have sunk Malharro; but remember, Pettoruti will survive all of you». Ingenieros' indignation did not lag behind, and his jokes were caustic.

This exhibition, wavering between the hilarious and the tragic, made me feel enormously dejected. I was used to respecting my fellow men and I couldn't understand what had just happened, it failed to adjust itself to logic. I felt immensely sad upon realizing there were so few real artists: no–one of good faith would have perpetrated such an act against a colleague who wished them no harm, and much less against a man who always ran to greet them with open arms.

By a whim of fate, I was forced to act in a narrow–minded environment for twenty–nine years, something that would have damaged many vulnerable souls.

I once mentioned I have always been reserved, that as a child I had no companions, that I didn't play football; it was at my father's request, who perhaps thought me defenseless, that I took boxing lessons, surmounting the repugnance this kind of exercise aroused in me. I overcame my reserved spirit, born of my timidity, meeting young people my age, and above all, talking to older people, both benevolent and bright. This doesn't mean my introversion abandoned me; in important circumstances it even caused paralysis.

It was the need to confront the hostile world that helped me; the urge not to be a lamb among wolves that pushed me to act with increased courage. A new nature substituted the old, without any other motive than the need to protect myself.

Knowing that people would have devoured me if I had let them, I became as hard as a bone, preventing anyone from sinking his teeth into my flesh. But this attitude wasn't arbitrary; it was conducted lucidly and applied exactly, directed towards men that rank or social position rendered arrogant, towards the corrupt and cowardly beings that hide their hand when throwing stones, but never towards men of good will, whether rich or poor. This explains why I have been able to make and keep so many friends, some the most valuable men on earth; it also explains why I am loved by those who know me, while the conceited, insignificant men, the simulators and the servile who never penetrated my intimate life openly detest me, especially if circumstances obliged me to put them firmly in their place.

Chapter 21

First years in my home country

The months following my arrival were hectic. People perpetually surrounded me, and I myself had many friends I wished to visit and was always taking the last train back from Buenos Aires, sleeping only a few hours. Because my mother saw me so busy, her maternal tact discreetly eluded the problems that worried her. She asked for details of my life in Europe which I had already forgotten, and we commented the interviews that were being published; the articles and the criticism upset her, for she was used to receiving those from Italy, where I was generally very well treated. I then had to calm her down, convincing her of my confidence in my fate. The only day I saw her happy was when she learned that three paintings of mine had been accepted at the National Salon, as she had grown accustomed at my being rejected year after year.

I was barely back that I committed myself to preparing a large painting, «My family», for it to remain in La Plata. It would portray my father and the rest of us, and I performed separate studies of each member. I worked on my mother's portrait, on the one of my youngest sisters, Carolita, and on mine. Unfortunately, everything came to a standstill.

A room in one of our properties, situated on 54 Street, served as studio. One day, however, my mother called me, revealing a delicate family problem. As a result, this house had to be sold immediately. The cause of this state of affairs, that could no longer be brushed aside, had been my father's improvident spirit: he had listened too benevolently to the whining of others, real or simulated. She asked me to remain a while longer in the country in order to help them economically. I couldn't refuse, and postponed my trip to Europe, fully conscious that this delay would cost me dear.

I first thought it would be a question of three months, in addition to the six months I had estimated. Obviously, I had no idea as to the sluggishness with which certain matters resolve themselves: houses that take forever to sell, the lifting of mortgages that charge high interest rates; everything required effort, and months went by briskly.

I wrote Nella a letter, telling her that unforeseen difficulties prevented me from returning to Paris on the projected date, and that I therefore didn't know when I would be back. I told her about my brothers, two of them married, the others studying, of my need to lend my family a hand until everything was back in order and of the difficulties I experienced in selling my art. I didn't tell her I had had to cover my paintings with glass because people spat on them, scribbling insults on the canvas, nor that I felt ever so lonely.

In effect, I knew that from an artistic point of view, communication was practically impossible: I spoke a language different from that of the rest of the people. There was no connection between one way of thinking and the other. For instance, I remember saying, standing before the 1925 «Self–portrait» study, that I didn't know whether the color of the hair I had just painted was brown, since color doesn't exist in painting. I was looked at with skepticism...How to explain that a painter doesn't actually see color, but rather, an infinite variety of hues and that it isn't reason alone that composes them, but rather, instinct and all the other senses: eyes, ears, intelligence, smell, touch? Of course, we are talking about touch related to reason, which is what guides the artist to see and arrange colors, and reject those that seem inadequate to him. Since light decomposes and fragments color, it is it absent in painting; it is thus necessary to create it.

So many reflections and opinions falling on deaf ears! These advanced ideas were dangerous, for they spurred animosity. I realized that since there existed no tradition of consolidating and debating opinions. To speak with clarity, to be frank, meant being envious.

It was taboo for me to speak about Mexican painting, which the philosopher Vasconcelos so praised through the means of an infinite number of leaflets. All of America celebrated it in unison; I suppose that in our milieu the only jarring cry was mine. Because I had said that this painting was no art to me, but rather, propaganda on walls or canvas, many people, including friends and connoisseurs, accused me of arbitrariness and even spite. I thus learned that only a handful interprets reproductions, especially when they come in color, rendering them artificial and empty. At any rate, I didn't base my opinion solely on the objective drawing that described aspects of Mexican painting, but rather, on the observation that their pictorial tradition established itself upon a decadent Spanish art, which was then applied to historical, indigenous and revolutionary motifs.

Mexico possesses excellent drawers. I believe that one of the reasons is that their artists actively participated in the Revolution: through drawing, they propagated the drama of misery, the revulsion towards exploitation, the revolutionary fervor and all that would lead to the liberation of the Indian and men of mixed–blood. Without any qualms, I said all this and much more to Clemente Orozco when the moment came, pointing out that all he showed me in his studio were drawings; not one painting was present.

Summer in Buenos Aires was sweltering. Most opportunely, the president of the Pueyrredón Club of Mar del Plata invited me to hold a show at their beach resort. The conditions were favorable, providing an excellent occasion to see that city again. As I was about to leave, the «Razón» newspaper entrusted me with the portrayal of some famous figures that were vacationing there. When I ran into Alfredo L. Palacios on the promenade, I suggested creating a caricature. This pleased him greatly, on condition that once it was published, I would give him the original as a keepsake.

We saw one another often; while enjoying a stroll, we would talk about innumerable subjects. Finally, we agreed that I would go to his hotel in the course of the following morning. That night, thinking about the caricature, I had the suspicion it would cause sensation in the political and intellectual milieu. I described my idea to Palacios the following day, certain that he would approve of it: only for once, I wished to portray him without his proverbial mustache.

I should have kept my mouth shut! He frowned, grabbed his mustache as if to protect it, and asked me if I meant what I said; when he realized I did, he categorically refused to pose. It was futile to threaten him by telling him I would draw the caricature from memory, even if I promised to portray him with his mustache. He wouldn´t be persuaded. Probably for a while, he held me to be the devil himself, terrified that I would play a prank on him.

In truth, despite the commotion that my name generated from Chile to Mexico, in spite even of the Latin American phenomenon I represented, life back home wasn´t easy for me: it was rendered worse by having to produce extra–pictorial work, thus creating burdensome commitments. Determined to return to Paris as soon as possible, my principal interest was to guide the family boat with a sure hand, for it had a tendency to sink, and I wished to keep it afloat. In the meanwhile I painted, attempting to enlighten people on modern art as much as possible. In order to do this, I continued talking and writing on the new tendencies, as well as holding exhibitions. To me, work has always been a way to lay problems aside, for I believe that any difficulty that oppresses our minds, either moral or physical, is unhealthy. In a nutshell: I do not believe that we can grow spiritually if we accept the negative aspects of life; rather, we have to discard them, and work is a powerful ally.

I continued living in La Plata and traveling to Buenos Aires to meet my friends. I attended the Saturday gatherings organized by Oliverio Girondo rather frequently; many national and foreign writers frequented these reunions. Among so many other poets, I met Vicente Huidobro, Federico García Lorca and Pablo Neruda, at the time the Chilean Consul in Buenos Aires. These were very entertaining gatherings: Norah Lange highlighted them, improvising new situations on every occasion. We would often dress up, for no reason at all. Very pleasant too, the parties that Norah organized at her mother´s home and those that the blonde Rojas Paz threw at hers. And then there were the dinners, more intimate, at the homes of Policho and Carmen Córdova Iturburu, which the latter enlivened with her charm and her beautiful songs in German, and the receptions, given by José María Castro and Juanita, attended by the most intellectual group of musicians.

Somehow, Buenos Aires always surprised or pleased me. The municipal office where Leonardo Estarico worked had been moved to the headquarters, and this is where I went to see him one afternoon. He told me a new employee was working for him, a pseudo–intellectual and talkative Spaniard, who boasted about being well–informed. This man confessed to whomever wanted to listen that he deeply admired the painter Pettoruti: the newspapers kept on talking about me, and he, who devoured all articles, always quoted them to my friend.

On the afternoon of my visit, having barely sat down, Estarico called his assistant to ask him for some coffee. When he brought the tray, my friend pointed at me, telling him affably: «Well, you now have the opportunity to meet the painter Pettoruti, the artist that you so admire.» The Spaniard suspiciously observed me for an instant; in his eyes I saw distrust, pity, incredulity, and finally, the satisfaction of someone who believes he is right: «You must be joking! Pettoruti, this gentleman!! Certainly I would recognize him...! Pettoruti is a sturdy young man, strong, arrogant, with such a penetrating look that no woman can resist him... And you want to make me believe...! Come on, Sir, don´t play those tricks on me!!» A long time went by before this good man resigned himself to accepting the image I offered him, instead of the one he had fabricated. As I recall this anecdote, I tell myself that if the common man is able to create such an exaggerated idea of a normal individual through the reading of newspapers and magazines, what can be expected from those people that are not prepared to understand new art forms?

One fine day, already feeling much calmer, I wished to visit my native city to witness the changes it had undergone and find out what effect this would have on me. I attentively walked through the old wood where so many artists of my generation had learned to paint, only to find out that the wood, as I remembered it, had disappeared. I recalled it was situated behind the buildings of the Faculty of Agronomy and Veterinary Sciences, between two almost parallel lines: that of Street 1 and that which, two–hundred meters beyond the railway tracks, stretched almost uninterruptedly to Tolosa. Both framed a compact mass of marvelous eucalyptus trees. From Tolosa onwards, the vegetation was less impenetrable, and from City Bell, it became even sparser, reaching the Pereira estate with only one or two trees.

The plundering had already begun before my leaving to Europe, something that Almafuerte had condemned a long time ago. A whole sector of Street 1 had been ravaged in order to erect the National School buildings: then, another sector to build the train station. Later, a beautiful velodrome considered the best in the country, and where my father used to take us to practice, was destroyed. The «Club de Estudiantes» football stadium replaced it, but, as the terrain occupied by the track seemed too small to the Municipality, more eucalyptus trees were felled to raise new constructions.

Always on Street 1, between 58 and 60, if my memory serves me right, they chopped down more eucalyptus trees to build official pavilions. But the nefarious practices went on, devastating the heart of the wood, and one after the other the immense eucalyptus collapsed. There, where once they had been kings, an artificial lake arose, excavated by the Melchor Romero Hospital lodgers. On its banks they created two Japanese gardens, sadly framed by a handful of hirsute eucalyptus. On the small island that lay on the side, a cinema was built.

Yet the destructive work did not end there. To design the Zoological Gardens, yet another sector was ravaged, sweeping the wild and lush vegetation, and a fine–looking arch, which served as an access to the city coming from Dyke 1, was blown up by dynamite. What harm had this arch done, I wonder?

As I record fragments of my life, on this gray Paris morning, I recall the Estate of the La Plata Governor, a majestic residence situated in the woods, in front of the Museum of Natural History. Not far from the Observatory and the Faculty of Agronomy and Veterinary Sciences, it was attended all year long by scholars. Tragically, this mansion disappeared overnight, when it could just as easily have been transformed into a library and a tearoom, a place where students and visitors, especially in winter, could have enjoyed a book and have had a bite.

Does this imply that no football stadiums, no artificial lakes, no Zoological Gardens, no National Schools should be constructed in a city? Far from it. What I mean is that progress shouldn´t be sustained at the expense of beauty.

We had lovely squares in La Plata. Some of them, such as «La Primera Junta», underwent frequent changes: streets appeared and disappeared, monuments were moved from one place to another, always depending on the whims of the municipal authorities in charge at the time. There was one square in particular, that some sensitive city–lover had turned into Eden. An infinite variety of magnolias and other plants blossomed there, and to read beneath the exquisitely perfumed shade in the «Plaza de la Policía», was like becoming inebriated in Paradise. Everything changed in a few years, and if my current information is exact, the rest of my city´s beautiful squares are now English–type squares. They are so bare it is difficult to walk through them when the sun cracks the earth in summer, or when the harsh wind blows in winter.

Another recollection: a stream, then called «Arroyo del Gato». It wasn´t striking, but the smile of water in the dry physiognomy of our flat landscape was a note of joy. The intelligence of man corrects or beautifies Nature when necessary; this explains why running water, crossing the urban centers, is the pride of both large and small cities of the civilized world, that lovingly looks after its largest rivers and tiniest brooks. This friendly «Arroyo del Gato» could have been eventually channeled into Dyke 1, enhancing the city and allowing its inhabitants to travel from its center to the River Plate, passing by Ensenada, the «Santiago» river, and further...But no: the city officials, taking asinine measures, silenced its course through the means of pipes.

Though the year went by swiftly, my problems were far from being solved. During its course I lost a dear friend, José Ingenieros, and I accepted a teaching post as a substitute art teacher for a few months at the Advanced School of Fine Arts of the La Plata National University. I produced a few paintings, among them my first «Small cup», some still–lifes, the first version of «The house of the poet» [23], the definitive version of «Young woman with green fan» [24], the «Portrait of the poet Alberto Hidalgo» and «Carolita».

In this period, my «Martín Fierro» friends that I saw most assiduously were Córdova Iturburu, Ernesto Palacio and Pablo Rojas Paz; at times we were all together, at a café, at times at their homes or visiting places. With Rojas Paz we used to go from downtown Buenos Aires to the Palermo Parks on foot, while he read me a chapter of his book about to be published; in Palermo we would sit down beneath the trees and he would read on; with Ernesto Palacio, our recitation sessions and conversations were held at the café. He was well–versed in European literature, especially in the French one. Córdova Iturburu, besides writing poetry, was interested in the fine arts; we talked a lot about painting, sculpture, and visited the exhibitions; if I´m not mistaken, he started out as an art critic not many months after my show at the «Witcomb» gallery. He wrote an article on my work, published in the «El Hogar» magazine, on 9 January 1925. That year, my friendship with the three men greatly consolidated itself.

From time to time I also saw Jorge Luis Borges, at his home on Quintana

---

23   This painting is owned by Leonardo Estarico.
24   This painting is owned by the Municipal Museum of Fine Arts, Buenos Aires.

Avenue, but mainly I talked to his charming mother, Leonor. I also held extensive conversations with Sibellino and Atalaya. Since I lived in La Plata, we always met at the cafés. The conversations with Estarico were exclusive, for he didn't want to share them with anybody, and I would often dine at his home. Xul I saw practically every day, and he kept on inventing things that he considered practical, but that didn't work without additional and complicated methods. He composed a new horoscope, so intricate that in the end not even he could figure it out.

In the course of the year I participated in the First Communal Exhibition of Industrial Arts, where I was awarded the First Prize, the Gold Medal and a thousand pesos in cash. I also held two other exhibitions, the first one in La Plata, the second one in Buenos Aires. On the opening day of the first exhibition, my city was welcoming Edward, Prince of Wales; I particularly remember this event because my brother Oscar, who was fifteen at the time, was too embarrassed to say he wished to witness the spectacle, and threw a tantrum. The second exhibition was held in the month of October at the «Amigos del Arte» Association, and only landscapes were displayed. I sold some of the paintings, despite the fact that a critic, just arrived from Europe, labeled them «ice–cold». He didn't realize that his vision was shaped to the «more or less» of Fauvism and perhaps of Impressionism, and that it was he who couldn't adapt to any composition that was constructed or measured. If one had to believe this critic, then all of the great Italian painters of the 13th and 14th centuries would be considered «ice–cold». However, bear in mind that all great paintings have this indefinable severity that reflect the creative will: the will to express things clearly.

One afternoon, I arrived particularly early at the gallery. I was told that the painter Fernando Fader was inside, and that he had been there for a while. I looked in, and noticing he was absorbed looking at the paintings, I felt reluctant to distract him. As I had to meet someone a few minutes later, I went up to him, for as Fader lived in Córdoba, I figured I would perhaps never be able to thank him for his visit again.

After having chatted for a while in the most agreeable of manners, he made a comment that probably reflected something that bothered him: «You don't paint directly from life». I answered that of course I didn't, that I drew my studies from life and composed the painting in my studio later, to which he answered that a landscape had to be created surrounded by Nature. He was so convinced of this, that in order to paint without getting tired, a studio–van had been built for him, in which he drove to the fields. I argued that the Venetians, as for instance Claude Lorrain, Magnasco and so many other great landscape painters, didn't paint their landscape when out of doors: the elaborate preparations and the large canvases didn't lend themselves to the open air. As he didn't seem satisfied, I added: «Do you truly believe,

Master, that Benozzo Gozzoli, in order to paint the landscapes that adorn his frescoes, transported the palace he had to decorate to the countryside?» Fernando Fader turned around and left, without saying good–bye. I felt very disturbed at my impertinence, and learning he was ill, I couldn't fall asleep that night.

In the year 1926, Dr. Benito Nazar Anchorena, President of the National University of La Plata made me an offer; as we often spoke about the teaching of art while traveling by train or during lunch, he proposed to create a chair of Composition and Landscape at the Superior School of Fine Arts especially for me. As he was nearing the end of his term, he believed it prudent to await his re–election in order to create the two new subjects. Unfortunately, when the moment came to vote, elections ended in two draws, and the third round revealed the outgoing president had not been re–elected.

We continued to meet at the famous «Royal Keller», a literary café, on Corrientes and Maipú Streets, to discuss the contents of the «Revista Oral» magazine, whose creator, Alberto Hidalgo, was an old friend of mine. The founding members of this magazine, published every fifteen days, were Macedonio Fernández, an admired figure by the literary youth, and Jorge Luis Borges, who, together with the author of «Don Segundo Sombra», Rojas Paz and Brandan Caraffa, directed the «Proa» magazine. Then there was Leopoldo Marechal, Eduardo González Lanuza, Norah Lange, Raúl Scalabrini Ortiz and myself.

We campaigned intensely to impose avant–garde art, as much in Buenos Aires as in the provinces, thanks to the then Secretary of Education, Dr. Sagarna, who provided us with tickets to travel, and to our friends in the provinces. We took our magazine with us wherever we went, and presented our views by reading modern poetry, excerpts of good literature, and slides of paintings commented by a lecturer, almost always the poet Marechal. This system awoke such curiosity, that a vast public attended our meetings...and for this to happen in La Plata, it was something extraordinary, to say the least.

The night when Hidalgo read his magnificent poem, «Ubicación de Lenín», stunning the public and greeted with rapturous applause, another surprise awaited me: a telegram from Marinetti. He had sent it from San Paulo, announcing he would arrive in three days, together with his wife Benedetta. The news spread like wildfire, and many people in Buenos Aires were excited.

Our reunion was very tender; hugs and kisses; I was truly happy to see them both. We practically weren't able to see each other on the first day, for so many people surrounded them; journalists, photographers, writers that wanted to greet the «Father of Futurism». I introduced him to some intellectual groups: in the first place, the «Martín Fierro». The members of the group prepared him a gastronomical evening that almost everyone attended, and the magazine dedicated a large part of its June 8 and July 8 numbers to him. Moreover, the «Amigos del Arte» Association organized an exhibition for him, with architectural projects by Prebisch and Vautier, and paintings by Norah Borges, Xul and me. Marinetti opened the show with one of his handsome speeches in which art counted very little, but where the word «Futurism» rumbled like thunder. He also spoke in a large theater overflowing with people: the «Coliseo».

One day he asked me when I would take him to my friends´ studios; he had noticed they were, without exception, men of letters. His question took me aback: I told him that our country differed from Europe in the sense that the interests of the artistic youth, far from supporting my art, were decidedly against it. Marinetti listened to me in complete astonishment.

He was often invited and they left the country very pleased. I, on the other hand, felt extremely sad, for I knew they were leaving for an exciting universe that I had once been a part of. I really didn´t know when I would go back, since I couldn´t even see the light at the end of the tunnel, and couldn´t even dream of boarding a ship. The memory of Nella mortified me. I therefore wrote her this would perhaps never happen, and that henceforth my letters would be shorter and more infrequent. She replied promptly, adding as if in passing, that she still had our friend in common at her side, her study–mate who had always wanted to marry her. That is exactly what happened.

Meanwhile, I received an invitation from the province of Córdoba to exhibit at the «Fasce» gallery; I accepted since it didn´t involve any expense –which I couldn´t have dealt with anyway. This allowed me to divulge the concept of modern art in other areas, and return to some of the places where I had painted in 1912. I was also attracted to the idea of getting in contact with Deodoro Roca´s group of intellectuals and meeting other people.

I had barely arrived to Córdoba, that the writer Oliverio de Allende interviewed me for the «Voz del Interior» newspaper; I realized by the tone of the article that scandal flitted about. I met many intellectuals from Córdoba, as well as the Governor, Dr. Ramón J.Cárcano. Jurist, historian, and politician well versed in classical culture, he was open to new conceptions. In our first interview he engaged in a long conversation, and I got the chance to see him on other occasions, during which he never ceased to ask me questions, desirous to confirm, as far as art was concerned, all that he knew through reading.

On 9 August 1926, date of the inauguration of my exhibition, I was taken by surprise: the streets were crammed with people and standing in front of the gallery, a cavalry troop awaited me, in my honor. The door to the gallery was closed and its director came to tell me the Governor was about to arrive.

A few minutes later Dr. Cárcano arrived, accompanied by his Ministers, by the Rector of the University, and by professors. Once the large retinue had entered, it was necessary to shut the doors in order to prevent the crowd from getting in. I accompanied my host in his tour of the paintings. To my surprise, Dr. Cárcano stopped in front of «The dancers», and after a few instants made this pertinent, if not exact, remark: «I notice here, Pettoruti, that movement is not conveyed through the dancing couple, but through the lines of the floor». The visit prolonged itself because this gentleman, due to his knowledge of traditional art and his natural sensitivity, was in condition to understand the new art without any difficulty. Standing before the paintings he wanted me to answer his innumerable questions, at once sensible and tricky.

When everybody left, the doors were opened to the general public, who invaded the gallery; more than half had to wait outside. The crowd was so dense and the noise so deafening I had to leave the gallery, for I felt I was about to collapse. Some said I had left because of cowardice, but it wasn't long before I returned, only to witness the arguments that had arisen and that by the way, nobody confronted me with directly.

From the following morning onwards, the press published their articles. I was either virulently attacked or adored. But when the Governor of the Province acquired «The dancers» [25], the press almost unanimously expressed its disagreement. The headings said it all: «Futurism worth a thousand pesos». What a scandal! If one believed my detractors, the acquisition of one of my paintings was money down the drain, and an offensive manner to encourage bad taste. Others affirmed that buying a Futurist piece of work wasn't only a waste of money, but an insult to the young artists of Córdoba.

The scandal that broke out gave rise to an editorial in the «La Nación» newspaper of Buenos Aires; it highlighted the unprecedented act carried out by the Government of Córdoba. Very appropriately, it was observed that it was perhaps the first time in history that Futurist art was paid a tribute.

As can be observed, everyone mentioned the word Futurism to describe my work, either to defend or attack me. In short, since opinion was divided, the Governor was at times bitterly blamed or highly praised; I know he received telegrams from university associations around the country and from Montevideo, congratulating him for giving modern art a predominant place in history.

Whether jeering or applauding, the public was being exposed to the new art in spite of themselves, while becoming interested in the debates it generated: my stay in the country wasn't pointless after all. Though the mentality of the conventional artists did not change, the attitude of the people that were not biased underwent a modification; many times I explained to them, both verbally and in writing, that if the art that I practiced decomposed the laws

---

25   This painting is currently at the Museum of Fine Arts of Córdoba.

of the visible world, the latter was recomposed according to other laws. This new way of tackling art, I said, had nothing arbitrary: by modifying reality, you could erect a totally new and more intense intellectual certainty with the same pieces.

In Córdoba I made excellent friends, among them Carlos Astrada and Oliverio de Allende. One evening, walking around the square as we usually did, we suddenly came up with the idea of producing an artistic and literary magazine. We planned it out the following day, and on 30 August, the publication «Clarín» saw the light.

In the month of October I exhibited sixty–nine watercolors, all of them on sheets of a travel notepad at the «Amigos del Arte» Association. To my amazement, all of them were sold the day before the opening. I learned that Benito Nazar Anchorena had purchased fifteen of them, and that Mr. Güiraldes, father of the writer and a known collector, had acquired twenty–two, meant, as far as I know, as wedding gifts for all of his grand–children.

My eyesight preoccupied me as much as ever. I went to see the doctor who had performed my operation, asking him to examine me again, not without informing him about all the other ophthalmologists I had previously visited. In his opinion, it was better not to touch my eyes again; whatever was lost, was lost, and according to him, too many years had gone by already. I looked at the originator of my misfortune, and walked away, wishing to strangle him.

Dr. Amadeo Natale, who had operated on me in January 1927, held a different opinion. Though the operation was successful insofar as the position of the eye was concerned, my vision, as he had forewarned me, did not improve.

That year, I painted «Harlequin», «Song of the People» and «Quintet» [26] among others. During the winter, Estarico and I were very busy creating and organizing the «Boliche de Arte», an exhibition hall directed by him. It operated, with a bulletin for each act, at the «Cooperativa Artística» on Corrientes Street that gave rise to several events that somehow contributed to shake the rather stagnant artistic milieu. We were full of ideas! Yet we weren't the only ones who struggled: Barletta, with his «Teatro del Pueblo», and Juan Carlos Paz with his music, had their own difficulties to face. The group desperately attempted to interest the public in the new music; to make matters worse, people left the auditorium as the musicians were playing, while critics scorned them. I have to admit that we were not personally upset by the situation, for we felt that the repudiation was a price we had to pay in exchange for our creative freedom and dreams. As far as criticism was concerned, we did not pay any heed to it. I recall that one day, commenting on the situation, Paz told me: «Criticism doesn't harm us, I know that; but undoubtedly it slows

---

26   This painting is owned by the San Francisco Museum of Art, California.

things down. I feel sorry for the public, for hey will die without having found out all that we do for them».

It is not easy to convince an apathetic mass, often nostalgic of traditional art, to adhere to new ideas; in Buenos Aires they were still talking about traditional art and classical forms in order to criticize my painting: as if the representation of reality had always existed and had to continue to exist, as if it were a secret that the schematization of the images dated from the Stone Age.

It was always necessary to explain to the neophytes that it is not by starting off from reality that the symbol is reached, but that on the contrary, the tendency to abstraction —and this is confirmed every time a discovery is made— has existed since time immemorial. The pre–historic artist substantiated expression to the fullest; all works made my Man until the pre–Renaissance and before waver between the figurative and the abstract. A battle by Paolo Uccello is as abstract as it is figurative; if we carefully observe the composition and distribution of the masses of color, we would notice that all great painting of the past and present is equally valuable, because the artist doesn't copy Nature. Although he paints exterior reality, he expresses the inner wish to sublimate it and reality is idealized, as occurs with the landscapes of Leonardo. Those painters that best copy reality are called «minor painters», whether considered «intimists» or not. This is not said pejoratively; rather, I wish to put certain things into perspective.

Moreover, there was an incongruity I decided to combat whenever the opportunity arose: people's tendency to accept the new and profit from all that implied betterment and comfort, but rejecting it when it comes to the Fine Arts. As far as technology and science were concerned, changes that took place over time were admitted, and progress praised; but this was frowned upon if habits and conventions were involved. In other words, the advantages of the railroad were appreciated, for one no longer had to use a horse and cart, or electricity was valued, for candles had become obsolete. However, no–one could conceive that the creative conscience could alter its state. How to teach people that the new art, just like modern architecture, like atonal music, were all manifestations of an identical era, of an identical state of mind? I don't even wish to recall how often I have mentioned this!

I needed money for obvious reasons and my paintings were not selling. As usual, people who could have bought them remained indifferent and those who were interested had no money. Talking about this with my friend Estarico, he suggested I sell them by monthly installments; he said he had some candidates willing to purchase them that way, and as a matter of fact, it wasn't long before he took them to my studio. The installments oscillated between twenty and fifty pesos. It was thanks to this system that the year 1927 ended without pressure and that the year 1928 began with a monthly income I estimated secure until 1931. In the short term, it allowed me to face a transitory situation; in the long term, it agreed with my plans magnificently. But obviously I am not an expert in business matters, since I have always experienced difficulties when dealing with them. In September 1930 the Revolution broke out and my buyers, old and new, were either fired or had to flee to neighboring countries. I was therefore left without my paintings and without my installments.

At the end of 1927, invited by the «Asociación de los Amigos del Museo» of Rosario, I held an exhibition at the Municipal Museum of Fine Arts. The preface to the catalogue, written by Estarico, was printed with corrections I will never understand, impairing the text to the point of expressing the opposite of what the author had intended to say.

The exhibition led, as usual, to several manifestations, but without the enthusiasm and sharpness adopted by the citizens of Buenos Aires or Córdoba. This didn't prevent the Commission from being violently attacked by the press, something that is difficult to understand, since the purpose of the Commission had been to bring a show that had drawn the attention of many people.

One afternoon, the members of the Commission got together so as to exchange impressions on the possible purchase of a painting. One of them, Juan Zocchi, whom I got along well with, brought me the news that two of my paintings had been bought: «Portrait of Xul Solar» and «Outskirts of Milán» [27]. Through Zocchi I learned that a painter that formed part of the Commission had cast a vote against the sale, something that didn't surprise me in the least.

Not even to my closest friends did I mention my return to the Old Continent; the subject disconcerted me, and besides, I now had the chance to leave sooner, thanks to my family's improved economy. Yet it wasn't the best of times: the specter of the World Crisis spread its shadow across the earth, and I found it awkward to ask Rosenberg whether he was still willing to receive me at such grave moments, especially after a silence that had lasted years. Friends that wrote to me from Italy painted a bleak panorama: loans had collapsed, all sectors of public and private economy were hampered by a generalized depression, food was reduced and the art commerce paralyzed.

The end of 1928 was nearing and it was imperative for me to do something; inertia drove me crazy, and I felt it would end up asphyxiating me. Friends from Brazil had spoken about exhibiting my work in Sao Paulo, under very favorable conditions. As I had set my mind to go, I thought the first move could be Rio de Janeiro, where I had some friends. I wrote to Da Vega Guignard, with whom I had always remained in contact, asking him two precise questions: whether I could exhibit there, without having to spend too much, and if there was a possibility of selling my work. He answered my first question by assuring me that the galleries were already mine, and my

---

27   Both works belong to the Municipal Museum of Fine Arts of Rosario.

second one with an ambiguous reply; he believed that given my reputation and Marinetti´s, who had always backed me up, a miracle could be accomplished. I would be well surrounded by a select group of friends, he said, and a large portion of the press would be in my favor.

After having dispatched two crates full of paintings, I boarded the steamship that headed towards Rio. My meeting with Da Veiga Guignard was worth the trip; it was truly exciting, and I believe we both cried when recalling our days in Munich. As from the following morning, we set off to retrieve the paintings held by customs. This odyssey was indescribable. Suffice it to say that after two weeks of unsuccessful procedures, after running from office to office, after fifteen days miserably lost, I dispatched the two crates back to Buenos Aires. I had had enough.

At any rate, my time spent in Brazil had been productive; the newspapers took heed of me and I met many intelligent and pleasant people. I often saw the poet Ronal de Carvalho: he aspired to be posted Ambassador to Argentina and spoke Spanish fluently; I also met the magnificent xylographer Osualdo Goeldi, the poet Álvaro Moreyra and his wife, the great writer Joâo Ribeiro, the painter Tarsila Do Amaral with her husband, the poet Oswaldo de Andrade and so many other friends that I remember with affection.

I learned some things, among others that our books are very expensive over there; artists and intellectuals also deplored the lack of cultural interchange between the two nations, albeit so close by. And I don´t believe the situation has changed over the years.

While in Rio, I received the strangest of telegrams from Buenos Aires. An excellent friend had sent it to me and it only read: «Kiss me, Dora». I thought she had gone mad, for I could not comprehend such an extraordinary attitude. Some days later I received a letter from one of my brothers telling me that my mother was gravely ill, but that I should in no way return; they would keep me abreast of the situation. The sense of the telegram revealed itself to me at once: it was an expression of condolence, simultaneously transmitting the terrible truth that the letter did not want to disclose [28].

For fifteen days I was trapped in a state of stupor, vacillating between sailing to Europe and returning to La Plata. If I decided on the first alternative I could not have chosen a worse moment, in view of all I was leaving behind and the stormy clouds that darkened the world. It was the month of April 1929.

---

28   The author refers to a pun: "Kiss me", in Spanish, is expressed as "Bésame", and a manifestation of condolence is a " Pésame": the difference lies in the letter "P".

Chapter 22

Appointment, Dismissal, and Replacement at the Museum

A European, especially one who lives in big cities, would find it difficult to understand how tough it was for me to live in Buenos Aires, and how painstakingly hard I found it to carry on with my work. Without museums where I could seek refuge, in intimate correspondence with great creations, without artists that followed the same tendency, without anyone knowledgeable about the new expressions, something that would have allowed me to sharpen the blade of my creative lucidity, without any «marchands» and buyers, my life as an artist was extremely painful and solitary.

This doesn't imply that as time went by the artistic environment of Buenos Aires did not undergo a modification. Although the Northern «Costumbrismo», the snow–capped landscapes, the gauchos, the goats on the crags, the rodeos, were still the main attractions of the collective shows, some of the artists that came back from Europe timidly imposed themselves on the official academic art and those advances were progressively gaining ground.

The panorama was certainly not brilliant. Yet this opacity couldn't darken the immovable faith I had in my art, for I was certain that only modern art speaks to us closely, moves and touches us, paving the way for new horizons. My path was defined and well traced; I only had to follow it, trying each time harder, progressing, destroying, producing and destroying again, for the artist who does not «burn» his work and sleeps soundly forgets that a signature means nothing in order to establish the value of a painting. Fortunately, courage and intuition were always of great help to me. Since childhood I had learned to get by with very little, and I still believed in this philosophy.

In spite of the penury the country was going through as a consequence of the worldwide crisis, all that I had planned with my parents worked out and my family was finally steered towards a safe harbor. Although some of my brothers continued to study, some had found a job and earned a living; others got married or were about to. My worries lessened and I plunged into intensive work, discovering new aesthetic problems in their most hidden facets. There was one theme that obsessed me: the Cup. I produced several versions of it that I would later take up again either in a continuous or sporadic way up until 1939 or even later.

Someone might ask why the Cup preoccupied me. In truth, it fascinated me, not so much because its shape lent itself to various interpretations, but because of its symbolism. Since rainwater created it and cascades eroded the stone, until it was adapted to become a chalice, what a wide array of form and usage! Core of belief and imagination of Man, the cup is present in huts and palaces, in sanctuaries and cathedrals, in tombs accompanying the dead in their passage, taking on the shape of an urn that contains their ashes or placed upon their tombstones, protecting the flowers that are offered to the deceased.

Symbol and familiar motif transposed to baked clay, iron, copper, marble, jade, gold, crystal: everyone uses the cup and with it we celebrate the most intimate and collective events, with it we receive the Holy Communion, in it we drink the sacred wine of friendship. To me the cup forms part of heraldry, and I have spent years trying to reduce it to complete abstraction.

From the moment my mother passed away, I lived between La Plata and the city of Buenos Aires, without settling in either one; Botana offered me his home on Sarmiento Street. I went to see my new place and it seemed to be fine: I could probably stay there provisionally. A very pleasant couple took care of the building. I settled in the rooms on the first floor, two of which I used as studios. In one of them some young painters worked under my supervision; among the studies I had them carry out, I included several copies of many of my paintings with modified colors. I wanted to oblige them to paint without the model before them, to remove facts from their memory.

In the course of time these copies became a major headache, because I often had to call the Municipal Bank to verify or deny their authenticity: I know that in La Plata there exists a horrible copy of the painting «Young woman with green fan», though I have no idea who owns the work.

I did not stay long at Botana's home, for as the month of November 1930 was coming to an end, I was appointed director of the Museum of Fine Arts of La Plata. At the time I was holding an exhibition at the «Müller» Gallery of Buenos Aires and the first issue of the art and criticism publication «Argentina» saw the light. María Rosa Oliver, Córdova Iturburu and I had founded it. It was a period in which I often saw María Rosa Oliver and other friends at the reunions held at her old Plaza San Martín home.

At that time two events took place: the arrival of my old friend Anton Giulio Bragaglia, whom I had last seen in Paris in 1924, and almost simultaneously, the arrival of Margherita Sarfatti. Bragaglia had been invited by the Argentine Institute of Italic Culture, of which I was a member. He brought with him a display of models for the stage, which he exhibited at the Salons of the National Committee of Fine Arts; in addition he held a series of lectures on theatre that we coordinated for him in Buenos Aires, in Córdoba, in Bahía Blanca and in La Plata; María Rosa Oliver introduced him to several people and I did the same. One evening, after having dined at the «El Pescadito» in La Boca, together with other acquaintances, I took him to a gathering that my friend Juan de Dios Filiberto was holding at his house. The reception in his honor and the popular music performed for the first time by authentic interpreters delighted Bragaglia.

Margherita brought with her an exhibition of Italian contemporary art, which was displayed at the «Amigos del Arte» Salons. She asked me to manage the show, in part because she knew I was capable of handling the situation, and in part because I was in good terms with most of the artists that exhibited. Knowing my friend and her authoritarian nature, I evaded the situation alleging I was short of time, which in fact was true. However, I ended up accepting, on condition that no–one, not even she, would enter the halls until I had finished my work: it was my Trento adventure all over again.

The agreement was respected. On the day of the opening, Margherita was told that at eleven she would be allowed in. She arrived at noon, amazed to find out that a massive marble bust of Mussolini, created by the sculptor Adolfo Wildt, a favorite of the regime, was not being exhibited. In effect, I had discarded it, not only because it was Mussolini but because it was a repulsive piece of work, pretentious, impersonal, out of tune with the rest. The scene was dramatic. Donna Margherita, beside herself, kept on crying out: «Il Duce, il mio Duce!!»

I remained inflexible, and both Doctor Marotta, president of the Institute, and the president of the «Amigos del Arte» Association, were on my side. Since she had to choose between dismantling the show–something I was ready to do and she knew it– and sacrificing her Duce, she opted for the last alternative.

Those visits from my friends abroad absorbed a great deal of my time, but at the same time they reminded me of my past existence, they revived dear memories and encouraged me to work full of hope. I showed them my art and noticed how surprised they were I could progress despite such a hostile environment.

I was ambivalent about accepting the direction of the La Plata Museum of Fine Arts; two reasons impelled me to reject it; the first one was that in spite of the bleak European panorama my mind was set on traveling, especially after my mother's death, and the second one was that I didn't want to deprive the young woman currently in charge of the Museum of her salary.

It had been Dr. Zavalía, then Secretary of State, who had thought of me to activate the Museum. He was connected to men of letters who at the same time were acquaintances of mine. Through the lawyer Pedro Blake, he invited me to come and see him at the House of Government, where he offered me the post, not before knocking down every objection one by one: a public post was not a chain around the neck, and if I actually did travel, I only had to present my resignation. As far as Miss Rivademar was concerned, since neither she nor her colleague (a painter from la Plata) had done anything productive over the years, it was necessary to either replace her or to close down the Museum, something the Government was envisaging with satisfaction, for an economic plan had been put into effect. He gave me a week to reflect upon it, insinuating that the responsibility of the decision would concern me directly.

I exposed the dilemma to some people who were aware of the situation; in their opinion, the only way to save the Museum was to put aside all sentimentalism and to give up my trip for a while. I accepted and started to work.

I won't dwell on all my eyes saw from the day I began my duties; suffice it to say that while walking through the halls I noticed a dent in one of the paintings. I made no remark, but as soon as everyone had left, I carefully examined the painting. What I feared was true: in the middle of the dent there was a crack caused by the constant fall of a raindrop. No doubt about it, the roof was in poor conditions; but it would have been enough to move the painting to one side in order to avoid the damage. Nobody had. No inventory had been kept of the books, among which there were novels. Only the titles were mentioned. Everything reflected the same negligence.

When I began revising the notebook –I can hardly call it a register– in which all the works of the collection had been jotted in numerical order, I noticed that the works our National Museum of Fine Arts had loaned were included in the list of paintings. I started out by classifying the works; those loaned I removed from the list and returned, for they were mediocre. With poor didactic criteria our museum had sent work it did not wish to exhibit to the provinces, thus deforming the vision of the regional public.

I also classified what was left of the La Plata Museum's property –a hundred and thirteen pictures in all– dividing the total in three parts: the good works, the ordinary, and those that should never be exhibited. Among these there were two paintings donated by someone whose name I cannot remember, one of which was attributed to Tintoretto and the other to Goya; two mediocre paintings any nearsighted person would spot a hundred meters away; I classified them as belonging to the schools of Tintoretto and Goya.

I took the necessary steps to obtain better halls in the Dardo Rocha Passage, that is to say, to locate the Museum in the city center itself, under the very nose of the public, of the intellectuals, of the university and Fine Arts students (who nonetheless kept on walking leisurely by, while inside fist–rate cultural events were taking place).

The newly obtained halls included an immense auditorium in which to exhibit the paintings, a stage, a few storerooms, and two offices. One of them was quite beautiful, and reserved for the Director, while the other became the porter´s lodge. The delicate money–related problem immediately arose: we were in dire need of capital in order to move. As this was a difficult task, I personally went to see the head of the City Firemen, who most amused, put his trucks and uniformed firemen at my service. This is how the move was carried out in January 1930.

We needed funds for the installation of the Museum; partitions, electrical devices, lights, furniture and tables for the Library, chairs for the auditorium. I attempted to obtain those funds, while petitioning for money for the publication of the «Crónica de Arte» magazine, meant to divulge the activities of the institute. When it came out, it was in fact the only official voice of the country linked to the arts.

I also sent a circular to all the directors of the newspapers of the Province of Buenos Aires, notifying them that henceforth, the Provincial Museum of Fine Arts of La Plata would be, as its name indicated, the museum of the whole Province and of each one of its inhabitants. Moreover, its program of cultural activities, already prepared and especially dedicated to the people, would reach all centers, even the out–of the –way ones, through the means of a novel system: the Art Wagon. I asked every director for his collaboration, telling him it would also benefit his own readers.

Additionally, like someone who battles on all fronts, I sent a note to all the county administrators, reminding them that the Museum, being a Provincial one, had to be considered their own; the personal contribution of each administrator would therefore be precious. The incentive was, of course, to motivate people to familiarize themselves with all artistic manifestations.

Almost all of the newspaper directors responded; of the municipal administrators, only two: Vicente Solano Lima and Aníbal González Ocantos.

As the procedures to obtain the necessary funds were evolving slowly, I wrote to the two administrators who had accepted my proposal; I offered to immediately present the first cultural event in their county. Mainly I addressed myself to Solano Lima, of the San Nicolás district, for having been the first one to answer; I suggested mounting an exhibition of Argentine artists opening on 9July and he accepted. People received it with great enthusiasm, and the show gave rise to various cultural manifestations, among which an act at the «Gran Teatro». The theater filled itself to the brim and several people gave a speech, including myself. Local newspapers delightedly commented on the event, influencing the Buenos Aires newspapers; I then realized how avidly people of the provinces wished to experience a cultural life.

Having verified this, I took it upon me to spread the view that it was a fallacy to believe that the arts were difficult to understand if one didn't possess a certain degree of sophistication. Since the arts relate to sensitivity as much as to intelligence, they can reach people in a myriad of ways. People would thus understand modern art, which is the art of their time. The position to adopt with regard to painting would be to look at it without wondering what it represents; to contemplate it in a receptive state, without trying to judge *what* it says nor *how* it says it; to appreciate it without making comparisons. This would open the spirit to delight and emotion, as well as to aesthetic pleasure.

From the moment I took charge of the Museum, determined to turn it into a work of art, I had little time for myself. My sense of responsibility obliged me to concentrate on work. I settled in La Plata, for otherwise I would have never found any time to paint. Once established, I practically no longer frequented the cafés, and traveled to Buenos Aires City only once or twice a week, at the most. This way of life was partly interrupted to satisfy the wish of my friend Delia del Carril, who wanted, together with a group of students, to study drawing with me.

On the same block where years later I opened my «Atelier Pettoruti» [29], Delia obtained a large hall from her brother, with enough room for at least ten easels. Besides my friend, the other members of the group were Stella Morra de Cárcano, Dora Cifone, Elena Videla Dorna, Fifa Spragón and other young ladies whose names I cannot recall. The art critic Atalaya attended one of these classes, and basing himself on all he had seen and heard on that occasion, wrote an extensive article in one of the issues of the «Alfar» magazine of Montevideo. He named it «The artist and the teacher».

In the month of July 1931 the first issue of the «Crónica de Arte» magazine, the organ of the Museum, was published, and it was well received by the local and foreign press. On 2 September the second issue saw the light, yet it became impossible to publish the third, already diagrammed, for though the work was done in official workshops, as I couldn't afford the paper.

That year, due to the intense rhythm of work, I was hardly able to paint. Nevertheless, I accepted an invitation from the cultural group «La Brasa» of Santiago del Estero [30], directed by the writer Bernardo Canal Feijóo, in order to exhibit my work and give a lecture in the capital city of that province. My sister Carolita accompanied me on my trip: the exhibition opened on 9 October. I must confess that I seldom saw such well–mannered and interested people walking past my paintings. Even school children led by their

---

29   Situated on Charcas Street, between Rodríguez Peña Street and Callao Avenue.
30   A Northern Argentine province.

teachers paid special attention, which proves my point exactly: even people with relatively little education are not frightened by modern art when unbiased. In most of the provincial cities my work was seen with naturalness and pleasure by people belonging to different social classes, who had never been taught to think that art must be this or that, for the truth is neither here nor there. The so–called educated people are those whose minds depend on clichés. My lecture was equally appreciated, though a heated discussion arose at the end with an educated local priest. Unfortunately, he was prejudiced, and felt that advanced artists were unavoidably anti–religious. He wasn't attacking my art: he was attacking my alleged atheism.

The Museum was working despite the fact that all we had asked for had not yet arrived. A carpenter I had spoken to frankly and who trusted me, accepted to do the work and collect his pay later. Though the brand–new partitions were lined with the appropriate cloth –obtained on credit– and the first twenty–five chairs I had designed were ready, the museum section could not be inaugurated because the electrical installations were missing and I had not found anyone who wished to work without immediate compensation. Yet obstacles were overlooked, and the opening presentation was very beautiful. The journalists visiting the Museum illuminated the halls with their flashlights, taking splendid photographs in spite of it all.

The course the Museum wanted to take was clear: it wished to become a place where painting, sculpture, engraving and drawing by Argentine artists could be studied. No museum in our country had reached this objective, not even the National Museum.

In my opinion, we had to acquire works by artists, Argentine or foreign, from the Colonial times to the present, whose works could be obtained at a relatively low cost. Once this goal had been achieved and all the gaps filled, my intention was to keep up the collection by purchasing contemporary paintings on a regular basis. In short: I wanted students to have immediate access to Argentine art, tackling it in a comprehensive way. This objective attained, my attention would then turn to the arts of the American continent. As a result, I came up with the idea of mounting a Latin American Biennial, for that allowed us to purchase and become acquainted with the works of the authors of many American countries.

Today, I still think those ideas were commendable and practical, had the Province possessed men fond of culture and willing to contribute to progress. But the patriotism of those who could have made a difference did not manifest itself. How can a country grow when led by narrow–minded men?

Because of bureaucracy and lack of funds, my hands were tied. The museum only counted with a meager monthly stipend, which was used even to purchase books. I set aside some of this money so as to pay the carpenter who had so nobly done his work.

During the whole twelve months of 1931, the museum remained closed, always waiting to obtain the necessary funds for the installation costs. What I did achieve, thanks to patient negotiations, was to obtain a hundred more pesos, thus increasing the inadequate stipend.

On 27 January 1932, the new Provincial Inspector, a lawyer named Meabe, dismissed me without even thanking me for the services rendered, in disdain of all civil service protocol: he immediately appointed a friend of his, a guitar professor from the Province of Corrientes named Luis Verón.

The news spread throughout the country at the speed of light and an unprecedented press campaign was launched. Under large headings, newspapers of all tendencies denounced the exceptional event, and telegrams of protest, even from abroad, flooded the House of Government; cultural and artistic associations throughout the country sent notes complaining about the measure, demanding my recall. The only institution keeping an enigmatic silence was the Society of Argentine Artists of La Plata, my native city.

Why this commotion? Because now that people had witnessed a cultural action that benefited them, they were not willing to give up the opportunity. No other explanation exists. Moreover, what also caused indignation was the fact that a guitar player had replaced a painter. Those newspapers hostile to the Government naturally took advantage of the situation in order to criticize the decision and to question the level of culture of the responsible party.

The day that my successor presented himself at the Museum in order to accept the post, he did so in the company of three people that I knew: the painter Gaspar Besares Soraire, from Buenos Aires, a Spanish sculptor and an Italian priest–painter, both from La Plata. At first I thought those three men had come especially to tell me how sorry they were I had been dismissed; but when they notified me they were the new director's «advisers», I called José González, my good–natured clerk, ordering him in a loud voice «to throw those three men out». Turning towards Mr. Verón, I let him know that if he indeed needed advisers, it was best he ask the President to appoint them.

I requested the presence of an accountant, and inventory in hand, showed the men the works of art. It was a comical scene, for each time González read the information pertinent to that painting, especially if it was described as being «a pastel», the brand–new Museum director would blush, believing I was pulling his leg [31].

Two days later my replacement presented a note to the local newspapers, admitting to be overwhelmed by the debts the Museum had run up. Little did he know that the debts he was alluding to already existed before my arrival. I immediately clarified the situation through the means of an open letter, which was published by the newspapers.

One day Mr. Pedro Cavello came to see me at home, solemnly announcing, on behalf of the elected Governor, that I was to be reinstated, so

---

31 "Pastel" in Spanish also means "pie".

as to repair the «error» that had been made. This is how, two months after having been dismissed, I was once again head of the Museum.

At the suggestion of Mr. Cavello, at the time Secretary of the Interior, I went to greet the Governor on the day following my investiture. I was taken aback, however, by his cold reception, for he had expressed his wish to repair the arbitrariness with such generosity. His first words were to tell me that he had learned, from people with sound opinions, that I hung the paintings upside down, and in deadly earnest he was asking me not to do this again. This might seem unbelievable, but every word is true.

I replied that these reasonable people were misinformed, and that if he only cared to walk with me to the Museum, he would find out for himself. Those were the magic words that changed his attitude. Right away he invited me to sit down and chat, as if he at once had forgotten that the antechambers were swarming with politicians and all kinds of people. Only wishing to hear what I had to say, he did not even notice Mr. Cavello, who anxiously kept walking in and out of the office.

A little later we received the necessary funds to pay off the debts and get the Museum going. However, in spite of my many efforts, I never managed to obtain the paper for the publication of the «Crónica del Arte» newspaper.

A large dinner was organized in Buenos Aires to celebrate my reinstatement. The Trocadero restaurant brimmed over with people. I do not believe any friend was missing, and perhaps only a few acquaintances were absent. There also were people who, sympathizing with my cause, wished to shake my hand and express their solidarity. Indeed, it was a colossal dinner.

Chapter 23
My first painting at the National Museum

Carefully weighing my words while I speak, I ponder about the curious duality of the place that became my home for over a quarter of a century. I was nearing forty, eight years had already gone by since my return from Europe and all doors remained closed.

The crisis had barely subsided in the Old Continent that the horizons darkened once again with the reigning dictatorships, their persecutions, their alliances, their exigencies and their war threats, and my idea of leaving progressively faded. So much so that I decided to settle in Buenos Aires, reflecting, among other things, on how useful it would be, while in the country, to teach young artists all that I had learned in the course of twenty years. Unfortunately, this never happened. Later, when I was forced to teach as a result of harsher circumstances, I had to do so in national and industrial schools, where it was impossible to carry out anything interesting and I lost my time; but never was I given the opportunity to teach in any academy in Buenos Aires or La Plata, my native city.

My paintings were not selling, in spite of their reasonable prices, for different reasons: 1) the collectors did not like them 2) everyone believed them to be expensive 3) the critics of the major newspapers, whose opinion the public respected, declared I repeated myself, and that I focused only on my way of painting. As if Goya, Rembrandt and many other artists hadn´t concentrated on «their way of painting», understanding that it is the cohesion of the art work that gives them definition. After having declared I was a «Futurist», it turned out I was not, that I was a Cubist and a follower of Picasso on top of that, or that I copied Juan Gris; others went as far as saying I followed «Severini´s luminous trail». This was the usual response of most critics in Argentina in 1932 and subsequent years, except for outstanding people like Estarico, Atalaya, Payró and Rinaldi; the others were not interested in the history nor in the evolution of the arts beyond Impressionism.

Never had I heard in Europe that Gris imitated Braque or Picasso, nor that the paintings of Metzinger, Gleizes, Marcoussis and so many others plagiarized them: in Europe history is still vibrantly present, and art is a continuum in spite of the opposition. The geometrical style we name Cubism did not break with tradition nor was it invented by anyone; Cézanne naturally evolved towards it, only to have other painters continue to pave the way, the way Giotto did after Cimabue, and El Greco after Michelangelo and Tintoretto.

As far as I know neither Picasso nor Braque have ever claimed having invented Cubism; they both knew that the common predecessor was Cézanne, whose influence was beginning to be felt as from 1906, right after his death. Serusier, Derain, Vlaminck experimented with it, as did the novices Léger and Lhote; only that these painters were impressed by Cézanne's austere palette and stark drawings, whereas Picasso and Braque favored the cubic simplicity of Cézanne's last works, painted at the foot of the Mont Sainte–Victoire.

All artistic movements contribute something to the arts, yet it is important to keep in mind that the majority of these movements cannot be called as such until after the works have been achieved and a name is given to them. The artist does not follow a program; he searches without knowing exactly what it is, and creates his work, whether sublime or poor. The only movement lasting half a century that had a name and a program was Futurism. That is perhaps why its promoters produced very little, although exerting an important theoretical influence that extended itself to numerous spheres of modern life.

The Cubist movement, for instance, just like the Futurist one –and before that the Impressionist, the Romantic, and so forth– belonged to everybody, for in all creative periods the air is loaded with ideas of renovation that each man seizes and develops according his sensitivity. That is why it is utterly ridiculous to accuse a Cubist to copy his peer; in that case one would have to accuse Braque and Picasso to imitate each other, so alike are their paintings belonging to the analytical period.

My compatriots were in fact more eager to criticize my paintings rather than attempting to understand an expression that baffled them. They didn't realize my work was deeply rooted in the past, and insisted on evaluating it with respect to the work of Cubists and Futurists to whom they tried to link me. Classifying it arbitrarily as one tendency and then another, these men pigeonholed my painting as soon as they saw it, without considering the period in which the work was begun, separating it thus from its context. If critics had taken their time to examine it comparatively, browsing through pictures (mine and hundreds of other reproductions of paintings created by known painters), they would have noticed the parallelism in the diversity and not have written so much nonsense.

Cubism, a tendency that only began to define itself in our hemisphere around 1930 or even later, had become a synonym of rebellion. My art was furiously criticized in the artistic milieu, especially if I were to be rewarded by the National Salon. My colleagues, some of them members of the jury, did not dare to reject my art, though several would have gladly done so. What I could be assured of, when sending my painting to the Salon, was that it would be given the worst possible place and that it would never obtain a prize. Not only did I never receive any national or consolation prize, which does wonders for opening doors, but no artist, among the large number of young and old ones who in the course of twenty–five years were members of the jury, ever voted for me.

Perhaps it is not pointless, at this point of my account, to digress and reflect on the contemporary nature of art. Many people have said they saw similarities between my work and that of Juan Gris. I do not agree with this suggestion, for our art has nothing in common: not in composition, not in color, not in technique, not in spirit. Whoever has seen art created by Juan Gris and knows mine, cannot be fooled: we are children of the same era but that's another matter. The same ideas nurtured our generation, but only the more receptive manifest them. This much said, I must add that while working in Florence and later in Rome and Milan, the name of Juan Gris rarely reached my ears, and if it did, it was only after the war, when I had already achieved paintings such as «The shadows», «Light–Elevation», «Friend by the window», «Woman at the café», «Self–portrait», «The blue cave of Capri», «Young woman with green hat», to mention only those that were better known.

It is true that in those times, international news were slow to spread around the globe. The names of Braque and Picasso, however, did reach Italy during the war, albeit only in very restricted circles. Only a few people knew about Expressionism, Kandinsky, or Mondrian, for only a handful were enlightened.

I ask myself whether people like to live in confusion, whether they have a manifest desire to destroy all that stands out or whether they are naturally inclined to creating problems. I notice, in effect, that the new generation of critics, jury members or professors, have not changed: they claim that many art students blatantly imitate me. Yet these students had simply studied under my guidance, and learned a technique based on simplicity and cleanliness of execution, for I had obliged them to work only with primary colors.

I tend to believe that those intellectuals pretend not to see that a long chain establishes itself on the basis of each discovery and each style: the thousands and thousands of paintings executed in the last few years, that follow the trend of Tachism, Informalism, Impressionism or Abstract Expressionism, were made by clusters of young painters from all over the western world who blatantly copied other artists. It is my belief that the measure of value has been lost not only in our midst but also everywhere else in the world. Either it no longer counts or few are those who notice it; the question is that a caricature–like painting with an ancient patina, or an exaggerated harshness of German Expressionism are seen as ultra–modern pictorial manifestations, when actually they represent a perpetual collision with what has already been achieved by more inventive artists.

Today it is said that painting is mediocre because there critics attempt to demolish it; I say it is poor because no–one knows how to paint, nor are there teachers that can guide. Painters are fully aware that individual pursuit and personal expression have always been the most appreciated values. The great contemporary artists are great precisely because they have disregarded the old norms and the vestiges of academicism; what critics do not seem to know is that the magnificent artists of our century, in order to reconstruct that which had been destroyed, have used a science and a technique that to them remain hidden.

To destroy is easy, but to build, and on top of that to renovate, is impossible if the laws of construction are not paid any heed to. Those who think that the notions of art and craft are contradictory are profoundly wrong; one cannot make art without being a craftsman. They who despise this view deliberately deceive themselves. Has a musician ever neglected the scale, in his longing to renovate music?

The Cultural Association of Azul invited me to hold an exhibit and give a lecture. Both took place in the month of May 1932 and were very much commended. However, it was not my reputation that mattered to me: what I wanted was to shake off the lethargy present in the provinces. Once challenged, something was set in motion and it seemed the public bought more books, attended museums more assiduously, or discussed art more vehemently.

In Buenos Aires, together with a group of friends, we founded the «Signo» Association with the purpose of mounting exhibitions and cultural events. A bulletin was printed and on Saturdays we held lectures. I directed the Association the first year, and Leonardo Estarico the following ones. It functioned in the basement of the «Castelar» Hotel, and the owners agreed on allowing artists to dine there at a reasonable price; we also organized reunions and dances. It was a way like any other to foster interest in people, and we reached our objective. Many people wanted to participate in the events and gatherings, and we got full support from the press. Interviews were requested, in order for us to explain the aim of the Association. Raúl González Tuñón, our beloved companion who shared all of our moments, signed one of the most beautiful articles ever written on the task performed by the «Signo» Association [32].

At the time, Leónidas Barletta ran his «Teatro Moderno», a rather modest looking building, on Corrientes Street. He wanted to transform it somewhat, without having to spend a lot. One afternoon that I went to visit him he told me about his plans. I promised him I would bring him my project, briefly anticipating what it would entail: «The idea would be to entirely change the aspect of the Theatre, highlighting the façade. Everything will remain quite simple and above all, economical, since you can perform a great deal of the work yourselves with a little willpower and just a few pesos».

I immediately proceeded to explain how to embellish the rachitic columns so as to give them an appearance of solidity and even stateliness. He had to paint them black, I told him, doing the same thing with the roof and illuminate the hall dimly, so that the grays and the whites... and so forth and so on.... We agreed the project would be ready in two weeks.

The term was not over yet when a gentleman I knew, and whom I ran into at the door of the Association, stopped to greet and congratulate me on the transformations the «Teatro del Pueblo» had just underwent: Barletta had told him it was my doing. You can imagine my surprise. I ran to see the novelty, only to find out that the Theatre had indeed been modernized: Barletta had done it all by himself, interpreting my idea brilliantly and possibly improving it, for the decoration produced quite an effect.

This anecdote reflects the intelligence of our people who achieve work through a great deal of personal effort, while the governors in charge of education sleep like moles. It is a tribute to the great Barletta who has always worked so hard, directing his energy towards the Argentine theatre without respite, in spite of the political, economic and professional drawbacks.

A little later, Luigi Pirandello and Massimo Bontempelli visited the country. The latter had been invited by the Argentine Institute of Italian Culture to hold a series of lectures, and the former had come with his troupe to present a few plays.

I received my two friends the best I could; Bontempelli managed very well on his own, but I had to spend more time with Pirandello than I could afford: barely disembarked, he begged me not to leave him on his own during his interviews with journalists. He was terrified about all they had made him say against Fascism on his previous tour and he told me about the hard times inflicted upon him by the regime when he returned to Italy. Pirandello was very shy and he only trusted me. We devised a program that we followed to the letter and he arranged for interviews on the days that I was free. One af-

---

[32] "Crítica" Magazine, 27 June 1932.

ternoon I took him to see the «Teatro del Pueblo». Pirandello was delighted at the wonderful work Barletta had achieved and congratulated him warmly.

In spite of all the obstacles, I continued to paint. As from 1932 I resumed working on the cup series, but that year I also painted two portraits of Alberto Hidalgo that I named, with one title only, «Man with yellow flower» [33] and a still–life, «Pears and apples». I completed two versions of «Gray cup» and two of «Green cup», and several sketches that later became paintings.

I kept on sending my work to the collective shows for the sake of discipline and for the public to see them: people always noticed them, no matter how poorly they were placed. Some new tendencies –all of them only slightly differing from the traditional viewpoint– were slowly making way into salons and galleries. Social, Abstract and Oneiric Realism found worshippers on the banks of the River Plate.

Seduced into making social art, some artists faithfully described the misery of our Northern provinces, or that of the high plateaus of Bolivia, through a painting both shallow and conventional that heavily relied on academic formalism. Others, more due to a lack of artistic culture than conditions, imperfectly assimilating the lessons of abstract art, yielded to a pseudo–abstraction which, not having originated from within, generated contradictory feelings. Others still became admirers of pictorial automatism and transported imaginary spaces and erotic nightmares to the canvas. In short, it was the anecdote that upset me, for it was irrelevant to the work. When I look at the portrait of Pope Julius II painted by Rafael, I do not see it as a portrait, for I do not know whether it resembles the model, nor do I care: neither do I behold the Vicar of Christ, the Holy Father or the Universal Shepherd; rather, it is the painting itself that interests me: the fusion of art and poetry is all that matters.

Good friends suddenly remembered that almost ten years had gone by since my return to the country. They wished to celebrate this event by attempting to have a painting of mine accepted by the National Museum of Fine Arts. But first they wanted to buy it from me. Roberto Rossi, Antonio Sibellino and Leonardo Estarico came to see me at my studio on 700 Corrientes Street, and chose the work that best suited their purpose: «Young Harlequin», painted in 1929, not before inquiring whether I would hand them the painting no matter how much money collected for it. I accepted. They entrusted the press secretary, who had offices and employees at his disposal, with the task of distributing circulars and to collect all contributions.

In the month of July my friends submitted the petition to the then head of the Museum, Mr. Atilio Chiappori, hoping the painting would be accepted before the end of the month. Yet an unexpected twist of fate thwarted their efforts. Mr. Chiappori had barely submitted the request to the National Fine

---

33 One of these paintings is presently at the National Museum of Fine Arts.

Arts Committee, presided over by the engineer Nicolás Bessio Moreno, that board held a meeting right away in order to establish that no work belonging to a living national author was to be admitted to the museum.

The ploy was too obvious. The press emphasized the impertinence to such a degree that the Committee could not but meet again in order to modify the decision. This time around, they established that works by living Argentine artists *could* enter the museum, but only if every member of the Committee was of one mind! The complications only changed their name and aspect: the point was to raise obstacles.

In a nutshell: the «Young Harlequin» was finally accepted, for the Committee voted unanimously. There was nothing they could do about that, and on 14 November 1935, one year and four months after the submission of the request, the Museum finally accepted my painting. If we consider that nowadays neophytes donate their paintings to the National Museum, and that this institution accepts them without objections, one can truly appreciate the change that has taken place.

Chapter 24

The treasure

The year 1934 defines my life thanks to a meeting, or should I say, a collision. I had an affable Chilean correspondent whose face I had never seen. She had written to me, congratulating me on a certain event relative to my art, lines which I gladly replied to; from time to time she would send me a postcard and I would send her another.

Towards the month of October I received two poetry books from this friend, «Samaritana» and «Rainbow», signed by an author whose name was unknown to me. A cluster of pretty photographs of children surprised in their games illustrated the book. The poems belonging to the first book were an affirmation of the expressive freedom of women, common subject among the female poets of the time and of these southern latitudes. The second book had character as well, and beautiful images.

I could not understand why those books had been sent to me, until I received the letter of my unknown friend, in which she announced that she would soon be traveling to Buenos Aires, where, perhaps, she would hold an exhibition.

The days went by, and I forgot all about it. October was ending, when suddenly, browsing through the «Crítica» newspaper I noticed large headings, in the sensational style that characterized the newspaper. It framed an interview filled with pictures, and in the middle of the page, was the photograph of a charming person that I immediately abhorred. How on earth, having been recommended to me, had she not even given called? Offended by her lack of courtesy I attempted to locate her through the «Clarín» newspaper, an easy task considering I knew the columnists. I called her at the hotel, and when I had her on the other end of the line, I gave her a piece of my mind.

I listened to her reply: sermons amused her a great deal, she told me, but she preferred to receive them in person. I accepted the challenge, and since we were not far from each other we agreed to meet a quarter of an hour later on the corner of Florida Street and Córdoba Avenue.

I went to the appointment with Ricardo Rojas Paz, not because I was afraid, but because I ran into him on the way. Night was falling. I saw an unusual silhouette advancing towards us: she was wearing a light gray coat with large lapels and a tight belt, and emerging from those lapels, a head with a long neck and straight dark blonde hair that fell onto her shoulders. Her figure was singular and pleasant: she truly was an athletic daughter of the Fjords.

We introduced ourselves and I presented Rojas Paz to her, while saying good-bye to him immediately after. Then taking her by the arm, I took her to a café where I intended to settle the matter. This is how my love affair began with my Chilean woman, my opposite and identical pole, discussing the sense and non-sense of actions in a dialogue full of antagonisms and agreements that revealed two similar universes situated in the antipodes, that we felt we needed to explore. Neither one nor the other wanted attachments, but as the way of the heart is full of snares, when we wished to free ourselves we found out we were trapped.

She was twenty-nine, quite sensible for her age and had a mind akin to a treasure. When I told her this, she answered that her true age was that of the Gospels, hence the impertinent weight of the «treasure» her brain represented. I noticed that the jokes she told were always at her expense, never at someone else's. She had a consideration for her fellow men that I judged excessive, a courage with regard to life that neared intrepidity, a self-assurance that gave her authority –kneaded with the yeast of pride–and an optimism that constantly contradicted my past experiences; such is the portrait of the complex human being I had before me.

In physics one speaks about the attraction of the poles; I appreciated them rather geographically, and while acknowledging the distances that separated us, I found it very tempting to draw her towards my geographical field. Perhaps the same thoughts went through her head, for there was between us, without manifesting itself overtly, the mocking defiance of contenders who believe themselves invulnerable. Seeking points in common, we talked about many things, and when we broached the subject of painting, I did so inviting her to see my paintings, with the secret intention to measure her culture and sensitivity through her reactions. She passed the test with flying colors, for nothing disoriented her. As was the case with Juan Gris, she liked the «Blue cave», which belongs to her ever since.

I showed her all there was worthy of seeing in Buenos Aires and its surroundings, including the «El Tigre» district, where we met the poet Alfonsina Storni quite by chance. They immediately took to each other, and in the course of the week I introduced my sisters Carolita and Lía Esther to her, as well as some of my closest friends, musicians, writers and poets. Among the first ones, I remember José María Castro, Ramón Gómez Cornet, Córdova Iturburu, Juan Carlos Paz and Oliverio Girondo, accompanied by their respective companions; Xul Solar and Sibellino had none.

Her first work came out in the «La Nación» newspaper in December; Eduardo Mallea directed the Sunday supplement at the time, and upon her arrival to Buenos Aires, had asked her to contribute. Strangely enough, her work came out in prose and I asked her what had motivated her to do so. She replied that she preferred prose to poetry because it provided a greater sense of security. «Through it one can become someone else. Poetry, on the other hand, is all nudity; lying becomes impossible. «And why would you need to lie?» I asked. After a silence as clear as bells, she answered without hesitation: «So that I do not have to reveal myself». In January, my enigmatic friend (I found her beautiful as well, but was careful not to tell her) was leaving for Montevideo.

At times, distance highlights unfathomable situations to us, and the roles we have played so far radically change. So far, I had believed to be some kind of protective angel to her, only to realize I was the one who was left forlorn. When she was not around everything seemed empty, and as soon as I could, I embarked for Uruguay.

The intellectual atmosphere of Montevideo, with which my Chilean friend was in contact, received her warmly and I found her surrounded by friends. I got to know them and introduced mine to her. My friendship with Luis Eduardo Pombo dates back to those days; he was a sensitive soul, a great poet without books, whose poems nonetheless hover in the ocean breeze of Montevideo. She and I also became acquainted with Edgardo Cadenazzi and with Guillermo Laborde and Alfonsina Storni, with whom we spent some wonderful days enjoying the beautiful Uruguayan shores.

Unfortunately, my stay in Montevideo was brief. Besides my work at the Museum, I was obsessed by the idea of a painting I had in mind, and relentlessly sketched the two figures, male and female, walking elbow to elbow along the paths of the world, as when illusion and disappointment at times unite.

When my treasure set foot again on the Argentine shores, I was painting «The travelers», which I had first carried executed on paper. When she departed, I was working on it with ardor and was therefore able to say goodbye without too much grief. My other drawings were meant to become two large paintings displaying three musicians, and my attention was fully taken up by my art, my life–long refuge.

Why did I let her go? Because there was nothing else I could do. Her hands had been tied for almost ten years and did not feel she had the right to liberate herself. That is why the exciting and passionate dialogue was filled with intermittencies, until it became possible to eliminate them forever. In order to achieve this, we had to wait six endless years: time flows slowly when two beings that love each other are kept apart.

Towards the end of 1934, invited by an intellectual and artistic circle of Bahía Blanca named «El Rincón», I mounted a painting and drawing exhibition in that city. It was held in the halls of the Rivadavia Library and, as usual, this helped to oxygenate the provincial air of the city a little, considering that cultural and artistic manifestations were rare at the time. That same year I created «The singer», a second version of the «The house of the Poet», which my brother Eduardo owns, and «Three Cigarettes».

In 1935, I produced «Wall and table», «Domino», «The pencil of the Master», two new versions of «The house of the poet» and finished «The walkers». As I have already mentioned, I also began two new paintings with three figures: «The improviser», and «Last serenade». With respect to «The walkers», here goes an anecdote: I had barely finished it that Sibellino, who had passionately followed its development, told Carlos Giambiaggi about it. The latter was a painter who had always raised a lot of objections with regard to my work. Curious about Sibellino´s «elation» he wished to see it, and one evening both came to my studio. I showed them some work and finally, let them see «The walkers», which they observed at length.

The following day Sibellino came to see me and this is exactly what he told me: «Yesterday evening, when you had barely closed your door, Giambiaggi said: «It possesses the strength of a Rembrandt!» This statement made me laugh, though I felt flattered, and Sibellino at once became serious, for he could not understand my merriment; it was only when I told him that Giambiaggi had never seen a Rembrandt in his life, that he shared my hilarity. Though I know perfectly well that there are artists capable of evaluating paintings through reproductions, there is nothing better than to see the original. However, I noticed Giambiaggi radically changed his point of view regarding my work; for ten years he had held heated objections against it whenever he found himself in the company of his best friends who were also mine. The latter defended it, and among these were Sibellino, Gómez Cornet and Atalaya. I have no doubt his conversion was sincere, for he told Sibellino he wished to see some of my earlier work that had been exhibited at the «Witcomb» gallery in 1924. I had no problem in showing it to him: I was sure that he, just like so many others, had never set eye on them before.

From the 11th to the 19th of October I represented my Province at the First Congress of Urbanism, celebrated in Buenos Aires, and some days later

I was overcome with joy to once again embrace my dear friend, Alberto Sartoris, who had become one of the most renowned architects. We continually wrote to each other and I was aware of all that he was creating. Already in 1933 some of his work had been exhibited at the Italian Architecture Show held in the Salons of the National Commission. Now he found himself in our corner of America invited by the Governments of Brazil and Uruguay and the Argentine Institute of Italian Culture of Buenos Aires to hold a cycle of lectures on modern architecture and aesthetics. [34] At the «Sur» magazine headquarters he held a personal exhibition dedicated to specialists, in which he included a series of his «progetti assonometrici a colori».

Physically, my friend had not changed, and seemed to be the same youth I had met in Milan fourteen years ago. It was great happiness to be together again and to exchange intimacies. Not once did we separate as long as he remained in the country: we saw each other at least once a day, for we always dined together. He did not wish to be in the company of anyone else, and together we went to see paintings, while talking about so many things we had in common. Art criticism had always been one of the activities related to his architecture. A good judge of avant–garde artistic currents in general and of Futurism in particular, he is the only critic qualified, in my opinion, to write on that movement and clarify the confusion regarding this subject. Moreover, he founded the first group of abstract Italian art, the «Como» group.

The Museum I was heading was not only functioning well, but had become much wealthier. Once the loaned works had been returned, very few paintings remained, especially since I had divided them in three groups: good, fair and poor, and discarded the latter.

Considering there were no funds to acquire more works of art, I had spoken to some artists I knew in Buenos Aires, and had written to some others asking them to help me form a museum of Argentine art. Without exception, they replied they would give nothing to a Government that never allotted part of its budget to acquiring works of art. However, they would be more than happy to personally hand me the work, with which I could do whatever seemed best.

Grasping the wish of the artists, those works were classified as if I had donated them. Later, the Provincial Committee of Fine Arts, upon publishing the only report it ever wrote in so many years of exercise, made the voluntary error to record them as having been donated by their authors. I wish to clarify this point in case any of these artists believes I betrayed his wish.

With the increasing artistic inheritance, in part due to those donations, and in part due to those acquisitions made during the Commemorative Exhibition of the Fiftieth Birthday of La Plata, there wasn't enough space in the

---

34 His lectures, ten in all, embraced several topics and were held between 8 and 25 November at the headquarters of the Argentine Congress of Urbanism, at the National Academy of Agronomy, at the Faculty of Architecture and Engineering, at the National Museum of Fine Arts, at the Argentine Scientific Society, at the Central Society of Architects, at the "Amigos del Arte" Association, at the headquarters of the "Sur" Magazine and at the National Center of Agronomic Engineers.

Museum to even hang one work belonging to each one of those authors integrating the collection. I then decided the display would function best on a rotating basis. For this purpose I divided the works into four groups that were exhibited every three months, reserving the main pieces as part of the permanent collection. It was a way to activate the Museum with periodical exhibitions that were bound to attract people, especially the Fine Arts students their teachers. Yet nothing like that ever happened: I never saw them set foot in the Museum.

Every time the exhibition changed, the artists would be sent a mimeographed note, as well as the list of painters, sculptors, drawers and engravers displaying on that occasion. Everything was thoroughly organized so as to avoid misunderstandings, and I saw to it that all was accomplished with the utmost fairness, something an honest employee cannot but aspire to. I can say, in all sincerity, that I never took advantage of the situation: inside the Museum I was the Director, while the painter Pettoruti waited outside the door.

Once the national and international card index had been more or less completed, something that allowed me to be in contact with numerous foreign artistic institutions and many foreign ministries of culture, including that of the Soviet Union (I regularly received magazines and information, before and after the war, until the advent of the «iron curtain»), cultural events took place at the Museum. Every semester or year was programmed in anticipation.

These events encompassed all kinds of cultural manifestations, including didactic exhibitions that displayed various aspects of our artistic milieu and, whenever possible, of the arts of Latin America and Europe (for these I naturally used good color reproductions). One exhibition followed the next: ten Argentine sculptors, three renowned painters (Centurión, Spilimbergo and Victorica), who had been awarded the Grand National Prize, five artists from La Plata, thirty artists born in the Buenos Aires Province, and so on.

Without exception, every Saturday a cultural event was held at the Museum. It was either a concert that had never been heard before in the country or in America, like the Wind Quintet of La Plata, or a voice and piano recital programmed by «Nueva Música», a Buenos Aires musical ensemble that attempted to introduce modern music into our country. There also were puppet shows presented by the «Teatro de Títeres». However, the lectures were priviledged, for all the lecturers were friends of mine; knowing that there were no funds available to remunerate them, they contributed in the name of culture [35]. Only years later did I possess a small budget that allowed me to reward each lecturer with a hundred pesos, which amounted to practically nothing.

---

35   Among the lecturers who brought their invaluable expertise I remember these names, (begging for forgiveness in the case of having involuntarily forgotten some of them) : Leónidas Barletta; Anton Giulio Bragalia, Mane Bernardo, Cordova Iturburu, Luis Cané, Ramón Columba, Alberto M. Candiotti, Leonardo Estarico, Gilardo Gilardi, Francisco Houlubek, Ilka Krupkin, Viscount of Lascano Tegui, F.T. Marinetti, Ezequiel Martínez Estrada, Nicolás Olivari, Julio E. Payró, Juan carlos paz, José León Pagano, Alberto Pineta, Julio Rinaldini, Marques Rebelo, Jorge Romero Brest, Honorio Sicardi, Juan Valmaggia, Amado Vilar, Javier Villafañe and Carlos Vega.

Very soon, thanks to a sustained activity and the competence of my closest helpers, the Museum of La Plata became a pilot museum known throughout the country, the American continent and other cultural centers of the world. I was permanently alert and kept in touch with the outside world through the shipment of catalogues that accompanied each exhibition and every ceremony: without exception these included the biography of the exhibiting artists and the intellectuals that lectured, as well as reproductions of paintings, sculptures or drawings. These catalogues fulfilled their role by spreading our values across the globe.

One idea guided me at all times: to take the Museum to the people, considering the people did not approach the Museum. Without respite I had warned that there exists no worse evil for a nation than its illiteracy in music, fine arts and literature, asking for a multiplication of spiritual manifestations in the country as well as for more libraries; I urged authorities for more lectures that would sharpen the artistic, musical, and literary vision. A country without a spiritual culture, without concepts regarding the arts and beauty, will never possess dynamic citizens.

Attempting to stimulate the public, I spoke about the great politicians of antiquity who were also patrons of the arts: their names were remembered because of their support. I insisted on telling them it was the people that made art —Michelangelo, Leonardo, Holbein, Goya, Cézanne and Van Gogh— though until relatively recently people had been kept away from the arts. For a long time, they hadn´t been allowed to enter the palace of Versailles or the Sistine Chapel, nor had they visited the frescoes of Rafael; the Church and the aristocracy had monopolized the best work. Moreover, private collections became public only a short time ago, as people became fascinated by images.

Chapter 25

On both sides of The Andes

In February 1936 I took a trip to Chile with my sister Carolita. I had never crossed The Andes before and we decided to do so «from within»; the «Transandino» [36] moved slowly, but the journey was fascinating. My Chilean woman was waiting for us: after a couple of months without anyone to quarrel with, the reunion was bliss. So much time had gone by our memory was in a blur and it was like getting to know each other all over again. Unfortunately, the more time we spent together, the more we found points in common; conditions or attractions that only but intensified our ties while knowing we had to let go, for we were only allowed to be friends. However, I could not imagine my future without her, and in my ear intuition whispered she was destined to become my wife.

Carolita and I spent some wonderful days, first in Viña del Mar and then in Santiago. My beloved treasure guided us around, praising the beautiful landscape. From Valparaíso to Maipú I met two of her seven brothers and some of her friends: painters, poets and journalists who received us most cordially. I particularly remember the sculptor Laura Rodig fondly. The avant–garde movements aroused great curiosity and I was frequently interviewed. My ties with Chile date back to those times and became very close in the course of the following decades.

The month went by too soon and the stay ended, like all things that come to an end. Unable to take her with me, I savored with abandon the last moments of her company. She accompanied us to a certain point of the Cordillera, where we awaited the passage of the train beneath the snow–capped peaks. The imposing scenery seemed to add solemnity to the separation and we felt so strongly united that being separated anew seemed

---

36   The "Transandino": Train that travels from Argentina to Chile traversing the Andes.

unbearable. Yet our love could not have any continuity: I had to accept the facts, since she did not want to face other possible solutions. I could sense her decision was dictated by common sense, but my reason wasn't always eager to contradict my feelings. Whenever these internal struggles arose we became trapped in one of those situations in which lovers reproach each other to be insufficiently loved or understood. Yet just like our letters that flew across the Andes, we would race towards each other, unable to stand the separation.

In the month of August the first issue of «Compás», the magazine that Estarico and I had founded came out. In spite of its warm reception, only two numbers saw the light. Around that time, I held an exhibition in the Salons of «El Argentino de La Plata» hotel, and received a letter from Marinetti telling me he was returning to Buenos Aires. He arrived almost at the same time as his letter did, but this time around I wasn't able to spend as much time with him as I would have wanted: I had to take care of the museum and organize the cultural events; I had my night classes at the Industrial School of La Plata; there was my painting and on top of that, another personal exhibition on the brink of opening. At any rate, I did I all could to render him homage. The «El Mundo» newspaper welcomed him with a dinner and I was in charge of decorating the table. Marinetti participated in the creation of the menu, enlivened by the music of a typewriter. Some dishes were frankly revolting: I remember his «Strawberries à la gasoline» perfectly well, which he was careful enough to spray with petrol.

While this was taking place, my exhibition opened at the «Nordiska» Gallery. The only objective was to display the painting «The travelers», but I also exhibited nineteen other works. Curiously, critics, including Fernán Félix de Amador in the «La Prensa» newspaper, noticed my painting was taking a new direction. Amador was a dear friend and poet who, like so many others, did not accept my art, and did not miss a chance to ferociously criticize my work, though this was done most courteously and reflectively.

While the exhibition at «Nordiska» was on, the last act of vandalism, at least as far as I know, was perpetrated against my paintings. The public was beginning to hold other views, and truth is that in general it behaved well at my exhibitions. I'm specifically alluding to the public of Buenos Aires, since people in the provincial cities almost always conducted themselves properly.

Everything indicated the public was beginning to comprehend the new forms of art, though national artists did not follow the trend. From 8 to 12 December 1936 an exhibition was held at the «Moody gallery» [37], displaying drawings and abstract engravings by Italian artists, the first abstract art show held in Buenos Aires. Pedro Blake, director of the gallery, presented it, and I wrote two or three articles with the intention to help the public understand the underlying motives of this new artistic endeavor. Indirectly my writing was also aimed at all art professionals, who still seemed unaware a new hu-

---

37   Located on Corrientes Street.

manism had been set in motion a quarter of a century ago. Though it seems unbelievable, the first indications of an awareness concerning avant–garde art did not arise in Argentina until 1944, twenty years after my homecoming and after holding twenty exhibitions.

As I recall all that took place that year, I cannot but mention an exhibition mounted in Bahía Blanca at the end of November. I presented some cups and still–lifes: among the former, two versions of «Enchanted Cup» and two of «Orgy», and among the latter, «Watermelon» and «Vino rosso di Capri».

I forgot to mention that my Chilean treasure came to Argentina in the month of October: she did not remain long for she had committed herself to holding lectures in the provinces of Rosario and Santa Fe. Her stay in Buenos Aires was so brief I had the impression it was a dream. In fact, not feeling that this had taken place at all, I traveled to Chile to see her, and went to the beautiful Colina Mountains for a rest, not far from Santiago. The sun shone like a diamond and the air was pristine. I painted quite a lot there before returning to Santiago, where she and so many friends were awaiting my return.

Back in Buenos Aires, I heard the good news that my dear friend Anton Giulio Bragaglia would soon be in town. He was leading a theatrical company composed of the best young Italian actors and they were planning on performing modern and experimental plays. I did not see Bragalia as much as I would have wanted, for we were both extremely busy: he had brought new plays that he needed to perfect and was absorbed by the rehearsals, and I was overwhelmed by my many tasks. I also spent pleasant evenings with Marinetti, Ungaretti and Mario Puccini when they came to Buenos Aires to attend the Pen Club Congress.

I have always worked hard, but looking back at the years 1937 and 1938, I find them particularly demanding. Moreover, my frequent traveling to Chile had me fulfill my obligations in the most efficient of ways. Without ever neglecting the activities at the Museum nor my classes at the Industrial School of La Plata, where I had begun teaching two years ago, I somehow found time to paint. Besides these four hours of classes, I was asked to teach Art History on a provisional basis in Buenos Aires from April 1937, at the Fine Arts Preparatory School of the Nation [38]. I had accepted the task because I knew that some teaching posts were opening at the end of the year and I had good reasons to believe I would be granted tenure.

«The improviser» [39], «Last Serenade» [40] (both paintings portraying three figures), the «Marú harlequins» [41], «The Soloist» [42], two versions of

---

38   Located at the time at 960 J.E. Uriburu Street.
39   Owned by the National Museum of Fine Arts of Buenos Aires.
40   Owned by the Museum of the International Business Machines of New York.
41   Owned by the Municipal Museum of Fine Arts of Rosario.
42   Owned by Dr. Carlos Vasallo, Santiago de Chile.

«Coparmónica» [43] and two versions of «Checkered Tablecloth», were all painted in 1937. «Romantic Serenade», «Man in my Time» and «The bell» were produced in 1938. And at all times, the memory of a woman's smile etched in my memory, lighting up my horizon or darkening it, depending on the tone of our epistolary communication.

My friendship with Julio Payró dates back to those feverish times, and is one of those unusual and close friendships that have embellished my life. I met him quite by chance on an evening I had dinner with Sibellino. We were leaving the restaurant and heading for a café when the latter let me know he had to stop by at the «La Nación» newspaper. He had to speak to the son of the writer Roberto J. Payró, whose commemorative medal had been entrusted to him, on the tenth anniversary of his death. It was only a matter of minutes, he said. I suggested waiting for him in the hall, but Sibellino invited me upstairs. Julio and I took to each other at once, and right there and then we agreed to meet at a café the following day to pursue our conversation. We realized then, to our greatest joy, that we had many things in common.

I had read some articles of his sent from Brussels, published by the «La Nación» supplement. They were interesting and knowledgeable, and displayed a thorough knowledge on art in Europe. When he returned to Buenos Aires, other texts confirmed that he was not a common writer. Critics that rarely make mistakes in their choice of artists, or who discover talents wherever they may be are indeed unusual. Speaking to him about the problem of painting, everything became clear: he was a painter himself, and had attended the Royal Academy of Brussels. He therefore knew what he was talking about, what a paintbrush was and how to use it. While we chatted, the afternoon turned into evening.

I soon met his mother, the incomparable María Ana and the rest of his family. But it was only later, when he reluctantly showed me his art he had painted both in Belgium and in Argentina that I realized this was the work of an outstanding creator. I asked him why he didn't exhibit his paintings like any other professional, even if that meant provincial or national salons. Julio gazed at me for a long time and changed the subject of conversation. Before long I learned why Julio kept so discretely silent: the obstacles, ah, the obstacles! It is naïf to ask oneself why they arise before the best artists.

When recalling a certain a period of one's life, one remembers it as either long, brief, calm or agitated. To me, 1938 was a hectic year, for it brought me at once unexpected satisfactions and setbacks. I traveled to Chile to meet my other half at the beginning of January, but not before confirming with José A. Merediz, head of the Preparatory School where I was teaching, that the selection of professors would not be held that month. To be completely certain that no error or omission would be made, I also consulted the president of the

---

43 Owned by the San Francisco Museum of Art.

Fine Arts Commission, the engineer Bessio Moreno. They both answered the same thing, that I shouldn't worry about a thing, for the selection, as usual, would take place a few days before the opening of classes.

Need I say that barely arrived in Chile, I was asked to return immediately. How many hindrances have I had to endure in the course of time! Perhaps it is that the passion of the artist possesses the rhythm of a torrent, and torrents alarm: smaller and calmer rivers are preferred. The reigning mediocrity isn't bothered by insignificant and compliant men.

When I returned to Buenos Aires I had already sent the chair and the rest of the academic figures to hell, and thought only about my work. The latter soothed the fever of love that consumed me, appeasing the inevitable everyday aggravations. There exists a pictorial instinct that leads one to see the world as a fabric of mass and values rhythmically distributed, and this instinct had always existed in me, but now, as a mature man of forty–five, instinct had become frantic and despotic. It couldn't be quelled.

When winter arrived, my Chilean woman came to Buenos Aires together with her sister Gloria, so pretty she seemed to have sprung from an antique print. They intended to stay a couple of months and they settled in a small apartment on 700 Juncal Street; my two younger sisters visited them, forming a lively quartet. The transitory yet stable presence of my better half brought me no peace of mind, however, for we were always in conflict; principally, the cause of unrest was that no future could be constructed. Besides, we were two diametrically opposed beings, and this reflected itself at times in our ideas, our concepts, but above all, in our reactions and our behavior towards life. Yet, forceful and hypnotic, love held us captive.

Gabriela Mistral, on her way back to her country, stayed in Buenos Aires for a couple of days. A friend of my sweet adversary, they spent some time together and I accompanied them on some occasions. It was a pleasure to exchange ideas with «this part of Chile» as she would say; her body was stout and her intelligence serene, expanding itself like the waters of a rising tide. The problems of the Latin American continent obsessed her, as did the fate of the Indian; listening to her words, I could not but remember Mariátegui.

In her daily life this exceptionally bright woman was as clumsy as a child. When María Rosa was with her, the former displayed a curious maternal spirit, calling the poet «mamita» [44]. On the day of her departure we accompanied her to the station, promising her to see her soon. Yet fate had it otherwise: fifteen years went by before we met again.

When the first buds on the trees revealed spring had returned, María Rosa and I escaped to the surrounding areas of El Tigre or San Justo, where we practiced horseback riding; those were Alfonsina Storni's two favorite places, and we often met her there.

---

44   "Mamita" in Spanish is an affectionate way of naming one's mother.

On the first days of October, the Municipal Fine Arts Museum, recently opened to the public, inaugurated an exhibition called »Three Expressions of Contemporary Painting», with works by Aquiles Badi and Lino Spilimbergo. I exhibited as well. Each one of us displayed ten works of art, and the show was very much attended. Julio Rinaldini dedicated two important articles to it in the «El Mundo» newspaper, and generally speaking, all the newspapers of Buenos Aires and the provinces wrote quite a lot on it.

It was the first time, and that is why I carefully registered it, that the critics of the country had a change of attitude with respect to my work, considered henceforth with due respect. The Exhibition of French Modern Art that came to Buenos Aires before the war broke out, accompanied by the historian René Huyghe, also contributed to end the stupid confrontations. At that exhibition, Cubist painting was amply represented and it was a stroke of luck that among the work on display, there hung one of the three musicians by Pablo Picasso; the public was thus able to see that it had been ill–informed, and that my trio of players shared nothing in common with Picasso's work. Moreover, there existed nothing that linked my art to that of other contemporary painters, if it wasn't for a certain family air that marks every period and purpose. In this case, I attempted to emphasize the noble structures of painting, granting its new forms a perfect sense of balance, also named the Divine Proportion. In any case, the experience proved fruitful. Most importantly, public opinion modified itself, and nobody ventured from then onward to speak about my being influenced by this or that artist or school, and my painting was never again accused of being cold or repetitive.

Before the exhibition closed at the Municipal Museum, the commission bought «Young woman with green fan», painted in 1925, to add to its collection. They also purchased «Carolita», a small painting that was never displayed –no doubt it would have occupied too much space on the wall. According to the declarations the museum's director published in the newspapers, at the beginning of May 1960, this painting, together with other important work, was stolen from the Museum's store. The media divulged the singular happening with large headings: then a total silence arose. To this day, those paintings have never been found.

The exhibition was drawing to an end when María Rosa decided to spend some days in San Justo with Alfonsina. Both had to leave on a weekday and I was to join them on Saturday. On the eve of the agreed–upon day, Alfonsina told us she was feeling a bit under the weather to go to the country, and María Rosa left by herself.

These were holidays meant to be ill–fated: Alfonsina exchanged her country outing for a trip to Mar del Plata where she put an end to her days, and only a few hours later my beloved had an accident while riding her horse in the morning. Before she was fully recovered, she had to return to her native

Chilean province, where less than three months later –20 January 1939– an earthquake created havoc, in which an appallingly high number of people lost their lives. All means of communication were cut off and the silence that ensued had us live hours of agony. Gloria was still in Buenos Aires and my sisters, who surrounded her lovingly, fully shared her sorrow. The news transmitted by the media was simply terrifying: heavy casualties and devastated cities were words endlessly repeated. The first news arrived from Santiago, notifying us that all of our relatives were safe and sound. My treasured Chilean woman, unharmed, was in Concepción working in the emergency ward, and couldn't leave until it was considered safe for her to do so: the ghost of the typhoid fever hovered upon the city in ruins.

I immediately left for Santiago, wanting to surprise her. Only one train arrived from the South of Chile every morning, so I had to be patient. Unaware I was in Chile, María Rosa was overwhelmed with joy. We fell into each other's arms, knowing this time it would be forever. The earthquake had not only shaken the earth, but had also severed her heavy shackles. She told me later that having seen death in the face and having thus understood the fragility of existence, she saw problems from another angle. Henceforth, the point would consist in finding the necessary inner strength to adapt her life to the new realities.

I returned to Buenos Aires feeling in a serene mood and months flew by. Yet my sorrows were far from ended. On an April dawn, the telephone rang while I was sleeping. One of my brothers was calling long distance from La Plata, announcing my father's sudden death. Shattered, I boarded the first train home.

The weeks passed imperceptibly. I was still immersed in my work, and continued teaching at the Industrial School. I mounted exhibitions, organized art shows and cultural events. The painter Ernesto Riccio, a friend from youth, came to see me at the office. He had recently become director of the Superior Fine Arts School of La Plata. He told me that he had always remembered a topic we had so often tackled: that of abstract composition, subject that I deemed important and even indispensable for a school of Fine Arts. As he was a close friend of the president of the University, Dr. Carlos Rébora, he wanted to know whether I would commit myself to teaching that subject, when the time was ripe. The offer delighted me: I was finally offered the chance to face young people at a Fine Arts school, revealing to them a hundred things with respect to contemporary art, the latter linked to our modern life and the incessant modifications of the world. Since my subject matter was to be abstract composition, the students would be told that form could be suggested rather than described. Form and color operate on their own, independently of theme and images of reality, without therefore disrupting the ties with a visible Nature, source of permanent inspiration. I promised Riccio that in a few days I would present an organic program of the course to him, as well as some explanatory pages, that could solidly sustain my ideas before any board of directors.

I set down everything in writing, handed Riccio the program, indicated possible counter–arguments in case objections were raised, and Riccio walked happily away. He didn't have the same expression when he returned and I supposed his attempt had not been successful. But it had; the board had listened to his arguments with the utmost interest and the chair had been created on the basis of my program; the only inconvenience was that Dr. Rébora had refused to appoint me and had offered the position to a friend of his, instead. As the friend in question hadn't a clue about the matter, the chair of Abstract Composition died without ever having seen the light.

As far as I know, in 1939 no official academy in the world taught Abstract Composition. Thanks to stuffy gentlemen who stifle progress, our country lost the opportunity to be the first to spread this kind of teaching. A few years later, when the movement of abstract art was at its height, our young painters were obliged to practice the new art imperfectly, copying it from the Europeans.

Towards the middle of 1939, I was invited by the Fine Arts Circle and by the National Fine Arts Commission of Montevideo to hold an exhibition. It was my first official retrospective [45] and was held 3 July in the National Salons of Uruguay. Articles had been written prior to the opening, and both the poet Luis Fernando Pombo and myself had spoken on the radio. Argul, together with the painters Bazurro and Laborde, also helped in organizing the show.

I can honestly say that the exhibition was a success. The art critic José Pedro Argul wrote a long and brilliant review on the show in the «El Plata» newspaper of Montevideo. Naturally, not all opinions were favorable, and mordant articles were published, while the authors concealed themselves under pseudonyms. However, I wouldn't let this bother me, for I knew it was the price to pay. What disconcerted me for a moment was Torre García's odd attitude, the old white–bearded painter with the compelling eyes. He marched into the salon followed by a group of students, glaring fiercely across the large hall and left, leaving all of us dumbfounded.

That same year I produced the first sketches of what was to become a long series of «suns». Since childhood I had sensed the Sun and the Light were shrouded in deep mysteries, and their secret nature fascinated me. When, as an adolescent, I read in art books that mystery lurked in the shadows, I mentally objected to the writer's opinion. Mystery exists in light, an obstinate voice within me repeated. Back in La Plata, and listening to that voice, I painted pictures in which sunlight formed part of the composition, like that basket filled with onions, next to a window. (The painting that I'm

---

45   The second and last lecture was held at the National Museum of Fine Arts of Santiago de Chile.

alluding to, I later destroyed). Mystery exists in light... I verified this when I saw the works of the great Masters in Italy: it was enveloped in a light of dazzling sweetness, and not in the gloomy chiaroscuro favored by Caravaggio! More than once I told myself that capturing that mystery in a single, violent brilliance, would be an act of magic.

«Lights in the landscape» is one of my first attempts to seize light with an aesthetic purpose in mind, whereas in «Light–Elevation» (1916) I try to concentrate light in a cluster. Then come «The blue cave of Capri» (1915 and 1918), «Window», «Solo» (1922), «Shadows in the window» (1924 and 1925), «The house of the poet» (1925 to 1935) and a couple of still–lifes. «Watermelons» (1936), however, is where I tackle light with greater audacity.

To seize the sun and bring it inside the home, something that has always been Man's greatest aspiration was only one step away, and I undertook the project with great determination. My attempts are visible in the 1939 sketches. Yet I struggled with other aesthetic problems, to which I found solutions that escaped logic: I placed the Sun, which I considered corporeal, within a room, where walls, doors and balconies existed. It not only filled this space with light and radiance that completely transformed it, but collided against the objects producing shadows, and in its double repercussion, luminous darkness. Objects became robustly alive in the sun's brilliance.

Attempting to capture light, with the sun as an «active form», took many years to complete. Today I still believe that it was an absolute creation and that if I had developed it in other latitudes (not in other times), its acceptance, and above all its repercussion, would have been wider. I possess only one painting that belongs to that series: «Blank book», achieved in 1946, and shown at every exhibition in Italy between 1952 and 1953. The following year, in Milan, we visited the Triennial Exhibition held at the former Palazzo Reale, and noticed several paintings by different authors that had the sun as the main figure.

It was in Milan that it became clear to me that a perfect work needs the balance of a thoughtful composition and exact hues. There are too many painters that are still unaware that color is an expressive instrument, as communicative as notes in music. One doesn't compose a requiem as one does a ballad, in the same way that elation is not manifested in sounds of pain. The various moods have different pictorial intonations, just as our voices have different timbres to express each cry of the soul.

A marriage is easily formalized; another matter is to annul it. The procedures in Chile were painstakingly slow, adapting themselves to the rhythm of the law. But now María Rosa felt morally free to establish other ties. Our engagement was a fact, and we were dreaming about our future together. In the summer of 1940, I saw the critic Jorge Romero Brest in Montevideo. As he told me he wished to meet Torres García, I offered to present the painter to him. I rang him up, and with his usual complaisance, the artist told me he would receive us the following day in the afternoon. On 11 February, day of the meeting, the «El Debate» newspaper of Montevideo published an article called «Pettoruti pioneers the new art», written by him. How to reconcile his attitude displayed six months ago with his present deferential behavior?

Another surprise awaited me that afternoon: the painter had invited a group of youngsters in order to give them a lecture on my art. No sooner had I introduced Romero Brest to him and thanked him for the article that he sat us down next to the other guests and began his lecture, illustrating it with paintings of mine he projected onto a screen. His presentation over and the youths gone, Torres García showed us his paintings. Among the most recent ones was a series of portraits of famous painters; I recall Leonardo and Velázquez. Yet they were so unlike his previous work that both Romero Brest and I asked him what had motivated his change of style. He gave us quite a few explanations, none of which seemed valid.

My first retrospective in my home country was held at the «Amigos del Arte» in the month of June. I had removed the glass that covered my paintings, for I felt encouraged by an increasingly respectful public. The show coincided with the publication of a monograph on my work written by Leonardo Estarico in French, and edited by «Il Milione» of Milan. María Rosa traveled from Chile to attend the ceremony, yet my mood darkened on the afternoon of the inauguration upon learning that Italy was at war, supporting Germany.

The public of Buenos Aires of 1940 was not the one of 1924; on the contrary, people looked at my paintings with respect, tired of superficial and hackneyed renderings. As usual, many art lovers and friends attended the inauguration, but few artists. In any case, from the day it opened to the last, many people, including students from several faculties and Fine Arts academies, attended the show.

One morning, I had the pleasure of receiving almost the whole student body of the Superior School of Art, whose spokesman told me the painter Emilio Centurión had not only recommended the exhibition but was asking me to speak about my work.

As Julio Payró was standing there, quite by chance, I introduced him to the students. I told them they were lucky to meet one of the finest art critics, and that if they so wished, he would perhaps say something about my work. Julio accepted willingly. I believe I have already mentioned that I liked Julio from the day we met, and this feeling became stronger as time went by. Never have I heard him speak in an authoritarian tone: rather, he reaffirmed what his interlocutor already knew. His discretion was bound to please me, not to mention his clarity of thought: I have always believed that unintelligible concepts are signs of intellectual confusion, if not sheer ignorance. Knowledge must be transmitted plainly and logically, and this also applies to the arts.

One noon, Rinaldi came to the show together with a friend. The latter invited us for a drink at his nearby home, and we accepted. Upon entering the living room, I noticed my «Self–portrait» I had painted in 1918 and had subsequently lost track of placed upon a white easel. The owner of the house told me he had purchased it some years ago, when he was still a Law student, at an auction at the Municipal Bank, for seventeen pesos. It was one of my paintings sold through monthly installments, and I have detested this method ever since.

While the exhibition was running its course at the «Amigos del Arte» Association, Julio Payró, Julio Rinaldini and Jorge Romero Brest decided with one accord to ask Mr. Antonio Santamarina, the new president of both the National Committee of Fine Arts and the Provincial Committee, to buy an important panting of mine for the National Museum. They chose «The improviser», (measuring 195cm x 140cm) portraying tree musicians. The Committee had the nerve to offer only two thousand pesos, alleging a lack of funds. Embarrassed, I accepted the sum, for I didn´t want to offend my three friends; moreover, I wanted no–one to think I was making a fuss over money matters, especially if I could serve my country.

The sculptor Alfredo Bigatti came to tell me a banquet was being planned for me, and assuming I would accept, had brought me the list of organizers. I gave it a quick look: it was long and would have taken me a long time to read. Bigatti pointed out that a certain painter´s signature was missing, but the issue seemed irrelevant to me. However, I was surprised at Bigatti´s concern. I asked him what grudges could this artist hold against me, and Bigatti replied the painter was angry at not having found his work at the Museum. So irked was he, that he had written the president of the Provincial Committee a letter of complaint. What Bigatti said was true: the artist´s work was not at the Museum, for it was mediocre and could not form part of the permanent collection.

Though the complaint had no follow–up, I was disconcerted, for the painter´s intention had been to harm me. However, nothing had come of it, for everyone knew I was a man of integrity: no vote of mine had ever been cast to acquire work sponsored by the Provincial Committee, except if I deemed it acceptable or worthy of a museum. Throughout my life I have always acted with the same impartiality, as I had quickly understood that the strength of the great is based upon the flaws of the weak.

I would also like to mention, while speaking about those years in La Plata, that its Museum could have easily possessed its own building. There stood a theatre on the island inside the woods, in front of the Museum of Natural History, that was no longer being used and I felt it could adapt itself to the needs of the Museum. I immediately went to see the government minister Roberto J. Noble, who replied that there wasn't any money for such expenses. I told him that if he helped me, the makeover could be achieved through the administration. I had carefully studied the theatre, noticing its large spaces could be used for storage. Moreover, it possessed two rooms, one for restoration purposes and the other for photographs, as well as many walls on which to hang the paintings. On the other hand, the stone, bronze and marble sculptures would be placed in the open, where they really belonged: the bridge, which connected the theatre to the woods, would turn into a drawbridge, requiring only a night watchman. I offered to design the plans, which would then be taken to the corresponding Ministry.

As had been the case with my friend Barletta, everyone showed understanding and good will. Noble accepted and assured me of his support. It goes without saying that I was overjoyed, and this happiness motivated me to work relentlessly. However, one day the Secretary informed me the project had crumbled like a house of cards. What extraordinary thing had happened? Well, Mr. Noble had met the senator Antonio Santamarina, and wanting to surprise him, had told him about my project. But the President of the Provincial Committee replied that he wished to construct a large ad–hoc building, with the sole purpose of storing works of art. Had Mr.Noble only paid heed to my request! That is why, almost thirty years later, the first Argentine province still doesn't have a permanent museum.

More than once have I suggested, in the course of these talks, that one would have to be an irate Jupiter in order to change our country's habits. If I were to mention all the lost opportunities I would need tons of paper, and if I were to reveal all the infamies perpetrated against me in the course of my seventeen years of public service as head of an art museum, it might sound unbelievable.

I have had to endure so many vexations, from the stupidity of some politicians, (often obliging me to give them a piece of my mind) to the malice of many pseudo–artists (I emphasize «pseudo», for real artists always possess a noble heart) that when I think about it, I wonder where I drew my strength of spirit. At times, I would vent my frustration by temporarily leaving the Museum, finding consolation in being around my father, my brothers Louis and José and my sister Catalina.

Chapter 26

Home and Friendships

On the day first day of fall 1941, my Chilean woman and I got married; at long last all the hurdles that had prevented our union were a thing of the past. The ritual was sober and no wedding party was held. Two loyal friends acted as witnesses, and after the ceremony, everyone left. Carolita and Lía Esther were waiting for us at our home to congratulate us, pleasantly surprising us.

From that moment onwards, though we frequented many people, as much from the capital city as from the rest of the country and abroad, only a handful of friends shared the intimacy of our home. Those who came to visit me or wished to see my paintings were received in the evenings, but otherwise María Rosa and I spent our days working, even on holidays. From time to time we accepted a friend's invitation to spend a day at the countryside or we took advantage of the weekend for a change of scenery.

Only Sibellino was allowed to join us, especially on those Sunday morning outings, when we would ride our bicycles along the Costanera Avenue or through the parks of Palermo. Sibellino would start off from his home on Baigorria Street and meet us at the Fishermen's Pier or elsewhere, so as to continue the ride together. Sibellino was my most receptive interlocutor in artistic matters and one of the most knowledgeable. When he decided to stay over at our house, he would invariably head for the bathroom where he would leave his toothbrush.

Here is an anecdote that illustrates the extent in which he had become part of our lives: one night, while the three of us were having dinner (served by Martina, our Chilean «bonne à tout faire», who ended up getting married in Paris), someone rang to invite us for dinner the following Saturday. I answered that unfortunately we were leaving for the port of Colonia on that same day and another date was agreed upon. Back at the table, conversation resumed where it had been left off. Suddenly, Sibellino became morose and began complaining about his bad luck. According to him, every time he made plans, an evil goblin shattered them. Completely in the dark about what grave and singular event vexed our friend, and feeling truly sorry, we asked Antonio what the matter was. He replied that he had hired a young model for that particular Saturday, but as she lived a long way away and had no phone, he would have to travel in order to tell her. «Tell her what?» María Rosa and I asked in unison. Sibellino opened his eyes wide, as if not grasping our question: «Why, I'm going with you to Colonia!»

The anecdotes about Sibellino are endless, and he was as good as gold, providing no one spoke contemptuously of the arts that ruled «the divine creation of things». With Margherita Sarfatti, in exile in Buenos Aires since 1939, he held vivid conversations about painting, often inviting himself over to dinner, and convincing our maid to prepare him a particular dish. He also discussed art with the critic Jorge Romero Brest. One evening, as we were sitting around the table at the painter Gómez Cornet's home after dinner, an argument concerning art criticism broke out. It is fair to add that when Sibellino did not respect an idea, he expressed himself rather offensively. On this occasion, he vehemently pointed out that it isn't the art critic who consolidates an artist's prestige, but the work of the artist himself. He ended his lecture with these words: «To discuss art, sir, one has to practice it».

A heavy silence ensued. Tears ran along the cheeks of the young critic who was still learning the trade, for he felt he had been unjustly attacked. Not knowing what to do in such an awkward circumstance, I rose and invited everyone to an ice-cream on the corner. Some days later, in the «Argentina Libre» newspaper, an allusive article was printed: «One has to practice art in order to discuss it».

This happened when Romero Brest still believed in artists as superior beings and felt deeply hurt by their inconsiderate behavior. He wished to get to know them closely, and I still recall how he attempted to reach out to them, and how dejected he would return, so petty and selfish had he found them. He couldn't understand how, in spite of all the obstacles, I never lost faith. The trick, I told him, was to shun pessimistic and sterile thoughts. Today Romero Brest no longer looks for authentic artists; he produces them at his convenience. Long gone are the years in which his heart and mind were sincere, though I have the feeling that when he is totally by himself, he misses those invigorating times. By the way, he was the critic who wrote the most about me: sixteen articles, I believe, were published between 1940 and 1948.

Sibellino was a good friend of the sculptor Rogelio Yrurtia, and the latter a bitter enemy of modern art. They both continually argued about my work, which the old artist refused to see: what he had seen in reproductions was sufficient. Not taking «no» for an answer, Sibellino harassed him to such a point that the sculptor became curious. This is how he visited my 1940 retrospective at the «Amigos del Arte». Not long after, he invited me to dinner. That evening he showed me his studio and his home. Walking through a room, he told me, stuttering as usual: «Th...th...this is ...is...a...a p... painting Pi...Pi... ca...sso...sso ga...gave me when I w...was in Pa...Paris. Do ...do you c...c...onsider this a... avant–garde art?» We then proceeded to have dinner in the garden, together with his talented wife, the painter Lía Correa Morales, and Antonio Sibellino. While we were eating, Yrurtia asked me to define modern art. Lightheartedly I replied it was best to leave those rather arduous topics for another day, since we were all enjoying ourselves. But he insisted, and Sibellino came to the rescue, quite graphically indeed. Drawing an invisible curve in the air, as if synthesizing the concept of movement, Sibellino explained: «Watch this, Master...Bang! The hare jumps, flees from the hunter, and runs off. The modern artist draws the animal with one stroke; no more is needed, whereas the old–fashioned artist wants to reproduce every little hair. Do you get my point?» Yrurtia didn´t reply but seemed to brood over the situation. Trying to ease the rising tension, I said a few words about my friend´s concise and humorous explanation, and the evening was saved. However, Yrurtia rang up Sibellino very early the following morning, asking him point–blank: «S...so I´m...I´m the one who draw... draws every li...little hair, y...young man? I ...I ex... expect you at...at... h...home this af...afternoon».

Sibellino had barely arrived that a violent quarrel arose. So violent in fact, that Yrurtia sprang to his arms collection, pulling out a saber; Sibellino, as swift as lightning, reached for another, and both of them ran around the table, dodging the blows. Yrurtuia was the first one to come to his senses when the situation became truly serious, as if he at once had realized the horror of it all. Shaking, he said: «My d...dear Si...Sibellino, we are p...playing, arent´t w...we?» To which Sibellino hastily replied: «Of course, Master,» and both lay down their sabers. «But», added Sibellino, when commenting the strange episode to me, «I didn´t lose sight of him, for that was no game! If I hadn´t seized the other saber, he would have split me in half, he was so furious!!»

Some time later, the «El Argentino» newspaper published three articles of mine on the teaching of art. I sent them to Yrurtia for I wanted him to see that both old and modern artists worked with the same amount of dedication. The old sculptor called me at the Museum, telling me he had read the articles. He wished to congratulate me, and not knowing how to better express his appreciation, he paid me the nicest compliment he could think of of, saying: «They a... are so g...good, Pet...toruti, they l...look like I w...wrote them myself».

At one point I mentioned that many Argentine artists, excepting perhaps one or two, had never attended my inaugurations. I could say of course they hadn't wished to disturb me at such important times, but unfortunately, that isn't the case. Because I like to be fair, I must add that when there was a dinner, whether to celebrate or to make amends, they came in throngs. Why this ambiguous behavior? This is something I no longer ask myself.

In general, my colleagues did not seek my friendship nor did they want it, though some I visited often and others I invited to my frugal table, something they gladly accepted, but did not reciprocate. They always seemed to be afraid of going too far, of breaking a rule. I felt that any attempt of getting closer represented an act of treason to them, like when one infringes a tacit agreement existing among brothers. To be around me was to appreciate me, and this would have meant recognizing my privileges. Undoubtedly, these reflections do not arise without cause, for I associate them at this very instant to an event that took place a long time ago. An artist was being honored at a ceremony, yet I cannot recall who it was. The National Salon awards had just been given out, and the painter Enrique Larrañaga, while regretting the jury had not taken me in account, wished to justify himself to me. In his usual confidential tone, as if addressing himself to a man that rises above the small intrigues of the trade union, he said: «You know, Emilio, how these things work: if we reward you, we get in trouble».

You can't keep someone permanently at bay without generating resentment. However, nothing of the sort happened, perhaps because I followed my grandfather's advice and kept my energy for more important things. Nonetheless many thought me bitter, accusing me of adopting unfair attitudes. They said my behavior was selfish and mean, and that I played down the value of great artists to the gallery owners and art critics, as if talent could be concealed simply through a conjuring trick. Many people are unaware that their work or their names often appeared at gallery presentations, in collectors' lists or in art reviews, thanks to an opportune intervention. I myself secretly bought, whenever I could, some small works of art that I later gave away or still own.

May this help to show that in spite of my fits of anger, I never responded in the same way to the unkind climate that surrounded me, and not once did I challenge the recognition my colleagues enjoyed. It was evident that if my work were praised, it would have meant public recognition.

If someone ought to complain about a vile and systematic opposition it certainly should be me. For instance, did anyone recommend me when the Argentine Pavilion, at the 1937 International Fair in Paris, needed to be decorated in a «contemporary» fashion? And did anyone say I lived in Buenos Aires when foreign delegations especially came to the capital city with the intention to get to know the art of the Argentines? It was mere chance if at times I ran into the representatives of those commissions, who couldn't hide their surprise to see me alive, for they had been led into believing I had vanished into thin air. I recall the rather clamorous meeting with the exquisite American thinker Lincoln Kirstein, representative of the «good neighbor» policy, recommended by Roosevelt. On his tour through the southern hemisphere, he acquired works by the most prestigious artists at the request of the Modern Art Museum of New York and other museums in the United States. That afternoon, on the eve of his departure, Kirstein was holding a reception at the American embassy. When the usher loudly announced my name, Kirstein literally threw himself upon me, expressing his surprise and pleasure to see me in Buenos Aires. Fortunately, two colleagues of mine with whom he was speaking were still present, and I answered: «Why, I live only a few steps away from the Embassy! You should have asked my excellent friends for my address and telephone number!» My statement produced such perplexity, that I realized I had hit the nail on the head. Kirstein gazed at both men as if demanding an explanation, but as they averted their gaze I understood I had been excluded in the nastiest of ways. And yet, I never paid them back in the same coin, especially when the prestige of the country was at stake. When other «good neighbor» delegates visiting our capital city came to see me —as for instance Mildred Constantine, in charge of organizing an exhibition of engraving for a museum in New York— as usual I set aside all prejudice and offense to make sure our nation was well represented.

Oddly enough, all those people who would have wanted to see me vanish into thin air acknowledged my presence. On one occasion, the painter Orlando Pierri told me a savory anecdote, which I faithfully repeat: one of the great Argentine masters of painting had manifested his enthusiasm about a marvelous formula a friend had brought from Italy, meant to improve the quality of the pigments used in oils. Pierri soon realized that he himself had given this person the formula while in Paris, the ingredients of which I had printed in order to save time and which in turn I had handed over to Pierri. The latter found it fantastic that a recipe «made in Argentina» had crossed the Atlantic twice as an imported product, and had told this great master he was using a «Pettoruti–made» formula. Whether or not this amused my distinguished colleague I have no idea.

With the exception of Antonio Sibellino and Lucio Fontana, who resided a few years in Argentina, the only artist who assiduously frequented our home was Ramón Gómez Cornet. Over the course of time we saw one another often, but these reciprocal visits decreased in frequency and our friendship weakened. Ramón, always so affectionate, did not explain why he no longer sought the opportunity to visit us: it was Sibellino who opened my eyes, revealing what the painter had told him: our friendship was costing him dear, for all his colleagues were giving him the cold shoulder.

As I search my memory, I try to recall which other artists came to visit us, yet it's futile task. Perhaps José Fioravanti, though his visits were sporadic, and his brother Octavio, whom I saw even less. Almost none of my colleagues got to know me. Those people that sometimes came to our house were motivated by interest, yet I did all I could for them, without any kind of resentment. Only one Argentine artist came to offer me something: Lino Spilimbergo. He wanted me to teach a course on composition in the province of Tucumán on a temporary basis. I turned the proposal down, however, for I never accepted anything that had to do with the government of President Perón. When the latter rose to power I was already head of the Museum for thirteen years, and that's why I stayed.

Quite by chance, as often happens, I noticed that the National Museum of Fine Arts didn't own a single painting by Ramón Gómez Cornet, whereas its halls were full of mediocre work. Determined to obtain one of his paintings, but lacking the money to purchase it, I achieved my goal through national subscription. After communicating my project to the artist and choosing the painting together (we decided on the portrait of his daughter Rosario), I mobilized my friends of the provinces, who appointed, just as I had done in the capital city, a committee in charge of collecting the signatures and funds. The cities of Bahía Blanca, Córdoba, Mendoza, Rosario, Santa Fe and Santiago del Estero responded favorably. The money raised fulfilled my expectations, and Gómez Cornet obtained more than a thousand pesos for his painting. As was to be expected, the Fine Arts Committee did not hold a session to prevent the entrance of an Argentine artist to our National Museum.

The Second World War, akin to the Spanish Civil War, brought many Spanish and Italian intellectuals and artists to our land, while many Argentines came back home. The last ones to arrive were Domingo Candia and Lucio Fontana, both natives of the city of Rosario. The former I had met in Florence, but we had become friends on his first trip to Buenos Aires, a few years back; the latter I did not know, and he introduced himself trough a letter written by a very dear friend of mine from Milan, Raffaello Giolli. Fontana told me that in Milan artists talked about me as though I still lived among them, considering me an Italian painter. This artist's cordiality elicited mine and I received him with open arms. At first we didn't see much of each other, for he settled in Rosario. When he moved to Buenos Aires, I introduced him to an environment he wasn't familiar with. His first surprise, and mine, was our colleagues' hostile response; they rejected him as an artist and made every effort to flaunt their antagonism. Imagining him forlorn and helpless, one of these artists insolently asked him to reproduce some of his pieces in marble, while another wanted him to pour plaster on one of his humongous sculptures. Fontana couldn't understand why they asked him to do such things. Vehemently I told him in Italian that they were taking advantage of him and that he shouldn't tolerate any humiliations. And since the merit of artists, as Sibellino had said so well, is consolidated by the artists themselves I took it upon me to let everyone know who Fontana was.

Eventually things improved and Fontana felt thrilled to be in Buenos Aires. Animated and cheerful, Fontana complained about artists constantly picking at each other instead of combining forces, considering the Government so neglected cultural affairs. Fontana believed artists had to reach for a common goal, attaining such a might that politicians would no longer ignore them. Fontana listened in dismay when I told him of my trials, especially when I warned him that in our country creative work was a solitary undertaking. I also warned him that his most commendable aspirations would be thwarted. Yet Fontana replied that it was a matter of imposing oneself. Laughing mischievously, he said I had to fight back, but that I was either too compliant or too old to do so.

I was fond of his candid nature, his childish way of dodging difficult situations. Completely baffled if asked a reasonable question, his fantasy embroidered adventures without paying any heed to logic, and there was nothing more amusing than the bizarre situations he had witnessed while still living in Fascist Italy.

Soon he got to know my everyday friends, starting with Sibellino. Both of them were good people, and they were bound to get along; our common conversations were always extremely pleasant. I remember that a little after Fontana's arrival both men sent their work to the National Salon. Neither one had ever sent anything before, for Fontana was living in Italy and Sibellino had never been motivated to do so. Fontana complained about the fact humorously: «Darn it, Sibellino, now that I'm in the country you compete with me for the awards. How about solving the problem with a bicycle race: the one who loses doesn't present any work at all». But immediately after Fontana added: «Now seriously speaking, don't worry if you take first prize; between us there is no possible rivalry, for we each seek something else». Sibellino wished to know what his colleague meant and Fontana answered: «I seek light more than form, expansion more than restriction. I work quickly so as to maintain my impulse and that is why I avoid marble; it is an exigent material and I enjoy freedom. You, instead, are measured.» «Yes», replied Sibellino, «I work in a relaxed mood. I like to do and undo, until I achieve my goal».

They say that good things, just like bad ones, never come alone. I was very happy with my new life, my treasured Chilean woman at my side, and my group of dear friends, when unexpected news arrived. Walking along Florida Street, I ran into Romero Brest and his friend, Luis Miguel Baudizzone, who worked together with Enrique Gil, representative of the

Guggenheim Foundation in Argentina. They told me a letter had just arrived at Gil's office: I was invited to visit several important American museums for a period of eight months.

The news left me euphoric; I had never dreamed of such a gift and wondered who could have been so generous. Thinking back, however, I recalled I had received the visit of three American people who had come to La Plata in order to see the Museum. They had inquired about its organization and operation, telling me they had traveled to many South American countries in order to visit their museums. Some time later, Grace Mc Can Morley, the director of the San Francisco Museum, one of the most intelligent, sensitive and charming people I have ever met, informed me this visit had long been been programmed, and that if they had paid me a last moment visit, it was because no–one had been able to tell them where I lived...

She saw my work and found out, because I told her, that I also directed the La Plata Fine Arts Museum. From that moment onwards, we became immersed in the fascinating topic of museums, and that evening we had dinner together so as to pursue our conversation. The following day she travelled with me to La Plata and I showed her the other facet of my activity.

In the course of time, the Museum had become a genuine museum. Thanks to my insistence, it was now located on the ground floor of the Dardo Rocha Passage, with its own entrance on 48 Street. It had offices for the increased number of employees, a large specialized library, large storage rooms, and many halls for the many works of art–it already possessed a thousand. Exhibitions were held twice a year and cultural events, every week.

Grace Morley and her three compatriots were favorably impressed by the Museum and its organization. Undoubtedly her opinion, very much appreciated in the United States, had a lot to do with the invitation. The host, as I soon found out, was the Committee for the Inter–American Artistic and Intellectual Relations, presided over by Mr. Henry Allen Moe.

I was barely getting over my surprise that I received another: the San Francisco Museum of Art invited me to exhibit my work at the main museums of the United States, assuming all responsibilities and costs from the moment my forty paintings left my studio. Moreover, I was told, my art would be insured against all damage.

In high spirits, I felt this double present compensated for so many years of struggle. As far as I was concerned, I would have left at once, yet something ignoble was being hatched by the ruling cultural entity of the Province; I sensed the danger and knew that in my absence no–one would parry the blow. I thus accepted the invitation, requesting a change of dates. Fortunately, the American organization accepted: I was to leave for San Francisco the following year, in September 1942. That city was to be the first leg of my journey, and my work was shipped a few months before my departure.

Grace Morley, with whom I kept continually in touch, wished my first exhibit to be held in New York. I understood that in order to avoid any friction, she was prioritizing this large city, but considered it my duty to decline this proposal. After all it been San Francisco that had invited me, and it was also fair to hold my first exhibit there. This is what I requested and this is what was done, though Grace Morley had already shipped my work to New York when this agreement was reached.

During that period I also met Mr. John Griffiths, the cultural attaché of the United States Embassy. We became good friends, and through him, I found out how some people, invited by his government, behaved. One afternoon, while discussing the details of my trip in his office, I noticed some issues of «Ars», an Argentine magazine, lying about. On the wall, there hung a pseudo–Realist painting, that I had seen exhibited in Buenos Aires some years ago. The peculiar thing was that a large V of victory had been added to it, in order to honor Winston Churchill. Griffith, who didn´t know how to get rid of the painting, told me its author, on whom an article had been published in «Ars», had sent him this material in order to seek «some publicity», as he was planning to travel to the United States. And as far as this gentleman´s trip is concerned, I have no idea whether he traveled or not.

Chapter 27

In the United States

I took a plane to San Francisco on 17 September 1942. In order to fly one needed a special pass and the flight was delayed because of the war. The pass prevented the military officers to take the passenger's place at one of the stopping points on the Pacific. My pass arrived at last; María Rosa, on the other hand, had to obtain hers in Washington through Nelson Rockefeller.

I arrived in San Francisco after the opening of the exhibition. Both the authorities and personnel of the Museum received it enthusiastically, and everyone was very pleasant. The show, wonderfully mounted in the two large main halls, caused an extraordinary effect. A memorable reception was held in my honor, and artists and intellectuals of the region had been especially invited to attend it. While at the cocktail party, I met many abstract painters of the Pacific who later became renowned, and I visited quite a number of their studios. The exhibit attracted large crowds, and remained open for two months. It then toured many other States, and many of the paintings were sold. Two years later, it returned to the San Francisco Museum.

As I'm reminiscing, the following anecdote springs to mind: some days after my arrival at the beautiful Californian city, I received a note from Grace Morley informing me that the Museum's Committee was meeting that afternoon to discuss the price of my paintings. She urged me to attend the reunion. The news greatly disturbed me, for I had heard that many Latin American artists raised their prices upon arriving to the United States, complaining later they hadn't sold anything. The only thing I had done was to change pesos into dollars, and it disturbed me they could think me unscrupulous.

Determined, however, not to lower the price of my paintings, I wrote some lines of apologies claiming to be feeling somewhat ill, and remained at the hotel writing letters. The following day, at the Museum, they showed me the new list of prices, and I realized with amazement they had been considerably raised: fifty percent in the worst of cases. Meanwhile, the Committee purchased «Coparmónica», for it to become part of their collection.

In her comfortable automobile, Grace Morley led me around to visit the area, sprinkled with beautiful parks: the Yosemite National Park was especially gorgeous. Together we attended the annual meeting of the museum directors of California, held in Los Angeles. Points of view were exchanged, and cultural programs adopted, and I myself had to give a speech with an interpreter standing next to me; some of my colleagues were surprised to find out I directed the Museum of Fine Arts in La Plata, and not the Museum of Natural History, famous for its fine specimens pertaining to the vegetable, mineral and animal kingdom.

I became close friends with Grace Morley, and when time came for me to move on to my following destination, we were sorry to part. The rest of the journey I spent traveling towards New York, visiting the large Midwest centers. I stopped at the Great Canyon, of breathtaking beauty, and many were the cities and the beautiful museums I found on my way.

María Rosa and I met in New York. We spent Christmas and New Year together, surrounded by our new and old friends. We were lucky Archipenko, Zadkine, René D'Harnoncourt and Henry Taylor, among others, were in New York. I had become acquainted with Archipenko and Zadkine in Europe; Taylor was head of the Metropolitan Museum of New York and had seen my paintings. He and his wife had often been our guest, and the four of us got along well. In New York our friendship strengthened; we didn't often dine together, but we had lunch regularly at the Metropolitan, where Taylor had a private dining room. He is the one who wrote the preface to the catalogue of my New York exhibition. As far as D'Harnoncourt is concerned, I had met him in Buenos Aires, and had been drawn to him by his exquisite charm.

We met so many Europeans in New York that it would be impossible to name them all. This city was regarded as a safe haven for many European intellectuals and artists. We mainly frequented French people, or foreigners arriving from France; this is how we became friends with the composer Edgar Varèse who entertained in his apartment, where many French people gathered. One evening he invited Fernand Léger and Geneviève Tabouis, the famous journalist, who spent the whole night talking, for she was so interesting her audience constantly renewed itself. The only Spanish–speaking intellectual I recall having spoken to was the Spaniard Federico de Onís.

While in New York, we frequently saw Archipenko and his wife. At night we sloshed about the wet snow, walking through the cold city and chatting away. Archipenko told us how he had been obliged to interrupt his trip to Japan on account of an earthquake and remain in the United States, and how, because of the war, his studio had closed due to a shortage of students. It was his wife who helped him out by working in a factory; this humiliated and mortified him. He was going through a hard time in which he doubted everything, including the future of his art, and had made up his mind to remain passive. María Rosa and I must have been convincing, for Archipenko began to work. A few months later he produced ten large drawings that I exhibited in La Plata and in Buenos Aires, but that is another story.

On an afternoon in January 1943, my New York exhibition officially opened at the National Academy of Design with a huge buffet froid; I had not expected such a vast and select public. We happened to be there quite by chance, because the exhibitions, organized by the San Francisco Museum, were held independently of my presence in the United States.

I had the satisfaction of meeting many old friends again. Among these was Lionello Venturi, who was quite moved by my paintings. However, this didn't prevent us from engaging in a major argument a week later, over tea at his apartment. At the time, he believed the greatest exponent of avant-garde art to be Rouault, who was inclined towards the gothic and the religious. Though I respect Rouault as an artist, I found him old fashioned, and told Venturi I preferred the art of the 12th century French stained glass. Our longest discussion revolved around the Fauves. We both agreed that if Braque's painting, mathematical and musical, was the outcome of a reasoning mind, and that if Matisse's art was significant, they both failed, however, to represent modern expression in its totality.

A short film was shot while the exhibition was on, and when the cameras began to roll I was in the halls with Zadkine and two American painters whose names I have forgotten. We all said a few words, and apparently the film was shown in the United States; in Buenos Aires it was announced on large billboards.

Like most refugees, Zadkine tightened his belt often. I was therefore surprised when he invited us to a cocktail party at his studio, for he had just told us he had no idea how to pay the rent that was about to fall due. Henry Taylor and his wife came to fetch us and together we went to the reception. Zadkine's studio was located in Greenwich Village, on the ground floor of an old building. As one entered, on the right hand side there was a small room. On a table, two or three glasses and a bottle of American whisky, almost completely empty. There also was a couch, on which Léger was gloomily reclining. He rose to greet us, and as soon as Taylor had left the room, he told us he was hiding there because he couldn't speak a word of English. On top of that, he had no intention of learning it. There were many people in Zadkine's large studio; the latter solicitously looked after his guests, showing them his sculptures as he had done in Paris twenty years ago, except that this time the visitors were almost all American. We didn't stay long, for we didn't know anyone. Later, Zadkine told us he had given that reception in the hope of selling something, and that he had managed to do so.

On the afternoon the show was closing at the National Academy, we were together with Archipenko and Angelina. At that point, Alfred Barr, director of the Museum of Modern Art of New York, showed up. He had come to purchase a painting. We had seen each other a couple of times and had had lunch with his wife, of Italian extraction, with whom I had held long conversations in Italian. There was a disconcerting silence when Barr arrived, for he and Archipenko were at odds. (At the time, Archipenko was in conflict with everybody, but then again, he had always felt that officialdom was composed of useless people). Magnanimously, Barr requested Archipenko's assistance in choosing the painting, occasion in which both coincided, if only about the selection of the work that had to go to the Museum. When the men in charge of taking down the paintings began doing their jobs, both Archipenko and Barr bawled at them. Indeed, they had burst into the halls ever so rudely. Why this team of uncouth men? We later learned that the draft had deprived museums of their specialized personnel.

We left New York to visit Washington for a few days, where the director of the National Gallery[46] warmly received me. It was a difficult time for Argentines on a diplomatic mission in the United States, for Argentina was the only country in Latin America that maintained its ties with the Axis nations. Yet the director of the National Gallery led me around the Museum most courteously, enabling me to fully appreciate its complexity. Everything was minutely planned: the electronic device that calculated the number of visitors in every hall and measured the level of humidity present in the breaths, the guards practicing shooting on the roofs of the building, aiming without respite at moving dummies, the complicated installation of an admirably regulated light that illuminated the works of art from nine in the morning till midnight. To my surprise, after my long and fruitful tour of the museum, its director invited me to a lunch attended by several artistic personalities.

I also met Mr. Roger Cahill, president of the WPA, who while the war raged on, assisted so many American and foreign artists living in the United States. He held a memorable dinner at a great Chinese restaurant that included over twenty different dishes...besides rice. The ambiance was ever so cordial, devoid of etiquette. We even imitated Velazquez' dwarfs when leaving, including D' Harnoncourt, which is no small feat, given his enormous stature.

With Nelson Rockefeller, assigned by Roosevelt to handle the Latin American cultural affairs (and whose Spanish is pretty good by the way), I

---

46   Also called Mellon Gallery.

held a lengthy conversation in his office about these matters. I expressed my thoughts clearly and explicitly, the way I have always done it. As far as my passage through so many cities is concerned, I can only say I was often surprised. For instance, I unexpectedly stumbled upon a Rodin museum in Philadelphia, entirely dedicated to his work, and where not one piece by this great French sculptor is missing. I also ran into a painting by Arcimboldo, in a town as small as Hatford. Due to the war, it was hanging in a dilapidated museum.

Back in New York, some gallery owners interested in my work were expecting me. When visiting Pierre Matisse's gallery, he was annoyed to learn I had already given my word to the «Bignou» gallery, in those days a branch of the one in Paris. It is never easy to negotiate from a distance, and the world wide conflicts made things worse. A year later I wrote to San Francisco, requesting that the paintings the gallery kept in its storage room be removed and added to the rest of the collection.

When we finally left New York, we had been in the United States almost six months. We had visited thirteen cities and we still had nine to go, all of them situated on the Pacific coast. We bid a fond farewell to Henry Allen Moe and his wife, such charming and intelligent people, to the Taylors, to D'Harnoncourt, and the rest of the people we had become friends with, like Edgar Varèse, who had invited us at his home. Saying goodbye to Archipenko was dramatic, because we were so fond of each other. He and his wife accompanied us to the station, yet we never saw her again. Archipenko we met again not too long ago in Paris, comforted in his widowhood by a very young wife. Good old Archipenko! Arm in arm with his youthful companion, he came to see me a spring afternoon at my studio on Rue Mabillon; it was in 1962, some days before leaving to Buenos Aires. My home country was about to pay a brilliant homage to me.

The evocation of our journey through the United States only brings back delightful memories. In spite of the hardships, of tense diplomatic relations, everywhere people received us in a friendly way. We were around the most privileged minds of America; I'm alluding to museum directors, university presidents, eminent professors and some artists, who, because of their age or whatever other reason, had not been drafted.

However, the cordial reception and the pleasant memories do not blind me, and today like yesterday, I condemn the economical policy and the unacceptable intrusions of the American Government into Latin America affairs. Americans would never accept any foreign interference, and they don't seem to realize that we are just as nationalistic as they are. If they see themselves as adults, and therefore able to protect Latin America, we too recognize the weight of maturity, refusing to be dominated. Let us never forget that many of us are children of millenary civilizations. There is no denying that

Americans have a lot to give, but unfortunately, what they offer us is not always beneficial. The proof is that some of our countries remain poor, while the fascist régimes they protect become rich and strong: how can oppressed people fight such power?

Don't think I speak forcefully because I'm no longer face–to–face with the Americans. In fact, I had no qualms about giving Rockefeller my point of view. I suggested that he stop squandering money by inviting Latin American people to his country, as was my case. A more productive policy would have been to have his compatriots visit each one of our nations, considering we already knew them, and they didn't know us. This awareness, I observed, would generate a radical change in their understanding about us. Fortunately, the Americans I met were cosmopolitan people, well–traveled, learned, greatly differing from the powerful bankers on Wall Street or the military at the Pentagon. If only the mind and spirit were educated in equal proportions, our rapport with the northern colossus would be different.

From the moment I arrived in New York I was stalked by reporters, who jotted down whatever I said while taking pictures of me. These interviews made me lose countless mornings, and only one got published. The head of press who coordinated the interviews enlightened me: the newspapers felt they could not cordially welcome an Argentine citizen, given that the United States didn't think much of Argentina at the time. This doesn't speak too well of the average American. Fortunately, it isn't the masses but the select few that transform the world, making it a more enjoyable place to live in.

We had barely arrived at our hotel in Boston, that the secretary of Dr. Edward W. Forbes, the director of the Fogg Museum of Harvard University, handed us a pair of tickets for a concert. She also told us Mr. Forbes had invited us for dinner at his home the following day.

The first thing I did when the cloudy winter sky cleared, was to go on an outing to Cambridge; at ten in the morning I was at the Fogg Museum, which is where future museum directors, art historians and guides are trained. It is simply incredible how much material this institution possesses in order to prepare these specialists; there must be nothing like it in the world. Such is the advantage that wealth provides, when intelligently used. While I was beholding the masterpieces this museum houses, I reflected about my country. With indignation, I remembered the years when a portrait by the Spanish artist Anglada Camarasa was valued at ten thousand pesos, when five paintings by Paul Cézanne could have been purchased for the same sum.

I will never forget the dinner at Dr. Forbes'. He spoke perfect Italian, for he had lived twenty–five years in Florence to study the Renaissance painters. I can still see his fine figure, his noble expression, his amiable and kind smile, his enthusiasm, his simplicity.

It was snowing that evening and our taxi got lost amid the residential streets of Cambridge, and we couldn't find the villa of our host. Suddenly, Dr. Forbes appeared holding a large umbrella, his trousers rolled up above his calves. He knocked on the window, asking me whether I was Pettoruti; his home was around the corner and he guided us towards it standing on the step.

That evening he had invited a group of Harvard University professors along with their wives, and during the meal the conversation was lively. We talked about art throughout the ages, attempting first to define what the term «work of art» meant. Then came the artists' turn. We discussed Van Gogh and his descriptive technique, and what I said at the time still holds true: that it had been a considerable error on his part to have applied Oriental concepts, especially having Rembrandt sitting on his lap! As a painter, he would have been more successful if he had paid heed to the call of his own origins and traditions, and I'm afraid this unfortunate association spawned the hallucination that led him prematurely to his death. If his painting lives on, it is because of his genius. Unfortunately, except for the usual imitators, he didn't leave any successors behind.

When Gauguin's name arose discrepant opinions were held. There were those who admired him and those, like Forbes, who in part coincided with my point of view. I admitted that it was a pleasure to look at his paintings, but I also made it clear that one didn't learn anything from them, and that they didn't even succeed in pleasing the eyes. It was the exotic motif that drew our attention, I said. More than likely, Gauguin wouldn't have emerged from darkness had it not been for this striking quality, independently of his talent. His wisest move was leaving for Oceania where he created animals and plants never before portrayed in painting, using bright, albeit not luminous colors, suggested to him by the tropics. Concerning the universality attributed to both painters, I pointed out that though they were known across the world, they remained local.

No–one dared to openly criticize those opinions, but someone wished to know whether I deemed Toulouse–Lautrec and Corot to be local painters. I replied both were painters of their time and circumstance. At least Corot's painting transcended. As an example I mentioned Piero della Francesca, definitely regional; yet he's an artist that earned universality through his art.

While speaking to Mr. Forbes about his Museum, he was surprised to find out I had visited it, and with a great deal of attention at that. We agreed to meet on the premises the following day. He showed me the hall where a team of specialists was studying the art of camouflage for war purposes (it so happened I had practiced this method in Italy during the First World War) as well as the storerooms, where thanks to a simple yet innovative system of sliding stretchers, paintings could be immediately and clearly examined. Upon leaving the storeroom, its doors closed hermetically, filtering out both moisture and dust. Dr. Forbes couldn't hide his satisfaction of finding himself before a person who not only displayed tastes similar to his, but also was well–informed about so many things. He hugged me on several occasions, telling me he hadn't had such a rich and varied conversation for a long time.

Besides speaking on the radio from time to time, visiting museums and institutions, and all that was worthy of attention, my wife and I wrote articles. She represented the Chilean «Zig–Zag» magazine. While in the United States, she sent her editor illustrated articles about life in the United States, whereas I contributed to the «Gente de Prensa» publication, of Buenos Aires. These reports were later distributed to hundreds of provincial newspapers. I also wrote some articles for the «El Argentino» newspaper, of La Plata.

From Boston we left once again for Chicago, stopping to visit the Niagara Falls. Of all the northern cities we traveled to, I particularly remember Minneapolis. As usual, everyone received us with open arms, from the Rocky Mountains to Seattle. Dr. Richard E. Füller, the director of the Seattle Art Museum, guided us around. His father had founded the museum, whereas he had created the art gallery. While in the city, Dr. Füller didn't abandon us for one second, and we had dinner and tea at his home, where I met his mother. He immediately hung a painting of mine called «Intimacy» in his beautiful museum, purchased while I was exhibiting there.

The last city we visited before returning to San Francisco was Portland. Robert Tyler, director of the Portland Museum of Art –which also owned a painting of mine– put me in touch with Peter Belluscchi, an Italian architect who thanks to his creative mind transformed the cities with his new constructions.

In San Francisco, Grace Morley was waiting for us at the station, very early in the morning. We hugged each other joyfully and spent some days together. She handed me a copy of a reduced version of the short that had been shot in New York. She also surprised me with the news that the Museum's Quarterly Bulletin [47], still at the printer's, was entirely dedicated to my work. She told me it was the first time the Bulletin focused on a single artist.

We arrived in Los Angeles, where the architect Raffaello Soriano was expecting us; born in Italy, he had lived and studied there. We visited his beautiful mansions, almost all of them in Beverley Hills. This exquisite artist had the particularity of taking only the commissions of those clients he had taken a liking to and who accepted all of his whims. Not only did this include the design of their house, but also the tablecloths and a music system he had created.

We also visited some movie studios, as for instance the Twentieth Century Fox and the Metro Goldwin Mayer, where we met many famous artists. Gary Cooper was one of them. Walt Disney left us a card, regretting he wasn't there to receive us on account of his trip to New York.

---

[47] Quarterly Bulletin, Volume III, Nr. 2, 1942.

In Los Angeles I contacted the «Datzell Hatfield» gallery, where I held two exhibitions. One noon, while at the gallery, we were pleasantly surprised to see Greta Garbo walk in: the «Divine» rarely made a public appearance, and therefore, very few people had the chance to meet her. On that occasion she was accompanied by a handsome man in his forties, apparently her physician.

The day we flew to Mexico, it was pouring rain. I had many things to attend to in this country: before leaving Buenos Aires on my way to the United States, I had received a telegram from the Mexican Ministry of Education, inviting me to exhibit in Mexico City. I had immediately notified our Ambassador, my friend Alberto M. Candiotti, who was posted there, asking him to arrange all my forthcoming meetings. In effect, everything was settled when I arrived, and that same afternoon I was able to get in touch with the right people. It was agreed upon that the Mexican authorities would directly contact those of the San Francisco Museum. Projects were planned while I was in the United States and I know the arrangements were carried out in a cordial atmosphere; but war prolonged itself and made it impossible for the plan to develop.

On the night of my arrival, my colleague Diego Rivera called the Embassy around eight o'clock in order to greet me. With my friend Candiotti's consent, I invited him for dinner at the Embassy; he refused, but instead, proposed to stop by after the meal for coffee. I was delighted to meet that pot–bellied giant, who so warmly welcomed me. We chatted till dawn, and it would be impossible for me to repeat all the gentle lies he told us with such artlessness and good humor; at one point he told us that he had never met Leon Trotsky. When I replied that it had been he who had managed to get Trotsky into Mexico, Rivera answered the press had invented everything.

I promised him Maria Rosa and I would visit his studio as soon at the end of our tour through the United States, and indeed, upon our return to Mexico City, we did just that. The day we went to see him, an erupting volcano had turned the sky. Rivera was extremely affable, and showed us some very beautiful drawings belonging to different periods. When I requested to see his pictures, he told us he was busy painting «Twentieth Century Woman»; he was producing different versions, for he wished to leave a typical twentieth century female figure for posterity.

Rivero's series were stunning: three detached female figures, perhaps four, life–sized, wearing the outfit of the sport they represented. I especially remember the pretty tennis player, holding a racket beneath her arm. Her short hair was blowing in the wind, and she was wearing a shirt and a pair of shorts.

After having shown us his paintings, he drove us in his van to visit the surroundings; he then took us to a brand–new gallery (we later learned it belonged to him), where only his versions of the volcano were exhibited, portraying its evolution. It was obviously meant for the American tourist.

I received many invitations to visit art studios, and our days were filled with radio interviews, lectures and receptions. We also visited museums and nearby archeological sites: Mexico fascinated us. I was lucky to meet the artist Clemente Orozco and the poet Carlos Pellicer: he and I became good friends. He showed us many interesting things, and we spent an entire afternoon in his large new studio, where we chatted a great deal. He had no paintings, so he showed me some drawings that he kept in several folders. One morning, standing on a scaffold inside a church, we looked at the ornamentation he was working on.

All I saw in Mexico in matters of modern art confirmed my view that the Mexican school of painting is a school of magnificent drawers. Yet it was its ancient art that dazzled me. Beholding the work of various peoples, such as the Aztec, Toltec, Zapotec, Olmec and many others, who lived as far back as one millennium before Christ, I realized that nothing has yet been said about the artistic audacities of those native people, about their original aesthetic values humanized by religious beliefs. They were accomplished masters of the art of sculpture, and the beauty and expressive grandeur of their statues, ceramics and jewelry is so admirable, that no European or Asian masterpieces created in the same period can surpass them. Hieratic or baroque, the boldness they display far outshines even the most daring of contemporary sculptors: their skill only compares to that of the greatest artists. Were these natives as savage as the Spanish saw them, or must History be rectified? The issue haunted me.

Towards the end of our Mexican journey, we traveled to the large valley of Teotihuacán, where excavations revealed the house of an Aztec hierarch, the perfect equivalent of a Pompeian mansion, with running water in the central fountain and hot water in the bathroom. When we finally arrived in Lima, there was a full moon. Together with the Peruvian painter Julia Cordesido, we explored the colonial city; there was no time to sleep for we were leaving at dawn. We rested in Santiago, where we slept, I believe, for two days on end.

Chapter 28

Years of hardship

A few surprises awaited me in Argentina. I took charge of the Museum and noticed that my friend Petarú behaved nervously, as if something distressed him. He finally unburdened himself and said: «Dear Pettoruti, some unfortunate measures were taken while you were in the United States. Firstly, the post you were meant to hold because of your seniority was given to the Italian drunkard we all know. Secondly, everyone's salary was increased except yours». The president of the Provincial Committee of Fine Arts was still Antonio Santamarina; my salary, from 1940 to the completion of my service, consisted of five hundred and fifty pesos. [48] Some days later, Perón rose to power in our wretched and troubled Republic.

One year went by that I would call of adaptation, if one ever adapts to misfortune. During that time, I focused as much as I could on the living reality of my love, on my painting and on my activities at the Museum. I exhibited Archipenko's drawings there, yet the public of La Plata remained indifferent to them. The exhibition was repeated in Buenos Aires, at a gallery downtown; no newspaper commented on it. Only the painter Jorge Larco bought one of the ten drawings for a hundred dollars, which was the uniform price established by the author when he entrusted them to me. Why this apathy? I still don't know.

Political convulsions tend to kindle people's inclination towards things of the spirit. Unable to receive the flow of cultural contributions coming from Europe because of the war, the country was boiling with curiosity. Both the war and the oppression disturbed the usual immobility of our life. On the one hand, printing presses prospered, as books no longer arrived to our shores, and publishing companies made rapid fortunes, offering us an even bigger

---

48   As Museum Director, my half pension consisted of 6,153 pesos, but my net income was 5,699 pesos..

wealth: enlightenment. On the other hand, people, hounded by insecurity and fear withdrew into themselves, finding time to read or look at pictures. Timidly at first, new names were added to the list of known marketable authors, and art books, always expensive and therefore inaccessible to the underprivileged pockets, entered lesser-known libraries. The «petits amateurs» burgeoned and small collections of national art began living an independent life not too different from those of the wealthy.

A cluster of young people, more informed about the European artistic movements than groups belonging to the former generation, attempted to reform values and concepts. (They were rather ignorant, however, about the immediate history of the country, since twenty years after my arrival, they still wanted to «break up with tradition» and «search for modernity in art»). Leading this group was the painter and commercial artist Tomás Maldonado. None of the members were older than twenty-five, yet believed without exception they handled the most advanced philosophical and scientific concepts. In fact they were so confident that it pushed them to decisively proclaim the presence of a new vision of space and time in the arts. One had the impression that those theories had never existed before them, much less based on such profound notions. To prove their point, they published a magazine called «Arturo», that saw the light only once. As always happens to those people who mix literature with art, the group no longer paid any heed to the latter in order to concentrate on the manifestos (which by the way have remained unchanged for over half a century). The objectives of the group, albeit well-intentioned, were therefore not achieved. A proverb of Chinese wisdom quoted by Jung reads: «If the wrong man uses the correct means, the correct means will act imperfectly». Indeed, the right means don't act independently: they always depend on the men who use it and never on the method itself. Likewise, the survival of new ideas depends on whether men turn them into mere slogans.

In our country, art and literature periodicals created by prestigious intellectuals had never lasted very long, and this magazine was no different. Incredibly enough, these young people proclaimed Argentine art had been enormously influenced by their writing. Though it is true that this group was committed, it practically had no members, and therefore it didn't achieve the significance some people would now wish to credit them with. The first exhibition, held at the end of 1945, opened at the private home of the psychoanalyst Enrique Pichon Rivière, and the second one, at the home of the photographer Grete Stern, in the locality of Ramos Mejía. We spent a most enjoyable time, listening to a musical performance accompanied by «elementary» dances.

Fundamental changes were operating in the country, involving its social, economical and political structures. Yet, those changes did not suffice to eliminate narrow–mindedness, and a new ignorance threatened us. After having experienced the feudal period, we lived in a totalitarian régime: the «alpargatas» [49] strived to replace books, jails readily opened up their doors to intellectuals, and the Peronist faith was becoming a legal requirement in order to lead a free life. Many writers and professors, among them a Nobel Prize, fell in disgrace because they had signed a petition against the new authorities. They were stripped of their privileges, no longer allowed to conduct research, teach, or hold any public office. When would all of this stop?

The Government controlled the provinces and Buenos Aires was next on the list. The La Plata Inspector, Dr. Juan Atilio Bramuglia, carried the list of people that had been dismissed in his briefcase, and these names he had to announce without delay. Mine was on that record, and it was read to me by a friend of the newly appointed supervisor, who in turn was a friend of a brother of mine. On the grapevine, I heard that among the weighty reasons for my dismissal were the accusations by the artists and intellectuals of La Plata: I was accused of being anti–patriotic and «anti–provincial», inviting educated people of the capital city as well as foreigners to hold lectures. Under their very noses I had asked Mexican, Cuban, Brazilian, and Russian artists (in allusion to Archipenko) to exhibit their work, even projecting a Latin American Art Biennial, and I was forgetting them!

The dismissal only worried me because I wondered how the Museum would fare and because, having amply exceeded the fourteen years of service as Director, there were only a few months left before my retirement, at which time the Province would pay me my retirement pension. I couldn't remain impassive while some wished to eliminate me, and I decided to defend my territory. I decided to go and see Bramuglia, bringing him all the official information I deemed important.

The inspector received me glacially. Yet when I told him that introducing the work of Latin American artists to Argentine colleagues was on the contrary a patriotic gesture for the latter wouldn't have to spend any money when traveling, his face softened. It lightened up even more when he realized, after having read the information, that the Museum organized exhibitions and salons for local and provincial artists in La Plata, Mar del Plata, Tandil, Azul, Pergamino or Bahía Blanca. At this point of the conversation, Bramuglia told me to take a seat.

As I had suspected, he was an intelligent, humane and understanding man, who realized I had selflessly defended the dignity of the Museum. He realized too how a handful of ambitious individuals who called themselves artists attempted to eliminate me in order to hang their own paintings at the Museum with the approval of the Government. We chatted for a long time. Watching the alarmed secretary entering and leaving the room, I was often on the brink of leaving, but Bramuglia always stopped me with an amiable gesture.

---

49 The "alpargata" is a popular footwear, made of canvas and hemp. In the text it is used metaphorically, to designate the uneducated man.

I later learned from my friend, whom I described our interview to, that Bramuglia had been told not to receive me. However, since all I had said was sound, the latter had been unable to send me away.

The dictatorship not only deprived the country of its freedom, but also undermined the morale of many of its citizens. I knew of a sculptor who in order to keep his post made so many concessions he became a spineless individual. Another painter, who had left–wing inclinations, ran to the police to declare he wasn't affiliated to the Communist party. Years of excess and injustice followed; taking advantage of confusion many people sought vengeance, and I became one of their objectives. I have no qualms about telling it just the way it happened, though I will omit the names of those who acted in the shadows or shielded themselves by means of pseudonyms, for I do not wish to soil the magnetic tape that records these memories.

The year 1945 had started. The vile passions that both my art and I had generated from the outset intensified, and people who I had never suspected to be my adversaries launched a press campaign that had me as target. Some openly accused me of not being democratic enough, or said I served the totalitarian state, because I did not resign as head of the Museum. Still others, crying louder than the rest, believed I was a Fascist and pointed at my friendship with Marinetti and Bragaglia as evidence. Once, a «sciocco», which, translated from Italian means obtuse, stupid or simple–minded, gossiped about my sinecure at the Museum, about the outrageous mismanagement of its funds, with which in part, he said, I handsomely paid my friends that gave lectures there. What these senseless men didn't know was that it was the Provincial Committee of Fine Arts that handled the funds and not the director of the Museum.

The sad thing about instigating anger in order to slay a man, is the dejection it creates, akin to bitter sediment. One then realizes the spirit of solidarity doesn't prevail in our midst, and how much circumspection, if I dare call it so, arises when time comes to take sides. Just like twenty years ago, but now with a greater tenacity triggered by resentment, the beaters pursued the deer to hunt it while onlookers watched without batting an eyelid, waiting perhaps to see blood run. Passive and cruel, a bookseller on Florida Street recommended to the irresolute: «Let him sort out the situation alone».

Alone I was, since nobody supported me. Peculiar reservations on the part of people who knew my political inclinations and my moral honesty, or who inevitably recognized both, either because they frequented my home and were perfectly aware of who my friends or companions were, or had witnessed my behavior at the Museum.

To my surprise, my inseparable, addicted and devoted friends, who knew about me almost as much as I knew about myself, remained cautiously aloof, as if paralyzed. I couldn't figure out whether they acted this way for fear of the dictatorship, or on the contrary, because they dreaded the eruption of left–wing forces in the world. War was bound to break out and all roads led to Berlin, while bombs were being dropped on the Nazi sanctuary. Triumphantly, Communism seemed able to develop untrammeled everywhere on the globe. By attacking me, I suppose that my detractors believed they manifested themselves politically. There are those who need to establish their own democratic reputation by sullying someone else's name.

My grandfather had made Ovid's saying his: «Friends will surround you while you are happy, yet when the heavens darken you will be alone». Through an associative process, I recalled a professor, who, calling himself my friend, had had the nerve to stifle Ernesto Bonasso's initiative, a young and noble ally, who had suggested leading a campaign on my behalf.

Yet, I cannot but commend some of my friends for their solidarity, who bravely defended me in private conversations. Others, like Basso, struggled to make the opposition see how unfair their attacks were. However, Julio Payró was the only one who publicly spoke in my favor, disgusted by the collective cowardliness. His open letter to the «La Vanguardia», one of the most offensive newspapers and voice of the unleashed mediocrity, refuted the ridiculous accusations. From that moment onwards, the aggressors vanished, fleeing like mice before the cat, and there were even those who approached relatives and friends to prove their innocence.

I continued to paint my series of suns, all of them rather regular in size, with which I wished to crystallize one of my cherished dreams. I chose a small sculpture by Antonio Sibellino as the principal element for one of these paintings, raising the figure two meters off the floor, as seen from the eyes of a seated man. I thus wanted to pay tribute to one of the greatest sculptors of our times. There are those who say Sibellino didn't produce many sculptures; I would like to remind them that there are artists who create an even lesser quantity; this doesn't prevent them from being great artists, for art is not a question of quantity, but of quality.

The night I showed Sibellino my painting, he was moved to tears; he then said I had enlarged his sculpture to the size he had had always imagined. Whenever he felt a strong emotion, he became euphoric and we chatted away. He praised my paintings, marveling at the light he said I had rediscovered, and which according to him, led me to an amazing abstraction. We were about to start a discussion, when an unusual peal of bells was heard coming from the outside. I then lived on Sargento Cabral Street, with the harbor nearby, and I opened the balcony windows. The ship's sirens gleefully mingled with the car horns, celebrating the end of the war. It had finally concluded, but under a bad omen, under the sign of an artificial dawn created by terrible forces that man had released. Were we witnessing the dissolution of the world? We embraced each other with both apprehension and joy.

Peace, at long last! Night was falling and Sibellino stayed over, in spite of having forgotten his toothbrush.

Though upset by the unjust accusations with respect to my idealization of foreign artists, I carried forth my objective to mount an exhibition of Brazilian and Cuban painting at the Museum, in addition to a show of drawings and sketches by the Mexican artist Clemente Orozco, with whom I stayed in touch by letter. Moreover, I was trying to organize a Latin American Art Biennial, which I believed could the artists of our republics.

The first exhibition, held at the Museum in 1945, displayed Brazilian painting, coordinated upon my request by the eminent writer Marques Rebelo; he selected the works of his country and traveled with them to Buenos Aires. The following exhibition, held at a later date, presented Cuban painting, and also upon my request, was organized by the writer José Gómez Sicre. The Museum's contribution –as I said before, everything in our country is achieved with a great deal of effort– consisted in the publication of a good catalogue. With luck, there still might be some issues in the Museum's archives.

Both the Ambassador of Brazil and the Secretary of Education of Argentina attended the inauguration. Striking while the iron was hot, I hastened to ask the latter to buy a painting by Cándido Portinari, included in the exhibition. This is how the painting was included into the collection of our Museum, though the artist never saw it displayed. On the other hand, our national authorities totally ignored the Cuban exhibition, inaugurated a few months later, in spite of my efforts to arouse their interest.

Marques Rebelo, responsible of the Brazilian show and true ambassador of the culture of his land, remained in our country for a while; we became close friends. He was invited to lecture in the capital city and in the provinces; he finished his long series in Resistencia [50], where the cultural institution «Fogón de los Arrieros» gave him a huge farewell party. As he set sail for Brazil, an airplane began to circle the sky, displaying an enormous Brazilian flag: Aldo Boglietto was on board, showering his guests with flowers.

One of the best and most serious monographs written about my work was published that same year, and the text included a beautiful analysis especially dedicated to my series of suns. I felt my activities and feelings had been wonderfully interpreted.

I traveled to Bahía Blanca accompanied by María Rosa, who had to deliver a lecture on Gabriela Mistral at the Rivadavia Library; I recall it interspersed with delightful anecdotes. When the lights were switched back on, I realized quite a few people had been crying.

The triumph of the democracies of the Second World War did not defeat tyrannies across the world. The Argentine political situation remained the same; in fact, it worsened, while the health of our fiscal coffers improved con-

---

50   Capital city of the province of Chaco.

siderably. We had so much gold and foreign currency that demagogy was freely exercised. Despotism became legal, prolonging itself indefinitely.

Just like many other responsible artists, I had stopped sending my work to the salons. Yet, as someone had sensibly said, if artists stopped communicating with the public altogether, it would favor a rise of the poorest of art forms. Therefore, a Salon of Independent Artists was suggested. The latter was held at the same time as the National Salon, in a hall on Florida Street, rented from the Argentine Rural Society. When I recall how openly we manifested our purposes in the catalogue, I still wonder how we didn't end up in jail.

Personally, I believe that in spite of my unavoidable contact with the dictatorship, I was rather lucky. For years, every time my checks arrived with the deductions imposed by the régime, I systematically refused to accept them. This implied I didn't believe in the government's «good deeds», thereby justifying these inadmissible deductions. Yet I was never sanctioned; to my surprise, instead of a reprisal, the check would return to me complete.

My gravest indiscipline I committed towards 1949, when refusing to sign a letter in which artist–professors had to recognize the First Lady's important cultural achievements and her equally important actions in favor of the Arts. I said I would never sign such a dishonest and obsequious note, and my categorical refusal was respected in spite of the pressure. I didn't care a hoot about my fate, so fed up was I. The worst thing was that in that letter, presented by those subservient men as a real gift of intelligence, two signatures were missing: Jorge Larco's and mine. Neither of us signed. On the eve of 17 October, date in which the letter had to be delivered, they looked for me until midnight. They wanted me to reconsider. In spite of the possible consequences, I told one of Pío Collivadino's cousins «no» for the last time. At the time, I believe I was a substitute teacher at a national school; I awaited my dismissal, but it never came.

My experience of the world and its rulers, many of whom use their power abusively, has taught me that in the long run courage is more profitable than cowardliness: absolutism surrenders before courage. All I can say is that I was never backed by any tycoon; however, I have my reasons to think that some believed this, abstaining themselves from hurting me in fear of reprisals.

I didn't have a lot of spare time and the little I had I dedicated to my painting. Luckily, due to circumstance —my work at the Museum, my trips to La Plata— I saw many people and they kept me abreast of the daily news, of politics and art. Since President Alvear had left office, the country lived in a state of abnormality; I felt it had worsened due to the action of a government that spoilt whatever it lay hands on. I sensed the whole country was out of kilter.

Juan Carlos Paz and Sibellino told me about their exchanges with the young musicians and artists. Self–assertive and arrogant, they were blasé, as if to prove no–one had ever created anything before them. They were the masters of a virgin land, traveling to the deepest layer ever imagined by Nature and tackling it fearlessly: the symbol. It was pointless to argue with them, for their knowledgeable was boundless. Speaking with Julio Payró about abstract movements, these superior beings assured him that in the United States they were démodé, just like Debussy´s corrupt music or Matisse´s painting. These art forms no longer embodied a «living experience»: only time and the space counted. Children of the atomic era, they had invented a sculpture and painting that time could not restrict.

I realized the words «a living experience» grouped them in the same category. Their plan was ambitious, for it comprised the entire universe. They would tackle it through the means of a thick six hundred–paged magazine; they had already asked Einstein and Kandinsky for their contribution, though Léger had been discarded as passé. However, professor Picard was welcome, and among the nationals, one of the most eminent physicists was on the brink of telling them the approximate date in which man would travel on energy beams.

The avant–garde group considered Sibellino and Juan Carlos Paz to be sufficiently worthy to adhere, but not without conditions. When they interviewed the former it was to tell him that the sculpture he would henceforth create had to be «temporal», the way his colleagues were already doing («a little piece of wood on the tip of a wire, swinging back and forth», Sibellino had told me). At one point, pretending to be meditating, he heard them say that Kandinsky, quite rudely, had not answered their letter. Sibellino then asked them why they hadn´t sent it to the cemetery.

Juan Carlos Paz was told that his music was old–fashioned –like all music that flows through time– and that the only way to modernize it was to compose spatial music, that could be played and yet remain static. Paz replied that music inevitably penetrates time from the moment a note is played, to which they retorted that it was his business to make it spatial; he had to figure out how to invent it, in the same way that they had invented the «present–moment» sculpture and the painting without a frame. At any rate, they had already decided that one of his works would appear on black paper in the first issue of their magazine, with the score printed in white. «I´m sorry», replied Paz, «but I don´t lend my name to such corny things».

What were those youths searching for, their gaze so frantically directed towards the future? Whether they were geniuses, martyrs, saints or heroes, it all boiled down to literary romanticism. Lucio Fontana, who often came to visit, talked about them. Then, during the months that preceded his return to Italy, he began to elaborate on the subject of an inexistent spatial sculpture to be projected in the heavens. It totally differed from the temporal sculptures for it transcended everything else. A sculpture, in his opinion, was real only in the mind of its creator, who could nonetheless project it onto the nocturnal and cloudless sky. Which means would be used? As usual, when asked to be logical, Fontana laughed wholeheartedly, like an ingenuous child.

The «Altamira» adventure takes place in 1946. I can't recall who came up with this Free Workshop project; what I do know is that it was organized by the editor Gonzalo Losada, and that the following people participated as teachers: Raúl Soldi, Jorge Larco and I were in charge of painting and drawing, Lucio Fontana of sculpture, and Romero Brest of Art History. There would be no director, and every professor would be responsible for his class. I got to know about the project, albeit belatedly, for they came to me because another painter had refused the offer.

The project was magnificent, liberal, idealistic, and can be summed up as follows: an industrious and generous man becomes a patron; an art school opens; a handful of professors works for free for enthusiastic students who will no doubt enroll; the amount they collect will be added to the existing funds in order for the artists to obtain their own building as soon as possible, so as to make «Altamira» a great art school. The professors, in the course of time, would own it as a fair reward for their noble efforts.

I accepted. As school began, students began to enroll. Contrary to what I had expected, most of them signed up for my painting class. When I realized that the large hall didn't have enough easels, I asked the secretary to please tell the students that for the moment the registration period had ended. Classes started and all began successfully; expectations were amply surpassed. Unfortunately, the building was requested, and «Altamira» disappeared. If there is something I regret, is that prior to the dissolution of the school, no meeting was ever held.

A few months after «Altamira» had closed its doors, I went to Mar del Plata on vacation, together with our wonderful friends Julio and María Inés Payró. While at lunch, Juan Petrarú called me from La Plata telling me I had been dismissed from the Museum. What a splendid occasion to celebrate my recuperated freedom! Since I was no longer wanted there, I would celebrate the new rudeness with a toast.

Personally, I wouldn't have left the Museum, for I felt committed to my work. It had entailed so much sacrifice and there were many more projects I wished to undertake; the Latin American Biennial of Fine Arts was to be held in Mar del Plata in December (San Pablo later took the initiative), and there were still some formalities pending. The most talented artists of each one of our countries were going to be present. Yet the funds to mount such an ambitious exhibition had proved insufficient, and I had turned to the ambassadors of the participating countries, who accepted to send me the works of those artists I deemed appropriate: this way no governments would be involved, and hence, no official favoritism.

On 13 February 1943, my dismissal was officially decreed. The statement read: «We hereby declare that the official number 7, Emilio Pettoruti, is suspended from duty». The letter bore Colonel Mercante's signature. I immediately ran to every one of the Embassies asking them to annul the procedures. I thanked them and apologized.

The point was now to find another way to earn money, and teaching crossed my mind. In Buenos Aires, as in Mar del Plata, I continually met people who wanted to study painting with me. Opening a studio seemed like a good idea, and I started looking for a place. In April, my «Atelier Pettoruti» was opened on Charcas Street. There were three shifts: morning, afternoon and evening, and if I may say so myself, everything was very well organized. Soon there were no vacancies left, for the three halls couldn't hold any more students. The evening shift always had students waiting for an opening.

During the five years that I directed it, all kinds of people attended the studio: from inexperienced and timid youths to graduate students from the Superior School of Fine Arts. Foreign painters wishing to perfect themselves in Buenos Aires also attended it, and among them were Brazilians, Chileans and Peruvians. At long last, I was able to teach Abstract Composition, something I had always wanted to do, and concentrate on my painting. No longer did I have to battle exhibiting artists, petty members of the jury, endlessly confronting ignorant high–ranking officials, or dealing with bureaucratic paperwork.

A climate of camaraderie reigned in the studio, and I truly believe that all those who worked there became fond of me. Yet my articulate teaching bothered many people; absurd stories were told, especially about my character. It was said that in a fit of fury, I smudged my students' work or pinched them wherever it hurt most. My infamous reputation gave rise to the following anecdote: the art critic Romero Brest wished to introduce his art student Samuel Oliver to me, as the young man wanted to attend the studio. I replied that the introduction was not necessary, since his sister, María Rosa Oliver, was an old friend of mine. Brest insisted, explaining his reasons: someone had told young Oliver that I punished the students and the latter wanted to know me before it was too late.

Chapter 29
My Trip to Europe

No longer head of the Museum, I was now able to start selling my paintings, since worries and agitation had become things of the past. So far, endless difficulties had demanded my constant attention, and I had been able to paint only during my free time. Now, however, part of my thoughts drifted towards other matters.

Remembering situations and attitudes, I realized, for instance, that many people who had wished to see my paintings and visited me at home in order to do so, had asked me about prices, to which I had answered evasively.

To put a price on my paintings, to hold a conversation about money, to imagine someone telling me my work was expensive, or even worse, someone daring to ask me for a discount, was enough to inhibit me, and this has always been the case. On account of this, and perhaps fearing I would sell my paintings at astronomical prices, people consulted me reluctantly; this prompted me to change the subject and nothing more was said. When I finally understood what was happening, I simply included the price of each piece of work on the catalogue of the latest exhibition. What a magnificent idea! Whenever someone asked me about a certain painting, I handed him the catalogue without uttering a word. So many people bought my paintings I had to stop selling them, for I needed a certain number of works for my exhibitions in Europe. From the moment I realized I could live from my art, the Old Continent once again became my aspiration.

Perhaps someone might wonder whether I received any signs of sympathy when I left the Museum and what happened to it after my departure. I mentioned the oppression in which we lived made people cautious; those were the days when Peronist gangs stopped citizens on the street obliging them to shout their approval of the régime. If one didn't comply, beatings ensued.

Just like people, institutions kept silent, until one day, out of the blue, I received a letter from the Argentine Society of Artists signed by its president, the painter Raúl Soldi, in which I was asked for details and facts concerning my dismissal. The Society wanted to «act in consequence». I replied by quitting, which I myself had founded, understanding that silence made more sense than a belated and wary proposal.

With regard to the fate of the Museum, this is what happened: they had barely ousted me that colonel Mercante's government began to appoint ineffectual people to fulfill the task. If, while I was in charge, every effort had been made to acquire more space to display the works of art, when I left, efforts were directed towards setting up offices. A point was reached in which there were so many employees without a specific task (who nevertheless needed tables and chairs to demonstrate they existed) that in the end the board of directors decided to relocate the Museum to an old people's home, situated on the Pereira's estate.

I had reached an agreement with the «Peuser» gallery to hold a retrospective there, and a date was fixed. I was counting on some paintings that had returned to the country after their long trek through the United States, but what I was far from imagining were the obstacles imposed on me by customs: my paintings were held for two years on a barge at the harbor.

I communicated my difficulties to the gallery, as well as my need to postpone the exhibition. Inevitably, those impediments caused them a great deal of annoyance, for they had counted on mounting an interesting show that would attract a new public. The Brazilian painter Cándido Portinari seemed a perfect solution, and I immediately sent him a few lines exposing the conditions to him: halls, catalogue and free invitations. He answered by telegram that he agreed to everything. Portinari would exhibit at the «Peuser» gallery during the winter of 1947, and my projected exhibition was programmed for August–September of the following year.

The paintings were returned to me just on time for my participation in the first Palanza Award competition. I was invited together with other nine colleagues and I presented myself, as the regulations stipulated, with five works achieved in the course of the last five years. Don't believe for one moment that I dreamed of obtaining some of the votes of the Academy members; if after twenty–three years of residence in the country and having turned fifty–five, I had not even received an Incentive Award, I could certainly not expect anything from them. Their mentalities had not changed, and it was futile to hope for a different context. The truth is, however, that I was happy with my paintings (and I say this without arrogance); they looked so fine that during the inauguration, Augusto Palanza, the donor of the prize and a collector of good art, greeted me affectionately. «At last, Pettoruti!» he whispered in my ears as he hugged me.

He wasn't the only one suggesting I would win the prize: the sculptor José Fioravanti, member of the Academy and therefore, a future member of the jury, was sure of it. After having heard his colleagues' opinions, he had no doubt they would all vote for me. So well did I know the grapes of my vine that I laughed in his face, assuring him he was being candid. Yet he remained firm in his convictions, which were also shared by the press and the public.

Once the votes had been cast, Fioravanti came to see me, apologizing for his mistake. I don't know why fate has always chosen me to comfort others for their inappropriate behavior: I found myself consoling José Fioravanti, for he felt ever so vexed. He told me that when the jury was about to debate the issue, he had risen and said: «Since the matter is already settled and we all agree, I vote for Pettoruti». Victory was short-lived.

The award produced a little incident: at one point during the first days of the exhibition, I received a phone call around two o'clock in the afternoon. It was the painter Raquel Forner, winner of the Palanza Award, who begged me to go the exhibition that afternoon because something diabolical was being planned against her: only I could prevent it. So great was her alarm, I asked her what it was all about. She didn't know for sure, only that there was a conspiracy. I then asked her who had said such a thing, to which she replied an anonymous person had spoken to her on the phone. To solve this spooky mystery I went to the exhibition, where I saw a student of mine, Oscar Capristo, walking about the halls together with other youths. I asked him whether he had heard of a plot, to which he replied without qualms that in effect he had. It was nothing serious: Ideal Sánchez, one of Spilimbergo's student, had called Oscar and the rest of the group, and unanimously they had decided to award the prize to me. Therefore, that afternoon they were determined to remove the «Palanza Award» sign from the wall and place it next to my works. Why refrain young people from expressing themselves freely?

At the end of the month of November the first issue of the magazine «Artes 9» appeared, which I had founded along with Daniel Devoto, Juan Carlos Paz, Fernando de Obieta and Alberto Morera. As was generally the case, we were only able to finance three issues.

With «Artes 9», my activity linked to the founding of magazines ended. Those who would follow my footsteps —I said to myself as I reflected upon the new failure— should do so responsibly; different times imply other attituded. Young musicians, artists, writers and poets had developed a taste for a hasty way of living, becoming inappropriately conceited. Friends had told me about their experience with the new generation of musicians and artists. However, I too lived amid youths who attended my Charcas Street studio, but those youths studied relentlessly. The others, though apprentices, already believed they could teach.

Because I demanded the best from my students, my usual detractors told everyone that I immobilized these future artists in straitjackets, their «natural drive» restrained through severe rules of conduct; in other words, my teaching left them lifeless. It was the dawn of a period of confusion that was to lead the arts to a standstill: the passion for novelty that had once convulsed the world had dwindled, and the successive waves of inventions, every time more banal, had driven us towards the Void. There came a moment in which no words were uttered other than «sensible content», «instantaneity», or «automatism», transforming the artist into a seismograph of his internal reactions, and draining him of all he possessed within through the means of signs whose sense he didn´t even master. Under the pretext of «creative license», trivial and ephemeral art reigned, conceived for an era in which Man rejected all permanence, in which attention and thought were no longer essential.

This period of unrest, still present as I revise these pages, ended up killing expertise. Everyone started painting subjects unrelated to this art, in the most rapid of ways. Tempera, prepared with different ingredients, became the latest thing, and it was proclaimed that only matt tones were chic. As they were being used in Paris, it was immediately adopted in our midst. We never asked ourselves whether painters overseas were perhaps trying to avoid the rigor that oils require.

Allow me a digression obviously not meant for technicians: matt tones are obtainable from tempera (and just as easily, if one so wishes, from oils) as long as one avoids layers. Pre–renaissance painting was executed in tempera, except that the artist then did not work negligently; he took his precautions. In fact, after finishing a painting, he varnished it carefully, which explains its luster and admirable conservation. Not everyone can perform this task, be it oils, tempera or water–colors. Before an artist even begins his work, a deep knowledge of tone is required. He must thus use color according to the density of the varnish, and this is wisely felt through his sixth sense.

There is a subtle skill, almost ineffable, in understanding the reactions of each pigment. Yet this is achieved only through love and hard work, which in the end is called experience. The green artist, therefore, applies color indifferent to what it will look like beneath the light glaze that will preserve his work.

Pigment, basic element in all paint, including that one used on walls, is always the same; what changes is the level of refinement, the wash and the media with which it is sized: oils or glues. Here lies the difference between tempera paint (made out of eggs and casein, among other ingredients) and oil paint. If the latter is deprived of its oils, what is left but pigment? In that case, it makes no difference if one buys it in the form of cheap powder and sizes it any which way.

However, if pigments are used without their oils, when they dry they nonetheless possess a virtue appreciated by all fast work addicts: they agree with all colors. That is why an oil painting lacking in oils (a contradiction in terms) or a tempera painting, both without varnish, will always seem harmonious. But coat them with a protector and each color becomes independent; some will give us the impression of volume, others of deep cavities; collectors who wished to protect their paintings lost them when they had them varnished.

I have said that the retrospective held at the «Peuzer» gallery was to be the last one I organized in my country. It was inaugurated on the projected date and a large crowd attended it. Though no colleagues of mine showed up, other people gave me deep satisfactions.

For this occasion, an illustrated a monograph–catalogue was printed, superbly written by Julio Payró. Massive reviews were published by many newspapers, such as «La Nación», «Clarín» and «El Mundo», and signed among others by José León Pagano (responsible of the Fine Arts column of the «La Nación» newspaper, this was the critic´s last article), Córdova Iturburu and the Viscount of Lascano Tegui. What surprised me was an article that came out in the «Crítica» evening paper. Measured and didactic, it was written by Héctor P. Agosti, whose name I had never heard of before.

One fine day, I was pleased to learn that the excellent Chilean sculptor and ceramist Samuel Román Rojas had come to visit. We knew each other from before and were bonded by ties of affection. Small and stout, his round face smooth and jovial, he told me he had come to see my work. He was staying at a hotel on the «Avenida de Mayo» Avenue that someone had recommended to him, yet most days he spent with us. One evening, however, something most unfortunate occurred, and you shall soon know what.

I introduced him to a few artists, but he didn´t take to anyone, except Sibellino; the rest he found petulant and rude. Outspoken, he told each and every one what he thought of them, whenever he got the chance. Though of humble birth, he felt like an aristocrat, and in many ways, he was. Coming from a free country, Samuel was in the habit of speaking his mind, expressing himself even more freely whenever he had had a drink. One night, however, something quite unfortunate happened. As usual, I had walked him to his hotel so as to prolong our time together, when the watchman, in order to be funny, made a comment about Chilean women, whom he held to be rather licentious. Samuel vividly replied that if one wanted to speak about female immorality, we only had to remember Eva Perón.

As in the times of Byzantium or Holy Russia, infallibility and omniscience ruled; reporting people was the tithe of the insignificant to ingratiate themselves with the powerful. The watchman called the authorities, and the police arrived. The artist was flung into a van, and taken to jail. I was notified at seven o'clock in the morning; at noon, the police report had vanished thanks to a watchful friend, and before matters got any worse, my friend was back in his country.

Every cloud has a silver lining and I do not wish to omit an anecdote linked to my painting «The blind flutist». I had promised it as a gift to Pedro, my brother–in–law, but already there were so many official instructions forbidding the entrance and exit of works of art, that I didn't attempt to proceed with the cumbersome and often pointless paperwork.

My wife, who was leaving for Chile, decided to cross the Andes by train, presuming that custom officers in the mountains would be less informed about imperial decrees. She therefore wrapped the painting as if it had been a common parcel and placed it on the luggage rack. As it was to be foreseen, the officer noticed it. She answered him the truth: that it was a painting made by her husband, who was sending it to a brother of his. The man knitted his brow while looking at the package and ended up telling the imprudent traveler: «It's alright for this once, but next time, Madam, it can't leave the country without papers. Imagine: it could have been a work of art!»

Many say my retrospective held at «Peuser's» was memorable. Meanwhile, the jury selecting works for the National Salon of 1948 was working at the National Direction of Fine Arts. I was awaiting a reply, for I had sent them a painting. One afternoon, Dr. Oscar Ivanissevich, at the time President Peron's Secretary of Education, burst into the halls and without preamble ordered the jury to turn down my work, accepting «full responsibility». He wanted no «degenerate painting» in the Salon.

If I had been a member of the jury, I would have thrown him out, without weighing the consequences of my action, but my old friend, the painter Quirós, more politically correct, amiably convinced him to go for a walk. As they chatted, he dissuaded him from getting involved. Ivanissevich finally drove away, and Quirós immediately came to see me at the gallery to tell me what had taken place.

The jury waited a few days before meeting again. Those were times of abuse, of vexations: in short, times of tyranny. To everyone's surprise, however, Ivanissevich desisted from striking anew, and my painting was displayed, or I should say, unobtrusively placed. I have always believed the finest spot in a Salon is where the best work is found; this is probably true, since my painting was noticed.

The fact is that a little before the Salon opened, the painter Raúl Soldi, member of the jury, told me on the phone that he and his colleagues were planning on punishing the Secretary by awarding me the prize of one of his departments; the problem was that those prizes, consisting of two thousand pesos, allowed the department to acquire the painting. As the tag listing the price of my painting read three thousand pesos, Soldi wanted to know whether I agreed to lower it. I replied that would be a self–inflicted punishment, and that I wasn't about to let that happen. What I didn't tell Soldi was that the bravest way to reprove the Secretary would have been for the jury to award me First Prize.

A month after this singular event, invited by the president of the Uruguayan Commission of Culture, the architect Juan Ramón Menchaca, I exhibited my work in Montevideo. It was well received by the press and many people attended the show. The sculptor José Luis Zorrilla de San Martín, whom I had befriended in Florence and was currently head of the Fine Arts Museum of Montevideo, came to see the exhibition in the name of the Secretary of Education. He wished to purchase a painting, for the State wanted it for its museum. This show allowed me to see my old friends again and make new ones. I was invited to some very enjoyable parties, like the one held at the home of Jannette and Arnó Mandello. The painter Costigliolo had decorated their house and Pombo had written the captions. Though Guillermo Laborde had already passed away, everyone remembered him vividly.

During the course of 1949, after having researched for years on how to introduce the sun as a fundamental element in my paintings, that is, a solidified sun, I wished to see whether it was possible to transfer the intensity of the light, achieved in some of those works, onto others that contained figures. I created «The indecisive» and later on, «Resistance», characters that, like all the rest, belonged to the Italian Comedy. In these paintings, the solid yellow of the sun wasn't present: rather, it was the general tone I was searching for that stood out.

Five exhibitions were held that year, two of them in Brazil, both displaying drawings. The one in Rio de Janeiro was mounted at the Institute of Architecture, and the one in San Pablo, at the Museum of Modern art. All of my drawings were bought on those occasions.

Chile, to which so many bonds of friendship tie me, paid me a most moving tribute. It was in 1950 and consisted of a retrospective of my work. Those were difficult times for such hospitality, for the Secretary–Poet–Physician, who delivered his speeches in verse and spoke about the degeneration of my work was still in office at the Ministry of Education.

Through forces of circumstance, because the invitation came from the Chilean Ministry of Education, the Chilean Ambassador to Buenos Aires had to forward it to our Ministry of Education through the Ministry of Foreign Affairs. Inevitably, it would fall in the hands of the madman.

Well aware of the situation and anticipating possible trouble, the Chilean

Ambassador Germán Vergara Donoso, not only a keen art lover and collector but also a very close friend of ours, decided not to take the official step without consulting me first. In turn, I knew the Argentine Secretary of Foreign Affairs, a writer in his free time, who strongly objected to his colleague's behavior. We decided to hold a dinner at home, where the Chilean Ambassador and the Secretary «Tuco» Paz would discuss the matter. Matters were so well settled that my paintings left the country without a moan by the Secretary in question.

The exhibit, which was subsidized by the University of Chile, was organized in Santiago by the Extension of the Institute of Fine Arts, in collaboration with the National Museum of Fine Arts. In the month of August, the works were displayed in three beautiful halls. I found out that the initiative, and the catalogue confirms it, had been suggested by the National Society of Fine Arts and by the Federation of Artists of Chile. I had reasons to be in high spirits; it was the first time after all these years that I felt the appreciation of my colleagues.

The show was very well mounted; everyone did his best, beginning with the head of the museum, the painter Luis Vargas Rosas and the Dean of both the Faculty of Arts and Sciences and the Faculty of Fine Arts of the University of Chile, Romano de Dominicis. The painters Isaís Cabezón, Marcos Bontá, García Herquinigo, Carlos Isamitt, Camilo Mori and Jorge Caballero formed part of the organizing committee.

I became friends with a man of letters, the Sub–secretary of Education Julio Arriagada Augier. I had already noticed his proverbial Chilean cordiality at the airport. He was a man of great culture, who received me with delightful simplicity. The public of Santiago was fully responsive, and the closing date of the exhibition had to be postponed. It was a continuous procession of artists and students belonging to the Faculties of Fine Arts and Architecture.

As far as the press goes, so many articles were published in newspapers and magazines that I'm afraid I haven't been able to collect them all. Academy students flocked to the «Últimas Noticias» newspaper, then run by the painter Byron Gigoux, to communicate their impression, which reporters later published. Soon, art professionals were consulted in turn: I still conserve many of their gratifying declarations.

Before leaving this generous country, I was invited by Amanda Labarca to return three months later to teach a course on painting at the Summer School of the University of Chile. This is how very soon, and greatly pleased, we were back in Santiago. Not only did art students enroll in the course, but also professional artists, among these an experienced painter who had studied in Paris with Lhote. This is not mentioned to show off, but rather, to illustrate the modesty of the Chilean people, who, instead of pretending to know it all, favor the possibility of learning.

I taught the course in an atmosphere of perfect camaraderie, one that is bound to comfort the soul. I believe they were taken aback for they were expecting a modern theoretician and instead, found themselves face to face with a painter who possessed a lot of practical knowledge. There, I got closer to the artists Gazmuri, Vergara Grez, Ana Cortés, Marta Colvin, Israel Roa, Montesinos, Susana Aguirre, Victor Carvacho, María Tupper, Aída Poblete and so many others.

With regard to my classes at the Summer School, a couple of articles written by Isaac Etchegaray appeared in the «El Mercurio» newspaper, informing the public about the way I tackled teaching. The stories generated curiosity, and among those people interested was Bernardo Leighton, Secretary of Education, who invited us to dinner to discuss matters more in depth.

On that occasion, I visited other studios. I recall one where two or three youths, enthusiasts of social art, worked together; I exposed my objections to them, yet they defended their points of view with such vigor, that I gathered nothing would ever change their minds. However, youth is fickle; soon I discovered that the most fervent of them all was painting abstract art.

Once the program had ended, we left for the south of Chile, up to Bariloche. Then we headed home. I recommend this trip to anyone who hasn't yet seen these pristine lands, certain that he will find it one of the most beautiful places on earth. Back in the capital city, I still had time to hold an exhibit in the month of July, before setting out on our projected trip to Europe.

We set sail for Haifa on 12 December on the «Río Bermejo». Imagine our surprise when we woke up in Bahía Blanca, to find out the ship was moored and loading up. That came in very handy, for it gave us the opportunity to greet some of our dear friends. Our cruise began from there; it was a beautiful journey, though I won't annoy you with details. Suffice it to say that in Rio we spent some lovely moments with our friends Rebelo and that the crossing was superb. Finally, we dropped anchor in Haifa and visited most of Israel by cab; the landscape of Palestine impressed me a great deal. We spent eight days there, sleeping on the ship at night. In those days, the country was going through turbulent times and food was rationed. Fortunately, we didn't need any vouchers, and every day we got off our boat loaded with fruit and anything else we had been able to obtain: this was welcomed by the people of the area and by those of a catholic redoubt. Israel was coming to life as a nation, and we witnessed the spirit that animated this state, its sacrifice and its idealism.

On a freezing winter dawn in January, I woke up still half asleep, sensing the ship was advancing with its engines turned off. There was such sweetness in this motion that it felt as though the ship was gliding on a sea of oil; I threw something on and went up on deck. Thrilled, I called María Rosa. We were entering the Grand Canal, and the Gardens spread out on my right, while the Campanile rose on my left: I was moved by such incomparable beauty. I had never seen Venice in winter, let alone covered in snow. The Bridge of Sighs, the Doge's Palace, St. Mark's basilica: I was overwhelmed by the magnificence. The transitory beauty of the stalactites enhanced the intricate architecture, forming a perfect counterpoint. This double splendor made us forget the cold and we set out to visit the enchanted city; we spent three wonderful days there. The museums were empty and we ourselves avoided them so as not to be turned into blocks of ice.

The only place I went to was Cà Giustinian, where Umbro Apollonio received me. He told me it was a pity I was traveling with an Argentine passport, for the Venice Biennale can only invite national artists to exhibit in their pavilions: foreigners were only invited through their respective governments. He then wished to introduce me to professor Pallucchini, at the time president of the Biennale, with whom I chatted for a long time.

I could have easily obtained an Italian passport, which would have been useful at times. However, I wish to point out that it didn't even cross my mind. I am not a dual citizen and only because of sentimental reasons do I keep every expired passport or document.

We left Venice to take the train heading for Milan. Giolli and Marussig were no longer there; my two best friends had passed away. I saw the others: Tosi, Carrá, Constantini, Funi, Ballocco, de Grada, Somarè, Radici, Sironi and Carpi, who had become the head of the Academy of Brera. I also saw Lucio Fontana, who was actively working; at the time he was finishing off the model of a door meant for the Duomo, which he was going to present at a competition. On 23 February the «Il Milione» gallery inaugurated my first exhibit in Italy, after three decades of absence. That afternoon, the gallery, albeit quite large, seemed too small to house so many visitors. Many people came: local artists that I knew, my old friend Aquiles Badi and the musician Juan José Castro and his wife. Though some Argentine painters were passing through the capital of Lombardy, they did not attend the inauguration, lest they lost their habit.

Three days later, the «Radio Nacional», in its program dedicated to the arts and presented by the writer Raffaello de Grada, devoted almost the totality of its show to the review of my exhibit, as well as to my return, which was considered definitive.

During the European spring of 1952, we visited a large part of Italy by car: the stretch from Rome to Naples, the Amalfi coast and Pompeii. Our dear friends Tomás and Hortensia Tarazi, who had moved to Europe, accompanied us. In Florence I saw my old friends again, among them Celestino Celestini and Giovanni Colacicchi, the latter now the director of an academy. However, Ferrante Gonnelli was no longer there; I only saw his widow. Sadly, many of my companions had vanished.

In Rome I saw De Chirico, Prampolini, Vittorio Orazzi, his brother and Roberto Melli, but above all, I was happy to see Bragaglia. He knew every nook and cranny, and guided us around the Roman ruins. The soft moon seemed so huge it seemed painted upon the pale blue sky. Meanwhile, the three of us chatted about a million things amid unknown passages that somehow always led somewhere.

In Naples we got together with Gabriela Mistral, whom we had greeted in Rome while she was giving a conference on the works of Alfonsina Storni. María Rosa disappeared for three days, as she wished to accompany her illustrious compatriot. Meanwhile, I visited museums and friends; there was Emilio Notte, an old companion from Florence, who had become the director of the Fine Arts Academy of Naples, and Guido Cadorin, the director of the Venice State Academy.

Gabriela Mistral was no longer the woman I had once met in Buenos Aires, where she was at the peak of her physical and mental capacities. Reclined on a couch, her words were hesitant, and at times she would lose the thread of the conversation. I realized it strained her when she talked to me, something which didn't happen when she chatted to María Rosa, perhaps because the affection they felt for each other led her towards more familiar topics. When dealing with things of the heart, Gabriela had no amnesia. As soon as I realized this, I left them alone.

Many were the cities we visited in Italy, many the memories that came back to life and many the surprises. I was interested to find out how Futurism was understood by the new generations, what they thought about this doctrine, in general so badly grasped. The movement had sought to unburden Italy of its heavy load of tradition; it was a cry of hope that had opened doors to a new artistic universe. In spite of its language excesses and errors, Futurism as the essence of creativity, turned out to be an excellent way to shock public opinion in order to activate it. In the period of philosophical, scientific and artistic relativity, it produced bold concepts, fertilizing the European avant–garde with its dynamism

I noticed that artists, as well as critics and art historians, (especially the latter), obliged by their profession to be informed about this youthful and healthy explosion that shattered Italy's reverence towards the arts of the past, possessed (and still do, unfortunately), a crass ignorance about Futurism, and generally speaking, about the Modern movement begun in Italy in the 1920s. Like bookworms, they quenched their thirst in texts, in manifestos, in catalogues; they recorded names almost alphabetically, mentioning the five signatories to the First Manifesto of Futurist Painting without any particular consideration. Moreover, painters who should have never been regarded as such were included, while others were denied.

History at times forgets or is inaccurate, and the foundations of Futurism, which embodied «a new concept of hierarchy, of order, of discipline in a world of artistic values» are resolved in a list of names, registered haphazardly in the catalogue of some trite exhibits. Yet, omitted are those names of artists, including mine, who had actively fought to impose modern art in Italy, though abstaining themselves from signing manifestos and sending paintings to the numerous Futurist exhibits. As extraordinary as it may seem, my name is not referred to in Art History texts published in Italy, in spite of my arduous battle fought in Florence, Rome and Milan. All that has been written in Italy from 1925 to date is perfectly invalid because of omissions and errors.

I visited my beloved Florence anew, where we had the pleasure of hugging our friends Payró, also traveling through Europe. They had come from Paris, after having spent some time in Spain and Belgium, and we were staying at the same hotel. One afternoon, Julio told us about his adventure with the bootblack on the banks of the river Tajo. The exact story would require too many details, but suffice it to say that the gypsy readily «dissolved» the two new rubber heels of his shoes, while swearing he was a man of honor. I have found many things hilarious in my life, yet never did I laugh as heartily as I did then.

Back in Milan, the crates containing the paintings were sent to a storehouse. We then traveled by car to France, taking our time. This allowed us to enjoy the landscape and stop off at some points to see old friends. We spent some very pleasant days in Lausanne together with Alberto Sartoris and his wife, the painter Carla Prima. Though we had renewed contact after the war had ended, it was thrilling to see each other again.

On 1 July we found ourselves in Paris, staying at the Hotel d'Alsace, Rue des Beaux Arts, in Saint–Germain–des–Prés, where Oscar Wilde passed away. Though Paris had changed since 1924, I realized that it was still the «Ville Lumière» that everyone dreams about, radiant on calendars, postcards and «Métro» guides; it is the only capital in the world where one can live and work in peace.

We spent a beautiful month in the capital of France. The Chilean novelist Salvador Reyes came especially from London to greet us, and he introduced the French writer Georges Pillement and his wife to us. In turn, the French writer introduced us to Frank Elgar, whom he described as an uncompromising, sincere and passionate art critic. In order to be operational, passion has to express itself clearly, and I discovered Elgar entirely satisfied a critic's first duty, which is to proclaim the truth no matter what; a valiant and dangerous posture when one thinks of the consequences. Emerson once said that artists, like the Greek gods, only reveal themselves to each other, and we soon became friends. Here and everywhere else, intimate friends share comparable talents and similar virtues.

At the end of September 1952, we were back in Buenos Aires, but only stayed for about a year. In effect, as the month of August 1953 drew to a close, we left for France, for I had obtained a permanent residence permit. While still in Argentina we had tied up all the loose ends, in view of a long absence, and I finished off several paintings, among these «Dark–haired Maula» and «The Ingenuous».

As I had done in the past, I left my Charcas Street studio to my students Mónica Soler–Vicens and Alejandro Vainstein. We said goodbye to everyone we loved, our brothers and friends on both sides of the Andes. We left on the «Augustus», while those who had accompanied us to the harbor waved their handkerchiefs. Inwardly we also said goodbye to those who had not been able to come, and who also wished us the best.

I left the country battered, for the ignoble dictatorship that prevailed had been difficult to bear, especially when friends suffered it in the flesh. Freedom of expression was impossible, and the situation was worsening. It was impossible for me to continue working happily in such a spiritually decomposed and morally distressing climate, where accusations had become ordinary business.

Not that I believed I was heading towards Eden, comforted by a compassionate humanity; the international situation did not tolerate such illusions. Much to the contrary, once the euphoria of victory had dwindled, the allied peoples of Europe lived in distrust and resentment, and already the fear of a new conflict hovered upon the continent. Yet lovers of peace and culture did not give up, building bridges to unite intelligences, creating a vital climate of friendship that allows men to unite. Hope was thus possible to imagine in the near future thanks to noble actions and ideas, while the only hope I had concerning my country was an unexpected coup d'état.

I left my home at almost sixty-one, after having given my country no less than thirty years of intellectual and physical energy; I moved at an age when most people would not dare to start from scratch and move to a foreign country. Thirteen years have gone by since then, so rich in spiritual life, in frank artistic competition, in events and proposals, that if I were to tell you about them, you might not believe me. However, that will be recorded some other time.

To tell the truth, I can't complain, for life has been overly generous with me: an excellent health, unconditional love, valuable friends and a renowned artistic position. To live from my art, totally devoted to it, without sensing it causes worry or jealousy, to look a man in the eyes while shaking his hand cordially are not minor satisfactions. If, as a human being I feel I can face the rest of my life with optimism, as an artist my faith and my desire to evolve are as deep as ever. But, how far can I go? Art possesses a unique dimension, the one of infinity. That is its mystery, something marvelously indefinite and undefined that lies beyond science, beyond our comprehension and our intellectual and physical truth. If I reach that point, my being, my strength, my faculties and my intellectual capacity will finally consider it sufficient.

Patience, my grandfather used to say, is one of the cardinal virtues, particularly useful when carrying out important tasks. I have believed this since I was a child, feeling that the idea of perfection, from whichever angle it is looked at, is a passion of the spirit: the object of our love must be perfect, for there exists a pride in loving those who deserve it. All of our existence we must keep the fire burning, for our work must be flawless. Passion and reason. A fire burning forever and a conscience that bears witness that such ardor is worthwhile.

Paris, August 1966.

The Pettoruti Foundation (Fundación Pettoruti)

The Pettoruti Foundation was created in Buenos Aires on October 21, 1987. The Board of Administration was composed of the following members:

President: Lía Pettoruti, the artist's sister
Vice-president: Raúl Soldi, artist
Secretary: Jorge Romero Brest, art critic
Treasurer: Oscar Fernández Brital
Active Member: Ramiro Casasbellas, writer
Delegate Director: Roberto Díaz Varela

In 1990 Roberto Díaz Varela is designated President of the Pettoruti Foundation.

Activities organized by the Pettoruti Foundation since its inception:

December 8: the Pettoruti Foundation introduces itself at the National Museum of Fine Arts.

Exhibition: " His image of cubism", General Consulate of the Republic of Argentina, New York, USA.

Edition of the book " Emilio Pettoruti: an avant-garde classic", foreword by Jorge Romero Brest. Out of Print.

Exhibition: " Tribute to Emilio Pettoruti", halls of the Pettoruti Foundation, Buenos Aires.

Exhibition: " Pettoruti 90", halls of the Pettoruti Foundation, Buenos Aires

Exhibition: " Emilio Pettoruti, 1914-1919", Universal Exhibition of Seville, Seville, Spain.

Exhibition: " Two Argentine masters: Pettoruti and Quinquela Martín", Colombo 1992, Genoa, Italy.

Exhibition: " Pettoruti, 1892-1992", in commemoration of the artist's hundredth anniversary. House of Government, Buenos Aires.

1995. Exhibition: " Pettoruti", National Halls of Culture, Palais de Glace, Buenos Aires.

Edition of the itemized catalogue of Pettoruti's work. Authors: Rafael Squirru, Eleanor Heartney and Jacques Lassaigne, Pettoruti Foundation Publishing Company.

CD-Rom edition of the " Masters of Painting" Collection: Emilio Pettoruti, Quinquela Martín and Pedro Figari.

Exhibition: "Modernism on the River Plate in the 20s", Surrogate Court House, City Hall, by invitation of Mayor Rudolph Giuliani, New York USA.

The Pettoruti Foundation presents the Harlequin Art Award to Argentine artists. Jury: Art Critic Fermín Fèvre, Professors Nelly Perazzo, Jorge López Anaya, Osvaldo Svanascini.

Launching of the internet site www.pettoruti.com

Exhibit at the II Biennial of Visual Arts of the Mercosur, Porto Alegre, Brazil.

Edition of the book " Pettoruti". Text: Fermín Fèvre. El Ateneo Publishing Company*

Edition of the book " Pettoruti". Text: Edward J. Sullivan. Espaesa Publishing Company*

Edition of the " Pettoruti" serialized publication. Text: P. Orgambide, J. Forn and M. Pacheco. Espaesa Publishing Company. Distribution: "Clarín" newspaper.

Exhibition: "Pettoruti, a painter before the Mirror", organized by the Picasso Foundation, Municipal Museum of Malaga, Malaga, Spain.

Launching of the television program " Art and Style", transmitted weekly by "Magazine".

Launching of the cultural program "Portal Informativo" on the Pettoruti Foundation website.

Re-edition of the autobiography of Emilio Pettoruti " A painter before the Mirror", originally edited in the year 1968 by Solar/ Hachette Publishing Company.

* The Pettoruti Foundation donated the copyrights for the edition of these books.

www.ingramcontent.com/pod-product-compliance
Lightning Source LLC
Chambersburg PA
CBHW020635220526
45464CB00001B/154